AF426646

CHAPTERS

WITH DISDAIN FOR DISCONNECTED INTRODUCTORY WRITINGS AND CONFUZZLED ORDER, I INSTEAD USE STRAIGHT-UP NUMBERED CHAPTERS.

DISREGARDING WHATEVER WRITING FORMAT PROTOCOL EXISTS OUT IN THE WORLD, I DO ADMIRE PRE-WORDS EXECUTED APPROPRIATELY.

QUITE POSSIBLY MAYBE JUST A RECREATION OF SEMANTICS, I DELIVER MY WHY AND SUPPLY SOME FOREWORDS, BUT DO IT MY WAY.

Cannot Fly

I've given up

But cannot leave

I'm fed up

But cannot quit

I'm tired

But cannot rest

I want to flee

But cannot fly

I want a new shadow

But this one's unshakable…

…pervasive feelings of incompleteness and fear.

I am engaged in a battle to save my own life, many of us are.
Many…of…us…are.

I attempt to live more like I desire and less like I do not, we all do.

Our frightening memories haunt us, we bleed quarts from past pains. The chain of yesterday is incarcerating, dragging around the weight of days gone by with us wherever we go. Us some teeter precariously, clinging to the thought of scary and doubtful tomorrows…even engulfed, overwhelmed and parttime breathless, held down and trapped within the shallow but deadly drowning pool of our here and now hopelessness.

If believing we have already given up, thinking our life is finished but we forgot to tell anyone, if breath even begrudgingly still swirls through our chest, well then and factually-actually, it's not over.

We all struggle with something, fucking all of us. We suffer amid a multitude of stupid shit…stuff we fear, stuff we dislike, stuff we doubt. Stuff we have, stuff we don't. Stuff we want, stuff we want to shed. Stuff making our walking and talking days harder than we think said days should be.

We all are stuck to something, something with more control over us than we have over it. Whether shooting dope or drinking the Devil's Water, working too much or over exercising, watching sports or judging others, even the act of worrying itself, if unable to turn it off and walk away at will, aka if unable to control our behavior, I call this stickiness addiction. We all have something clinging to us, scratching us, biting or eluding us, and perhaps a sum pile of that vexing crap sits atop our head simultaneously.

Yet after the hardest parts of life begin to settle, moments of relief arrive, always, that is if our hearts are open enough to let them in, always, fucking always. Hence still…following such stretches of goodness, pain visits us once more to be sure.

Life goes up and down, down and up, always, fricking always, like ravaging storm clouds rushing afront then aside the giving glorious sun.

All these here words thunk up written and edited hand-first by Roger Ray Bird.

A.I. cover art by Mister Damon Nawrozki, Mooresville North Carolina, USA, Planet Earth.

My breath embolden to the 10 friend family members saving my life thus far when me my lame-ass lowlife loser self was entirely incapable of doing so otherwise.

This here battered bird brain book, first edition and perchance last, September 2023.

Copyright (C) 2023 Roger Ray Bird, aka my kid's daddy BigBirdy-BigBoyd.

All Rights Reserved, so they say, whoever *they* quite possibly maybe bee-bee.

For all you peering and peeking creeper eyes outside thy nest other than my two darling baby birds my brood…no duplication, copying, plagiarism or ripping off my shit pretty please. I said please motherfuckers. No portion of this book may be reproduced stored or transmitted in any form flail or fashion without prior permission from Roger Ray Bird. I'm at rogerraybird@gmail.com and rogerraybird.com if you at all give a shit.

This here uncensored deep dive reverts not from my unreserved potty mouth, aka my sans-bowdlerization, aka the 631 *fucks* found within thine chivalry-abandoned 263 pages, uh, frick to the no, the gloves get thrown to the ice…do the math, just sayin'.

This here bird hatched within the bounds of Cleveland Ohio USA, Earthmass, Earthbomb.

This punk-ass bitch's tale begins in West Baltimore at four years old.

I smoked my first joint at 12 whatever who cares.

I sold my first bag of weed and a handful of amphetamines at 13 no bother no better.

I earned the illustrious distinction of high school dropout at 16 sans worry.

I slipped the drug needle into my arm at 18 lacking total fucking concern for what comes next.

Querying my darling daughter Birdy's formidable unknowing, these my bare all writings are for her, my lovely Lauren. Revealing a plethora of never before recognized truths concerning my addiction, I also dedicate this ramble to my son Travis aka Boyd awhile you my preciouses, you my beloved sisters and brothers of the world.

Sharing these here my lived knowings, I try to help. Help locate a sunnier path, or least shake the damn shadow. Help to find, see and embrace the straight-up factual possibility…it…is…possible you can do it, you can do it, I know it, you really-really can, I fucking know it, I know it deep in my heart, you are strong-stronger than you even realize, I believe in you, I am fighting for you and I love you.

One

~

Friendwords

A Word or Three From Those in the Know

Chapter One, Friendwords ~

I'm struggling, lost with no purpose, adding nothing of sustenance to this life, isolated. I don't know what to do anymore…I have never felt so ready to check out, I feel the ease of it becoming overwhelming right now.

I'm suffering at a rate that I can't control. Slap me around. Call me a coward. I'm starting a kick again, I hate it…sobriety is somber, the dope kills the pain, but I hate the dope. I can't win for losing.

Up-down, up-down, fight this bullshit, fight this addiction. I go full unsupervised in June on probation, but I can't even fucking look past the moment…I see no future Roger, none. You know people say oh you got so much to live for, yeah why don't you tell me what I have to live for? Because I sure the fuck don't know, I don't see it.

I should be helping, I should be giving back, and I'm sorry I'm not. I want to be better. I want to do better but I'm just fucked up right now, I have been for a long time. I wish I were there to do something for you. My greatest successes in life always come doing things for other people, never for myself, there's no foundation of self-love.

The day I was born my grandmother lifts me up to show my father and his first words are, "Put him back". That's where it started you know, he was 18 years old and he had a rough upbringing so it's generational, but it stops with me I assure you, I'd NEVER hit a kid, I just don't do that thing.

When he wanted me to come home he'd whistle, like I was a dog. He put me down my entire life, he was relentless with it and wouldn't stop. My mom would try to tell him to leave me alone, he'd tell her to shut up then he wouldn't stop, he wouldn't stop, telling me what a piece of shit I was at eight years old. I could never do that to anyone, I don't care what their age is. There's no sorry's that will fix that. I don't talk to him anymore, I don't have to like him. I was raised in the Baptist church with my grandparents while my mom and dad stayed home. They'd say I need to love my parents, I need to love my parents, but you don't have to endure pain, you don't have to endure bullshit just because of your parents, you don't have to do that.

Roger let's do something, something worth meaning, something that gives, helps, and sustains. Something talking about the pain, the stories riddled in heartache, bleeding despair and angst, identifying why self-medication was the only way.

~ The Masterful Mister Joshua Duke Sansing

Peaceful Understanding

My story, from where I sit today, has been one of facing and, sometimes, even overcoming fears, uncertainty, and vulnerability within myself and in the world. I say "from where I sit today" because this is a somewhat new discovery to me. I'm 30 years old, and I started using drugs when I was 17. So, as my mind was coping with all the life stuff that comes with being a teenager, I found this great escape in drugs. Of course, we also had a local mall, but for me and my friends, it was no comparison.

As time went on, the life stuff got "bigger", and the drugs got "harder" until I found myself in jail at 20. Prior to going to jail, I entered a six-month rehab. I also had the opportunity to earn an early release from jail by completing a boot camp. My life at that point had been shaped by my family, school, friends, TV/internet, to name a few. But none of these inputs had brought on any sort of self-reflection.

Now, there are plenty of issues with the Wisconsin as well as federal prison system, but they are at least making an attempt to offer programs to people who may benefit, and this is a trend in the right direction. Because of this boot camp, I was introduced to programs like CTRT (Critical Thinking and Rational Thinking), Narcotics Anonymous, and other programs. The knowledge from these programs introduced new ways of looking at my addictions and my relationships with my thinking patterns.

Since those days, I've been on a path to understand myself and maybe find a little peace along the way. I've had ups and downs, relapses and revelations, but at the end of the day, I see growth, and that is all I can strive for.

~ The Mindful Middle Way Tyler "TJ" Schmidt

Love Each Other

I had spent most of the last 10 years hiding. Guilt and shame had been both enemy and best friends. They kept the perpetual cycle of use, shame, and guilt twirling. An endless merry-go-round spinning, sometimes at ungodly speeds, and other times barely moving. This kept me alive, for how long I wasn't sure, but I didn't really care. I wanted to feel again. Alcohol and drugs kept me from feeling, something I was accustom to, something I longed for, but life had to have meaning. Right? I spent most of these 10 years in and out of rehabs, therapy, meetings, not really for myself, never really for myself. Always to appease someone else, but why?

"You either get it done, or you don't. And not getting it done is not an option." A phrase my father spoke, and my brothers and I seemed to strive to perfect. I speak for myself but I think it rings true for them as well, that all we wanted to do was be as smart, dedicated, and hardworking as him. As strong and endlessly gritty as my mother. As loving and caring for others as they both were. How had I staggered so far from such simple beliefs and values?

The need to feel competent at what I do, the need to feel authentic in my life, and the need to feel connected to others. These fit my values that had been etched into my soul. Even further distilled down, first things first. What am I going to do today, even if it is make my bed. I can still go drink after that, but what is the one thing I will do today to either better myself, or better someone else's life around me, today, just today.

I had identified my life with those around me, something I still do today, which is a terrible curse and sweetest blessing my mother has given me. But I have to take care of myself, to put on my life vest before I can help others. How do I find balance if life has no meaning? First things first. What can I do today that will better my life or someone's around me? Sobriety is something I never think about and think about everyday. Emotions are what makes us human, and it's okay to have them, but what is behind them, and if it's not the desired feeling, what can I do that changes that? Not dealing with life's terms is not an option.

Find beauty, be weird, have fun, be emotional, help others, build something, and love each other.

~ The Beautiful Creator Zak Siefkes

Finding Hope When There Was None

First I thought the world had a problem, not me.

If only the world would change I wouldn't have to alter my brain with booze.

By the time I knew it was on me, quitting seemed pointless.

I was in too deep to just quit, I was convinced I'd fail, so why try.

Then, I could only feel dull happiness from extreme pursuits, so getting sober appeared even more boring.

I gave up on life.

Finding hope when there was none is the hardest thing I've ever done.

Someone close to me told me that they loved me whether I drank or not, that I was a good person regardless.

For me, the letting go of the self loathing and shame removed the heavy burden and allowed me to care again, about both myself and the world.

Sobriety allowed me to feel again.

And now the tiniest, barely noticeable event gives me extreme joy and satisfaction, one that I will never surrender.

~ The Original O.G. Iron-Man, Mister John Stamstad

Kindness and Acceptance

There are many spheres to approach the concept of addiction- historical, sociological, cultural, medical, spiritual and inter-personal; all of which offer a useful spectacle of ideas but have fallen short to curb the global epidemic. One doesn't have to search very far to see how drug and alcohol abuse permeates through our society and although I recognize there are several kinds of addiction, for the purpose of this exposition, I am referring to drug and alcohol addiction.

I briefly worked in the addictions field, as many recovering addicts do and I have also been clean in twelve-step recovery for thirty-three years. I have heard the horrific experiences of many addicts and have shared my own. I have watched many addicts recover and seen others destroy their lives, their families and ultimately become human tragedies.

I am a recovery addict and the way I define that is, that I am free from the compulsion and mental obsession of drugs. I no longer have the need to use and my personal psyche has taken a fundamental shift. This doesn't mean that I have forgotten where I came from and where I could easily go back to. Therefore, my recovery is something ongoing, something that is a life-time process. In a word, addicts never graduate.

Experience has shown me that once I start using ANY mind or mood altering drug with the intent on getting high, I cannot stop. I fall into the abyss of degradation and I begin a slow, self-destructive suicide. What I'm saying is, my journey has been one of complete abstinence.

That's not to say that there aren't other ways of treating addiction. Some people use harm reduction therapy or medical assisted treatment and live functional lives. Although these other treatment milieus may work for others, I just felt that they wouldn't work for me. Whenever an addict decides they want a new way to live, I think it is a good thing; no matter where they get their recovery.

There is one thing that I would like to emphasize, addiction has nothing to do with one's moral character and is not a matter of weakness! People don't just decide one day they want to be an addict. Addicts are subjected to much stigma in our culture and many others. This makes it even more difficult to get help. Imagine the kid walking down to the breakfast table and saying, "Hey Mom, I don't think I want to go to school today because I think I'm dope sick." I just want to say to anyone that finds it easy to judge, try walking in an addict's shoes. There is an old adage that goes, "we don't know what we don't know."

Now the question is this, why did I become addicted to drugs and other people from a similar demographic to my own, did not? Is it due to a bio-chemical predisposition? Maybe.

Could it be related to the environmental, mental, physical and sexual trauma that I suffered as a child? Possibly. There are many variables I'm certain. Yet, I think there is a larger psycho-social phenomenon, that offers the most explanatory value.

Reductionism, or reducing the analysis to just the individual, is naïve at best. I believe in a society where we are often plagued by alienation and general disenchantment of the world is a strong determinant.

I lived many years, especially my formative ones, feeling like I was on the outside looking in. I felt like an outcast, a pariah, even around my family. Although I couldn't identify it at the time, I was feeling disconnected and I don't think that my experience is that unique among those who have suffered from addiction. And although the disease/ medicalization model has been clung to for almost a century, by the treatment center, industrial-complex, the model has some flaws.

Lately, I have been reflecting and I have come to my own conclusion. I believe it was my experience, that I was unable to connect with people in most social environments. Those spaces and places of kindness and acceptance, whether that be family, community, or societal institutions sort of eluded me.

In 2010, a social psychologist in Vancouver, British Columbia, Bruce Alexander came up with a convincing hypothesis, that addiction is mostly caused by dislocation from positive social connection. In his research he argues against the orthodox consensus, of the bio-chemical theory. The paradigm shifted further and was further analyzed by Dr. Gabor Mate', who has written extensively on addiction, trauma and connection.

To sum things up, I'm grateful for what Roger is doing. As a result of him exposing his vulnerability, he has opened a space for others to be as vulnerable. I believe this is the kind of connection that we all seek and it has the power to heal. Roger has exposed what is under the mask, which must be a healing process for him. As some have said, "we are only sick as our secrets". Roger is putting it out there. He is establishing a connection, within his circle and beyond.

This is extremely more difficult when we live in a society, more disconnected by technology, tribalism and fear. Our Nation is unkind and violent, the future is uncertain and our lives are short. That is why I think it is important for us to show our humanity, as Roger has done. All we can do is strive to be the best version of ourselves and sometimes it gets messy. Some say that our past struggles are our greatest strengths because we can pass our experiences on to others. This is particularly true for someone that suffers from addiction because they know what it is like to live in hell.

Pax,

(The Wicked Smart) Dennis Dodson

Asking Hard Things Of Us

I have heard something along the lines of "Your friends will know you better in five minutes of meeting you than acquaintances you've had your whole life ever will." Damn if this doesn't remind me of Roger the Bird. I met Roger a few years back while I was working in a small cafe on Willy Street in Madison, Wisconsin. He strolled in with his friend Brian, a regular in the cafe who owned a tattoo shop across the street. Brian introduced us and somehow Roger and I quickly started talking about music and how important it was to us. I don't remember who it was we vibed over, but I remember that afterwards, it felt like he and I had just done a secret handshake upon meeting. We just clicked. There was something in that brief interaction that made me feel understood and seen, even though I had shared no details about my story or any of the things in my life that had happened to bring me to that moment in time. Something about talking to Roger made me feel lighter, brighter, and most of all, like I mattered.

Roger and I became friends and began sending messages sharing music and thoughts about life. No fluff, just the larger than life music that captures a feeling so brilliantly it brings us to tears, and thoughts so deeply profound that they shape who we are and how we navigate our lives. Thinking about it now, I'm not sure that before Roger, I had ever had these sorts of exploratory conversations with anyone, let alone with someone I barely knew. I loved his writing and challenged myself to match his eloquence, surprising myself by what came out. No one in my life had ever really asked me the types of questions Roger did, the types of questions that I needed to really reflect on to answer authentically. Or maybe until that moment I had been too afraid to look at and talk about what I truly wanted out of life. At any rate, he appeared to me at a time where being vulnerable and talking about that shit felt needed, felt good. He sent me a copy of the book "Bring Your Life Back to Life" by Brian Andreas. This gesture made me feel ten feet tall. In the message I sent to him thanking him, I told him "The best part…This feeling that I feel right now, I get to carry this feeling around forever. I look forward to having this gift and this knowing and this moment to call on in times when I need a reminder of what I am capable of."

In the years since, I've started taking risks, betting on myself, and seeking out some of the expansive experiences my heart calls for. I've moved across the country two (soon to be three!) times, went to school in Sedona, Arizona to become a massage therapist, started a new career, and tried my hand at love. I have had a parent diagnosed with dementia and watched the disease rock my family's life as we knew it. None of it has been easy. But, as Roger will be the first to tell you, life is scary and asks hard things of us. And he is part of the reason I know I can do them. I call on my connection with Roger when I have trouble seeing myself as strong or capable, whatever resilience he saw in me that made him send me that book. I pull it off of the shelf from time to time when I need to know there is someone in the world who believes in me and gets it.

Full on secret handshake gets it. There is someone out there who has done really hard things and doesn't doubt that I can do them too. And I know it's not just me. Roger has faith in us all. And that's what this book is all about. That's what it's always about with Roger.

Roger Bird, thank you for seeing us and sharing yourself and your scars with us. Thank you for your words and their remarkable ability to remind us that we are not alone, never ever alone. Not even when we are swimming in the deep end, where we find ourselves more often than not.

~ The Ferocious Lucy Fucking Brown (as titled by Roger, of course)

In My Own Bed

If somehow left to dream

Still I am lost

Pretendedly released from the fear awhile tangled

My nightmare legs broken and crossed

Stuck wandering blindly

Under the noontime light

Shattering the terror

Doesn't make it alright

Looking for a friendly

A stranger hands me a dime

Powerlessly afall to a place without bottom

I might not reach out for a line.

Two

~

Running

Thine the Pain, the Fear, the Disallowed

With father bird the Father mostly off and about elsewhere, it was a total crapshoot where us four Bird kids would be at any given moment, yet every so often we collected together outside. One typically standard day, while also being a very particular mid-week afternoon, my sisters and I were playing together in our back yard, probably Whiffle ball or badminton, actually I think it was kickball. Anyway whatever…BigBird was at work during this particular mid-day moment and we were somewhat older, in care and in charge of ourselves, aka no adults around.

She was about fifty feet away…it was a true ambush from behind. The loud, slow, methodical and rhythmic rasp of her vocalized demonic tone caused us to spin twist in horror, then we took off screaming and running like mad to get the hell away from her, fast as we could.

Frighteningly, I recognized Patricia Lou instantly, especially because of her announced threatening demands. This wicked woman was demanding money, saying bad things about our father, and yelling for us to stop and come back to her, *right now*. Oh my god hell no, no way, we were losing our minds. We made a beeline for the side-mounted metal staircase, which was closer than running around to the front. Mostly we used the steep side steps to our second and third floor residence, knowing the mid-floor entry door was unlocked. We got up the clanging stairs and inside ok, but I am somewhat ashamed to admit I was so frightened I gave no notice to how my sisters were doing, I think Laura grabbed our littlest sister Christy's hand as we ran inside. Laura had things covered for sure, my older sister locked the door and immediately called our father at work.

Our frantic unified crying echo-pack-filled the inside rooms, while our mother's violent shouts penetrating the lock-her-out-lock-her-out windows and doors scared me close to seizure. I heard her try to come in the side door then the front, but both barriers kept her at bay, least for now. Patricia scavenged around trying to gain access to our house, I heard her traveling loud ramble. We ran about on the second floor bouncing between rooms, gawking through windows and trying to keep track of where the hell she was. I lost sight of her for about five minutes, that is until the cops came roaring up to our house side-curb. Their two squad cars barreled in full speed with lights and sirens ablaze and everything, the emergency vehicle scenario certainly in flamboyant effect. We viewed through the barriered glass intently because least for me, I wanted to make sure they were going to take her away…preferably far, far, and further away than she was held before. Awhile frenzied, I also immediately grew sad thinking we would have to leave our friends and move away, us trying to escape our mother yet again.

When Laura called our father, BigBird called the cops. I feared the police would demand we open the door and let them in, which might also let our mother in…*blech*, an unsteady notion almost making me throw up. The Baltimore City officers walked swiftly towards our house then remained out of our field of vision for a few minutes. Off-scale frightened, I still could not see my mother. Everything was quiet, then I heard Patricia yelling. Finally walking out into plain view, the burly four male officers surrounded mother Patricia and led her back to the curb. The mother-type person argued with police…*oh no, no way*…she quieted and it sounded like they were getting along. My concern was deliriously unsettling…I imagined she was convincing the cops everything was fine. I dreaded the police would leave our mother here, them driving away before BigBird got home.

Powerlessly, I could do nothing but restart my panicked crying.

Oh thank goodness…an officer opened one of the copper car back doors and motioned for my mother to get in, which she did. They didn't cuff her and once in view, I saw no physical contact between my mother and the cops. The car encaging mother Patricia left quickly while the second car stayed put. The remaining officers stood outside talking, and my tears slowed their roll. I was surprised they did not come to check on us, but not sure I would have favored letting them in without BigBird at home. My father might take an hour getting back from his downtown work but somewhat speedily, he was home in less than half that time. We watched eagle eyed out the windows, BigBird chatting with the two officers, then the remaining cop car finally left. The matter was ridiculously unfathomable to me that she found us. I believed my father purposefully tried to shield us from our mother in every way…how in the world did she track us down?

I can barely attempt describe how I felt after that, well, I guess…betrayed by an unknown force, tormented by a higher power, lied to, cheated, comprehensively flabbergasted on a horrific level.

Once more and much like before and before and before, my entire world upended. Mainly I pondered…how in the hell is anyone going to keep this crap from happening again? I thought she was gone like forever, and once she was locked up, we left, we moved away, we changed our phone number and everything. We got a different car, we were going to different schools…how for fricking shit's sake did she find us? How did she get out…did she escape, did they let her out? If they let her out won't they let her out again? How will we ever get away from her now? How will we ever be safe from our own mad-mad mother? Will we have to live our whole lives running from the monster mother? Door to door, our father was usually gone for 10 hours or more on a typical weekday. If our mother kept getting out, how could we possibly ever stay safe from her? Felt like the clock just rolled back…if her time in the mental hospital was supposed to help her, clearly it did not, no fricking way.

After she was committed years before, I maintained a fearful uncertainty we would be able to stay hidden away from her forever.

The while, I hoped she never-ever-never found us, and we could be free from the monstrousness once and for all, forever. So much time passed since she left, years long…regrettably, I had let my guard down. My mother was far out of my mind on this particular afternoon when she showed up. Mother Patricia was in the hospital under lock and key long enough that she also did not physically resemble the woman I once knew, but, well, I surely recognized her voice though.

We loosely learned she did not escape but they released her. Upon expulsion from her confinement, it appears no protocol existed to call her family but rather she then just set free unto the streets. From what I knew, the hospital did not notify my father the mother of his four children was just let out of her multi-year cuckoo's nest captivity. I do not know for certain but I believe she found us when a family friend told mother Patricia where we now lived, after Maryland Spring Grove state mental hospital opened the door and let her fumble free from her cage.

She went in and out of the hospital least a few more times, yet I tried not to notice. I kept moving far away from both mother Patricia and my father's house as possible. Sometimes I saw her before she saw me, both her hands carrying a plethora of those plastic shopping bags filled with who the hell knows what…and, well…I never knew better but quite sure this is where the term *bag lady* comes from. Alternative days she pushed around her crappy little vertical wire cart basket on wheels with varied sorts of random shit crammed inside. Regularly she wore her big trashy brown pleather purse over her shoulder, her same shoulder hand death gripped on the straps, and the main bag tucked under her same-arm side. Often, both her shoulders rolled inwards to clutch the faux leather sack tightly against her chest with both hands, trying to protect everything she owned in the whole damn world from the downtown Baltimore street punks. Most always she demanded money, and, well…when not demanding, she requested I hand over all I have, *right now*.

Years ongoing, immediately her jabber trash talking pelted BigBird, which radically offended me. Although defiant and resentful of my father, he was fricking all I had, and, um, well…least he wasn't actively trying to physically harm me like my mother was. All me and my sisters could do was run away, often sprinting for inside the stupid house then lock the damn doors when we saw the monster mother coming to get us.

The rather oftened periods stretched hours before BigBird finally got home after kooky mommy came to scream and chase us around. Those were tough times at home, very tough, least for me, and not so damn pleasant to clack-clack-clack about still.

                    Chapter TWO

I would not feel safe the rest of those days to go back outside, like she might be lurking in the nearby bushes waiting to reach out and grab me by the throat, so I didn't. Also I hated being confined inside, *hated*…quite the quandary for my becoming of a *PAB*, aka punk-ass-bitch.

When the veritable truth finally rested as obvious on my slow dumb ass bird brain, duh…that the system would not or could not hold her, my mother encapsulated the life of a ravenous street outcast, her going in and out of homeless shelters wherever, Baltimore City proper while sometimes venturing off to surrounding suburbs, mostly western. Although our prized Whitney Avenue house in the northwest Baltimore City *Pimlico* neighborhood first seemed steady for years, once my mother found us, I hated that damn house too. Immediately and forever more, our newer-to-us Whitney house was also shadowed, *wobbly*…like the Hillsdale Road monster house in West Baltimore before it, *wobbly*…like a rock was stuck underneath it or something.

I adapted and learned to somewhat stay alert, aiming to keep my eyes up and looking around for the monster mother, hah, pathetically she was not hard to identify as time went on. Patricia became increasingly disheveled and started to assume a rather weakened and hunched over stance as she shuffled 'round, like quite 'litrilly she could fill in as substitute bell ringer at Notre Dame. The reputed bird mother was without a car, without a job, and without an available roof to sleep under.

Predominantly her nature was horrifically aggressive, maintaining a forward-facing pre-pounce position, what I identify as her coming-to-get-us stance.

Maybe she learned better as months got by, and once we sheltered fearfully inside she might wander off, frequently the police would just shoo her away, hah…then only faint reprimands were tossed out of open prowler car windows as the boys in blue rolled by, the cops conveniently leaving momma Patricia to thrash about on the sidewalk, stuck there within her own darkness. For holy-crap shit's sake she would not stay away though, she kept coming back and back and back at us. It sucked, it really, really, really sucked. Despite her threatening physical advances, neither the police nor mental health facilities could squash her reign of terror, least not for long. The situation incipient kicked off as, oh hells bells…just the way it is. Precautionarily, BigBird gave explicit instruction to our schools that under no circumstance is the lost-all-marbles-mother allowed to contact us in any way, both while at school or en route. Our father told us same-same…the mother monster possesses zero rights to see us and we should make sure these facts are clearly known to all, if by chance Patricia corners one of us when we are away from the house.

Specifically, BigBird said that if in question, we should run away yelling FIRE at the top of our goddamn lungs.

Burning

Life's cessation creates no concern

The memories to ponder, just sit there and burn

Ending for better

Given up on it now

Live for the moment

Is all I can vow.

Discarded

I have three sisters.
I have one older sister.
I have two younger sisters.
Beth is one year younger than me.
Christy is four years younger than me.
It was December, around Christmas time, in west Baltimore.
Christy was a little biddy two-week-old newborn baby.
Beth was three years old.
I was four almost five, and our family had just imploded.
Mother bird was being held in a short term mental hospital.
Without a word, three of us kids were driven to Michigan, and left there.
Hastily we got dropped in the neighborhood where our father grew up, Dearborn.
We three younger kids remained in Detroit with BigBird's parents, for a year.

The circumstance of drop-the-kids-in-Detroit-and-run-away went down only days after mother Patricia collected Christy from the baby delivery storks. Immediately upon her return home from the hospital, my mother's mental health was violently out of control, and downright dangerous. Appearingly, no reasonable option presented except to then hold her outside walkabout societal freedom.

Notably…before sent away, my blood had pooled on the west Baltimore Hillsdale Road monster house kitchen floor, twice. Although my mother did not directly inflict the literal stitch-this-bird-boy-back-together lacerations herself, deep down I believed she was the mastermind of the attacks.

In Detroit I fought an nightmarish battle to even begin comprehending what the ostracized hell was going on. Maybe they thought we were too young to understand, and maybe so. I was extremely confused. The experience felt like we were lost in a ginormous store with mean yelling adults everywhere. Several times, Beth or I would ask our grandparents when our dad was coming back to get us. We got no answers, just lots of yelling, so we stopped asking. Our grandparents were not nice, not nice at all, and this truth was painfully real. Many times I drifted off asleep at night with my head on the dining room table, still in my punishment chair from dinner. I had to stay there long as it took for me to eat every single morsel of food put in front of me. Some of what my grandmother served made me sick, like certain kinds of soups and vegetables. I tried to eat everything, really I tried, but often couldn't entirely clear my plate, so I had to *just sit there and shut up*, aka no talking, no book reading, no pencils, no paper, no crayons, no nothing.

I vomited at the table a few times, which made my grandparents furious, like I was stabbing Baby Jesus with my dinner fork.

I learned attempted silence when gagging on food, secretly puking into my napkin. Once going to bed, finally but with begrudged scolding the grand birds dismissed me, *go, just go away, just go…*straight to my sleeping quarters. I was not being stubborn at all, really I wasn't, but carried a sorta psychogenic twisted-up tummy because of the familia unrest, well as holding an aversion to some foods, so I could not leave the table for hours. The dinnertime punishment sessions happened quite often, and although my emotional brain would claim they occurred 80% of the darn time, factually 50% of bird time is probably closer to the truth for the year we lived there. Regardless, it happened a whole-whole lot, by my measure.

There was no love from either of those two senior people and they yelled a lot, especially my grandfather. He was a very harsh man, he scared the shit out of me daily. We could not do anything right in our grandfather's eye, not a single darn nothing. Thurman followed Beth and I around much as he could keep up with us, then whenever escaping out of sight, we ran fast to get away before yelled at to come back this very minute, *or else*. Beth and I made a few part-time friends in the Motor City that year but got yelled at for leaving the yard or being gone too long, or something else, seemingly so they had the opportunity to have some *you are bad* hard rain fall down upon our little scared and confused pre-K noggins.

The arrangement in Detroit made no sense to me, no sense at all. Out of the blue, our father was gone, our mother was gone, and our sister Laura who is three years my senior, was gone. Our infant newborn baby sister Christy, well, she was held aside in our out-of-bounds grandparent's bedroom, so I believed her gone too, them all but Beth gone, gone like dead and forever more gone-gone-gone because what the hell did I know I knew a whole lotta nothin', no one told me fricking anything. There whilst then my disdain for grownups kicked into high gear, aka *Fuck The Adults*, although too young to realize what was happening around and within me.

The worst moments were at night, during the short time before falling asleep.

My desperation for BigBird to come back and rescue me was overwhelming. I prayed and prayed and prayed, hoping today he would return…please today, please today, please let today be the day, but I had not much a nothing to hold onto, not much a nothing by my standard. The only sign, the only response, the only answer showing itself was just my sadness that came to lay with me.

Although holding little to no understanding at the time, looking back I name it as heartbreak sad, supreme unfairness, and tired of the struggle, mostly fed up with the gosh darn dinner table decree. No way did I want to scare Beth, which was hard, but tried to muzzle the sadness deep within my pillow, not letting her hear me cry myself to sleep every single night.

Mirror-Mirror Why Do You Hate Me So?

Yes I see, yes Mirror I see the glass is clear yes I see...
Yet Mirror, why always same-same the seeing?

Storm clouds shower thy under-roof's nest
Sans shelter, sans safety, sans calm
A rare outing, apart thy guardian's wing
Some sunshine sprinkles atop thou's madness
Near here, only near here my dear, fear the mere moment
No-no, oh no, no-no-no, I hear thine momma bird's song a calling...

Mirror please, I hunger hearing no more
Mirror please, now cut off these ears
Mirror please, I seek seeing no more
Mirror please, forever fog thy darkness
Please Mirror please now forever blind these eyes.

Some Nests No Home

Once collected from Detroit, still occupying our first Baltimore area Hillsdale Road haunted home, after a while the bat-shit-crazy mother bird then nothing but gone from our family forever-n-ever institutionalized…*bye-bye mommy*, father bird removed his wedding ring for finality and we fled that damn monster house. Veritably, BigBird did what he believed right, both protecting us from our mother's insanity, while himself adjusting course to attend night school for another five years. The resulting edginess flooding my father seemed unbearable, even to me as a young ignorant seventh-year child. He was by far away more than home, and even when around, BigBird yelled into my perceived ears more than he spoke.

The wobbliness followed wherever I went, me invariantly unsteady within my own shoes.

Though a shaky roof teetered overhead, I felt relegated apart from any shelter, and far-far from whatsoever warmth or support. Maybe I was just being weak, a wimp, a little fucking biddy crybaby bird, IDK. With the familiar sheets of bitchboy downgrading rain pelting me, finding nowhere secured nor space zoned calm, I fled, I ran.

I ran fear filled and resentful
I ran then fell then ran til lost, castaway adrift and underbelly exposed
I saw, I saw only slightly…I saw only darkened skies
Darkened skies, darkened skies as the bare warm noontime sun shone

Not running to get un-lost
Not fueled by hope
Not desperate to find
Nor frantic to be found

Again fleeing the frights
Again eluding the yelling
Again pissed off mad I was, atmospherically disregarded
Again, again this catastrophic unsteadiness

I relied on nothing, I turned to no one but mine some the paltry resource crumbs
I sought shelter, I coveted comfort, yet still running, yet still lost
I then froze, I then froze and I hardened, I hardened cold like stone
I hardened cold like stone, immediately then the chipping away began

My self-belief fractured, factually crumbled, my-self succumbed to nothingness
Unbothered the nothingness, unbothered the skip-over, worthless even the bother
Worthless the breath, worthless the existence, this slur worthless the worry
Worthless…worthless to a lesser degree than even muddied parking lot gravel.

 Chapter TWO

Credits

The best I can be

Seems worse than this now

My hope has been shattered

I wither and bow

Happy ending, already over

No longer do I wonder or worry

My job done, my piece spoken

Nothing good left here~ end of story.

One Lived Within the Cuckoo's Nest
With ease, the horrified rising of detail visiting my mother at Spring Grove mental hospital surfaces, total terror…my memory all too vivid on the damn matter. Approximately, I would align the institutional encounter to, hum…think-think-think, my first way-inappropriate adult horror movie when I was too young to be allowed in the theatre. I was seven or eight years old at the time and the revulsion not so much my mother's bound behavior albeit horrible, but more so the screwed-up ostentatiousness…the aggressive maneuvers of the other patients. Following my first Spring Grove visitation, most adults scared the fuck out of me for months, maybe a year or more. Four peer inmate patients were talking to themselves loudly or shouting indistinguishable words, yelling wildly and lunging toward me as my father and sisters walked through the building to find our sick mother. I claim four patients because I remember with detail where the scary people stood or sat, as they lunged at me like a scattered band of demonized jack-in-the-boxes. I recall the faces lurching at me with visible malicious desires, and I see still what the off-kilter adults wore as their hands reached out aimed at my waist, my shoulders, my neck and my eyeballs. Two wore medical robes, two had smocks, two of them wrapped up tight with socks or slippers, and the other two wearing a second layer gown or medical shirt underneath and scary bare feet.

There it was and I within it…seemingly close to hell as I could ever imagine a place to be. I never wanted to go back there, ever, not even to visit my mother, no way forget it.

I considered the enclosed space a house of horrors, a place of purified evil, constructed and existing for one sole purpose…to scare all remaining life out of me.

I think to have only visited Spring Grove twice, at most. Perhaps it was just once and because of extreme fright I suffered the first time, such fear could be spilling over and flooding my memories. If I honestly walked into that bedeviled place more than twice, pretty sure I'm blocking that shit out.

As a youngin', I never went to haunted houses except one time in my late teens when I thought I could handle it, but left the place terrified and running towards the darn car. The anticipatory sensation of something or someone reaching out to grab me from a dark place was way too much for me to handle. Hum, wow, I never associated deep harmful fear of haunted houses and visiting my mother in Spring Grove until this minute, so weird. Perhaps this newfound realization of fright factories simply reinforces the comprehensive notion I was despondently scared when younger, well…maybe. I never went to another haunted house, ever. I rode a roller coaster in my youth but only once, it freaked the fuck out of me…I thought some mad monster was driving, planning to crash and kill us all just for fun. I rode a mini-sized sky-top rollercoaster on the roof of a hotel several times one night in Las Vegas when I was deep into adulting shoes, proving to myself I wasn't so damn scared anymore.

Scared of what, you may perhaps ponder? Lots.

I've never started watching a horror movie on purpose that I made it through to the end. Weirdly, I have attempted to watch *The Exorcist* a handful of times…I can't clearly explain why, perhaps entertained by the epic cage match battle of the angel and the devil, but I never finished it without pausing, walking away a while and returning hours or days or weeks later. That kind of intentional frightful shit deeply bothered me, it rattled me to my core, and honestly still does, thanks but no thank you very not so much.

In middle school one class-in-session day, I cut out and walked to the nearby Reisterstown Road Plaza by myself to see a movie, any movie, simply to kill time. I hurriedly chose a new theatre presentation featuring a swimmer and their big pet fish. I liked ocean life, so I paid the money but ran out part way through, walking home scared and fearing every little cavernous crack on the sidewalk and every poisonous leaf bellowing down from its tree. The next day I could not build up nerve to lie in the bath or sit on the toilet. It was actually a real problem that stuck with me for months…the movie scared the bejesus out of me.

Several times as an adult I have watched *Jaws* all the way through, demonstrating to the giant great white shark I am no longer afraid of him reaching up through the toilet and eating me ass-first.

Apart from my regarded movie and the terror faced inside Spring Grove state mental hospital, I remember my lack of comprehension at the time…why did my mother have to live in this place, in this place, loud and crazy, in this place, forbidding and grave? My immediate thought struggle also frantically wicked…simultaneously I wanted her held far away, her who supposedly mothered us. She must belong here for some reason and, well, um, well…I tried to suck it up, hoping she never comes back looking for me. And so it was, and so it became…my mother was angry at us all, very angry. Especially she was spiteful with my father who did exactly what he had to, once Patricia lost complete track of her mind. Much later, my mother's official diagnosis was sold to me as paranoid schizophrenia, her condition possibly brought on or somehow negatively influenced by childbirth, so I heard.

Our mother was entirely convinced our father the pastoral Father was the devil himself, literally.

The momma bird Patricia's behavior was dangerous, dangerous for everyone.

Bye-Bye Monster House

I do not remember what my father told me about my mother, at the time. Perhaps he did not say much of anything. My mother was gone, and I understood she would not be coming back. Once she left for good and it sunk in to my grizzled bird brain, I embraced the sans-mother notion as…just fine by me. My mother changed, she became someone I cared not to know. I did not want her back, no way no how, my mother scared me.

Once the monsterly mother was locked up for good, we moved, we left that haunted home…bye-bye monster house. I hoped the new Whitney Avenue motherless bird's nest was a *no-way-allowed non-monster house*. Perhaps unspoken, but I understood we moved so our mother could not find us…moved so she could not find us which was fine by me, perfectly fine by me actually. I figured we moved far enough. We landed several miles away to the north but more so east, still within the bounds of Baltimore City…hello big corner house on Whitney Avenue.

Digging into the reality of my youth for a minute, well…yes I was an asshole to my father but I was not necessarily mad at him, hah, no, I was mad at the world. Truthfully I was minorly fearful and majorly angry with all adults, my father just got in my way more than anyone else. Also I hated reading, or so I believed, well, I did not read, neither for fun nor assignment so honestly, I did not know what books contained for me, I knew no better.

I held the impression of being unfairly punished regularly, well…but maybe I was a predisposed supreme asshole and brought all that shit upon myself honestly, IDK. Mostly though, I was scared. I was scared and felt very alone. I did not feel safe and was fleeing my mother, even after she was locked up. Maybe I was a run-of-the-mill average punk bitch boy whitey kid but had a hard time settling down and resting within the truth of the matter, thus unable to see clearly. Or I was unable to calm slightly so I kept my guarded walls up high…hard to cipher, hard to know, hard to say.

Arid Scenery
After the motherly monster was released unto the world, then spent some additional bonus time back in the looney bin, once more they for fricking shit's sake let her out. After some while's time and rather remarkably, mother Patricia worked as a server at Howard Johnson's restaurant in southern Baltimore County. The motherly person also received a special deal on attached *HoJo's* housing, her one-bedroom secured roof motel residential being only a few-minute walk to the restaurant. We visited her a couple times both at her motel apartment room and as paying restaurant customers. BigBird was mostly on the go and balanced cautiously atop a thin fiscal line, so it was rare when we afforded the time and money to eat out, even at a quasi-truck stop diner like HoJo's.

                                    Chapter TWO

Remarkably times two…Patricia got her driver's license, bought a car, and was able to get some time off work. She wanted to take my best friend middle sister Beth and I back to visit her hometown of Zanesville. I did not at all want to go but the grownup units conspired. My father allowed the trip only if our twenties or thirties-something neighbor dude Tom chaperoned.

My mother agreed and off we went, planning to camp once we got to Ohio. Tom lived next door to us on Whitney Avenue and having him join us was one of the best choices available, I suppose. Tom's role was to make sure no harm came to Beth or I when around our mother. The roadtrip was 350 miles each way, so we made the drive easily in one day. This was the first time Beth and I ever stayed in the presence of our mother without BigBird nearby since she was long-ago locked up. In my mind, it was also the first opportunity for something to go horribly wrong.

Beth and I ran off and played whenever we could, me not wanting to be around the monster-mother for fear of what she might do or say. We briefly visited our mother's mother, the reduced Grandma Grace in Zanesville, then began our return back to Baltimore. The entire trip was unnerving while empowering, like cockily surviving inside a cage alongside a hungry untamed lion for half an hour, without being eaten alive by the snarling beast. I slept in a tent and sat in a car for days, not otherwise arriving home in a body bag, thus fictionally delivered back to my father murdered by this lady who assaulted me most my entire life, a situation as verifiably weird to me.

My mother and I had none-zero tender moments during the trip, not one slight minute of togethering time, which was just okey-dokey fine by me. We shared in no deep talks, barely engaged in surface conversation, and the strangeness of the journey now being difficult for me to describe.

> The woman driving was someone of supposed significance, but the nondescript feelings between us were as vacant and void as the arid highway scenery we sped past.

I thought not of what I missed or longed for from a mother. I held no hopes or dreams of make up or recovery with my mother, hell no, not none…I just wanted to get home from Ohio without Beth or I being physically injured by this woman who supposedly brought us to life.

Some weeks after returning home from Ohio, we got a phone call from HoJo's one day. My mother did not show up for work and restaurant management could not reach her. BigBird drove to the motel and with help of security officers they gained access to my mother's room. My father never told me what they found inside, but my mother never worked at Howard Johnson's again, she never lived in that motel room again, and she went back into the mental hospital, again.

Stay Put, and Lock the Damn Door
One off-target oddball day Patricia would be assaulting us, physically attacking us, and some rather reserve yet otherwise random days we tried to fake-play nice with her.

Although my deep-down hope was that my mother would grow to not ever want to hurt us again, seemed like something was foundationally wrong, like she forever broken…the monsterly mother bad-bad askew, possessing something infernal inside her, some dark thing never to be overpowered by no earthly human like never.

She landed a job, again, got a driver's license, again, and bought a car, again. The monster mother rented an apartment not far from us in northwest Baltimore City, technically her paltry place was in the Park Heights community. Our father who was trying to help us gain some sort of slight relationship with our mother, he took us to her apartment a couple times to visit the misaligned monstrousness.

One day at home after school, there was mayhem.

Weirdly, our father was in the house when Beth and I arrived home with notebooks in hand…BigBird intensely glaring straight at us soon as we walked in. He gave us no other instructions but to stay put inside, and lock the damn door. BigBird then sped off in his car. We had no idea what was happening. Based on my father's frantic out-of-sort emotions, I knew something was horribly, horribly, horribly fricking wrong. BigBird was physically shaking, a condition I never saw my father in before, ever.

Beth and I held so many questions, but no one to ask. Laura was not home from school yet. Christy was somewhere else, I do not remember where. So best we could, Beth and I tried to stay busy because the way our father left us, I knew better than to tempt him with disobedience and travel outside. I hoped Laura came home soon because I was sure she could help us figure something out. Around then, although we often picked on Christy, the other three of us Laura Beth and I seemed to get along ok. Laura was pretty cool and someone that frankly I looked up to, although hah, I would never otherwise admit it. Laura was a well-rounded young lady with strong academic skills and rather independent…I guess being the oldest of four alongside a single parent will do that to you. Laura was downright spunky, with a fire drive and energy that impressed me. Laura was also tough, physically tough, and no one seemed to stand in Laura's way with what she chose to pursue. Laura was later a lifeguard at a public swimming pool and went on to graduate from high school proper, she the only one of us four who finished the 12th grade, or maybe even 11th.

Back at home with the damn door locked, things got weirder. Our father was not home, he did not call, Laura was not yet home from school, and Christy was still missing. I do not remember the detail but surely Christy should have been home already. I confuzzled if Laura had gone to help with Christy, but the all-good-things scale was far-far off balance. BigBird was gone a relatively long time, an hour or more, and I for one became increasingly worried. I sensed true physical danger in the air…bloody, so I withstood the urge to go out and look around.

The bizarre feelings of not knowing why Christy was still off somewhere really bothered me, and I assumed an out of character protective attitude concerning my littlest sister. Finally, there was noise outside our house…a slight ruckus. The front door got flung wide open, I heard it slam into the wall.

Fast as she could, Laura ran inside screaming and crying frantically, absolutely fucking hysterical, like someone was chasing her, she rushed straight into her room and slammed the door furiously. Beth and I looked at each other in terror, I could not for the life of me understand what was happening. I barely saw my big sister run by, but her combined physical and emotional state entirely shocked me. My nerves, my frights, my fears, and my legacy nightmares instantaneously flooded me.

Something was tragically wrong, something really bad just happened, like someone was coming to take us away, like someone got bad-bad hurt or worse, I knew it, I fricking knew it.

Never had I heard saw or even imagined Laura so distraught before, not even close, ever. Beth and I froze, scared to speak or move, desperate for our father to come home soon and hoping like hell he has Christy with him.

 I heard more noises, then realized the front door was still open. There was additional commotion, but I waivered to go take a look. I started to get up but then sat back down protectively while purposefully, right in front of Beth.

Someone else was in our house.

The creaky front door closed slowly. Softly but with a pronounced latch-shut click, I then also heard the damn dead-bolt get locked, from the inside. A single set of patiently-placed footsteps came into the house towards us, almost tip-toeing…oh good lord.

 BigBird stuck his head in on us briefly, not even looking our way, somberly saying he is going to start making dinner. I did not know any better but his face-fractured voice sounded like someone just died. Our father asked if we were ok, he said we are going to eat early, then slithered off without even allowing us to answer his question. I knew better than to approach my father but I scooted closer to the kitchen and tried to listen in. BigBird picked up the phone and had a quick quiet conversation with someone, then hung up. About ten minutes later, Christy was dropped off and she came inside to play. I was highly confused but more so, genuinely relieved to finally have our littlest sister home safe and sound. Then when our father called us to the table, not even a place was set for Laura. Laura did not come out of her room the rest of the night. I do not remember seeing her out of her room for a couple of days afterward. I wanted to ask BigBird what happened, because I was too afraid to approach Laura, but for whatever reason, well…it seemed inappropriate to say or do anything, least for now.

 The zip and sparkle Laura carried around for all her days prior, wherever she went, whatever she did, *hum*, well, how do I say…it was gone, forever. I never saw the fire my big sister once had return to her, not even much later as an adult and mother herself. From what I perceived, something was taken away from Laura that day, something never to be replaced, never ever never. Laura hid after that for a long time, she hid from the world. Most everywhere she went, Laura hid. The timeline seems like a year or more…she hid, she irrefutably hid, cowering both emotionally and physically.

In a matter of mere minutes that afternoon, our mother removed Laura from school against her will. School administrators ignored instructions my father explicitly gave them, and they surrendered my sister to mother Patricia. The monsterly mother then restrained Laura, which I am sure was no small feat on its own and actually, I cannot even understand how the mother-monster could have overpowered my big sister. The full-blown malevolent-monster-mother-monster swiftly sundered my sister, and, well…truth be told it was, it was a dismemberment of sorts, perhaps inflicting the deepest of lacerations, a maiming to the likes I've never known, oh motherfucker wait a sec…I need to shut the fuck up now. Myself I was not there and I know not Laura's feelings, so I will detour any more dirty-assumptive emotional detail.

Knowing the players within this certifiable horror scene, the violence is hard for me to describe.

The monstrosity-of-a-mother drove to Laura's school and told education administration she was there to pick up her kid. Patricia said she needed her daughter to leave with her early for an appointment or some other made-up bullshit nonsense. As the story goes, Laura refused, and my big sister started freaking out, insisting in front of school personnel that this lady is not allowed to be near her, and the school needs to call BigBird. Patricia Swope Bird insisted they release Laura to her, and convinced school staff to help forcefully put Laura into the monster's car. I have to imagine it was a wild and physical struggle. From what I remember told to me, Laura was literally screaming and fighting them the whole way, fearful of what her momma-monster would do to her without the mighty poppa BigBird there to protect her.

After school administration watched the screaming hot mess drive off with Laura hysterical inside the car, someone mentioned like *hum*…debatably something was a smidge odd, you know, maybe something a wee-bit off, maybe just a little, maybe not, *so oh bother ho-hum*, they called BigBird at work to check in with him somewhat maybe. No one inspected the file to notice Patricia Lacey Lou Swope Bird is no way-no how not allowed to come close to Laura, something similar to what I imagine is a modern day restraining order. Evidently my father, who could curse like a goddamn motherfucking son of a bitch sailor when unraveled, my father the Father shared some choice toxic words with school administrators during the phone call, so I was told, then BigBird left work early to look for Laura, but found me and Beth at home first.

The site makeup of such-a familia crime impossible to know, can't exactly for-sure now say what happened, because the entire ordeal never spelled out to me in detail, nor was I fricking there. So much emotion was involved, and it seems some moderate physical violence occurred back and forth in opposing directions. Patricia drove to her Park Heights apartment and took Laura inside. It still baffles me how this warped woman was physically able to drag Laura around, I don't at all get it. Our father arrived and seeing the monster's car out front, he forcibly entered the apartment, collected Laura, and brought his damaged daughter back home to us.

                    Chapter TWO

Monster Pat may or not have bounced off a wall or two, might have even fallen down some steps during the exchange, so I heard, but impossible to know the factual deets. The malicious mother went to jail that night and maybe back to live in the hospital for a while, IDK and did not at all fricking care, she hurt Laura badly…very, very, very fucking badly. Months later as Laura began to heal, I would be slightly offended but still confused over the matter…when asked about her mom, Laura would simply say with nonchalance, "My mother's dead". My big sister's speak was delivered emotionless and non-descript with zero qualifiers, then Laura would just move on in the conversation. Our mother did not die that day, well, factually in Laura's mind or so I presume, Laura no longer had a woman in her life she associated with as a parental figure whatsoever.

We did not entertain my mother's presence remotely close to our family life ever again. Meaning, we would not visit or proactively engage with her. Also, the monster-mother would not pop by our house again for some time, after that ugly-ugly day when she yanked Laura from school. Maybe BigBird scared her when he showed up to rescue Laura, maybe my father even hurt Patricia physically, maybe my mother realized the severity of some of her own problems, IDK.

Maybe the motherly monster was in jail or held at the mental hospital for a long time after that, thus afforded no chance to contact us even if she tried, I'm not at all sure.

The next I caught sight of her, my mother operated unobtrusively downtown Baltimore as a homeless raggalady. Patricia never again rebounded in a fruitful way…she didn't have her own apartment again, she never drove a car again, and she never held a job again. That dark-dark day when Laura was physically brutalized by our *Mommy why can't you just love us* mother, it appears we all suffered some damage too, by my measure. Damaged how exactly, you might ask? Well…hum, pardon me my precious but sorry, I know not the words.

How horrible simply horrible…this hurt.
How quickly the warm blanket gets shed.
How forceful this damn darkness returns.

Center rests only on a razor-thin teeter.
Center weighs heavy on an unsettled mind.
Center been lost 'round here quite a while.

Maybe…on the verge of falling pushing or jumping.
Maybe one other day something else happens here.
Maybe someone where and else sees themselves a one sunny day.

Dark Face in the Crowd

Once Patricia Lou tracked us down after we years-earlier fled the monster house, I honestly felt like nowhere was safe, certainly not under any roof or behind any walls, not even at school. I believe such unsettledness regarding building structures and my mailing address pushed me not only deep into my head, but also far into nature. Any exposure in the woods felt safe to me, certainly safer than any house. The flexibility and freedom of being outside was pleasing and extremely comforting, even when it was raining. The more time I spent alone off and about was additional time I desired to move further and further away from wherever I sat emotionally. At home I had met thine the rogue villainess and I mostly chose to run, attempting to find sunny solace, or least, hah…separate myself from such dark-dark-darkness.

If accustomed to only seeing parents up close, if never required to pick them out of a crowd, it's kinda hard to explain. Riding my bike in proximity, I often encountered my mother downtown or plainly out and about. From blocks away, I quickly recognized the monster mother. Her shape unique, her frail stance clearly identifiable, her walk more like a painful shuffle. Carrying her life around in bags and carts, the crooked haunting haunch of the homeless mother bird eventually dropped her beam, then gazing straight down at the sidewalk wherever she went.

This my gift though, here my skill and one I am thankful for…the heads-up radar perception of my motherly person. Much less than half the time, I detoured around and she never saw me. My corrected action, my adjusted course, my evasive maneuvers all executed to self-protect…aiming to deflect away from the mother of monstrosity. However, not always existed a way around yet I would attempt to sneak by. Hah, no…she had the same even better ESP as I did. I think most parents have such gift, radar of their children.

I'd speed up when trying to escape contact with psychotic Patricia, splitting between cars in traffic, or frantically beeline for the opposite side of the street. Before even into her field of vision for shit's sake, I heard her deep resonating tone, "…Rooogggger…". Later into my teens this setting was rarely violent, awhile always confrontational. My primary aim…stay away from the menacing manifestation of the monster-mother.

For most everything she demanded or asked of me, I could not give her.
For most everything I desired or needed from her, she had nothing to offer me.

The atrociousness of the mother-son dysfunctionality quite frankly did not even reach a measurable amount of manageability, never mind approach anything close to reasonably livable.

Life was, well, oh flipping frick whatever…as it was. I tried to keep rolling best I could, running, sheltering within, and trying not to collect too much worked-up fear worry or loss concerning this woman who could have been a functioning part of my life, but no way wasn't.

It Being Said

The feelings of a motherless child
And a long-long way from home...

What does a motherless child actually feel like?

And does their house, any house, really feel like
home?

Well, I ask...how could it, factually?

Disallowed Dreams

I dropped my bicycle on the sidewalk out front and strutted into Mount Washington Pharmacy heading for the candy aisle. Barely did I catch a glimpse but that's all it took…the vivacious image entirely mesmerized me. Although a far-off unrealistic fantasy, then while there I absolutely fell in love with dirtbike motorcycles. Ablaze with colorful speeding adventure, I was drawn to the magazine rack, I had no choice. I dared not look away, the close-up racer dude image was intensely powerful. The sport came to life in a split-second, and my hopeful emotions splattered the page. The day's candy budget was blown on the magazine instead, and I zoom-zoomed home to explore its insides multiple times, cover to cover. Not possibly could I dare imagine to escape this dirtbike thing, the sport hooked me straight away. For years I rode my pedal bike speedily every month to buy a new gasoline-engined dirt bike magazine. The dynamic nature of the activity left me awestruck, factually an overwhelming sensation I struggle to now try describe.

Commandeering such a powerfully beautiful beast of a machine, one seemingly capable of going anywhere and doing anything…

Navigating such bizarre and treacherous terrain…the built and purposeful bermed turns, the tight twisty singletrack courses through the woods, the jumps oh the jumps, the gloriously huge send-you-airborne jumps…

The radical movement, the contrasting neon colors, the velocity, the presumed sheer speed, the ferociousness of the competition, all of this all of it more attractive to me in ways I could not even yet understand.

My love affair for the moto's however was restricted to admiration from afar. Not thus-then soon and perhaps at no time in the future would I ever own one, so I believed. A few neighboring Mount Washington guys rode their dirt bikes aggressively through the many offshoot trails alongside the nearby railroad tracks. Thereupon fucking hell the dilemma began…my truthful position spoke to me clearly, the motos drew me closer than close, but, well, true-truth these Mount Washington guys did not like me, so I had to stay back.

I never got too close, neither to them nor their machines, although there was nothing more in the world at the time and for years I desired more.

Dirtbikes, a device capturing me, carrying me off to a better place, setting me down softly amid a newfound land of prospect and dynamism. Truth clear 100, the chance of becoming a motocross racer was a desired escape for me from an otherwise unsettled world. Coveting greatly something different in my life, something better…yeah-yeah for sure, far-far off and apart from where I elsewise lingered dormantly, artlessly forlorn. I needed such dreams, I required such hope…somedays only selfsame the propensities kept me going.

 Chapter TWO

The motocross racing stars donning my mag covers and pages seemed larger than life…stronger, skilled, superior and moving with effortless ease like expert ballroom dancers, both extremely competent and confident. Every aspect of the sport appeared grueling while rewarding, and the attractiveness for such demanding endeavor moxie drew me in entirely, I had no choice.

One day beyond, this my drive…I will go somewhere else, do something else, be someone else, someone more secure 'n better than this little biddy shitty me anyway. Much more rumbles 'round me in such regard…some unique added sayings splay-showing what afforded me breaths to breathe towards such dreams, but so sorry My Precious-My Birdy-My Love-My Life-My World, I know barely some furthermore the proper tell-to-show words.

Affixed in my forward vision…this opportunity for me to do something, so I thought.

The chance for me to pursue an alternative life, so I believed.

Like perhaps spaceship off and discover a more conducive world, so I hoped.

I embraced dirtbikes in a way brand new, this and resoundingly…my number one big-ass cool thing. Back when around ten years old I informed my father I wanted to race dirtbikes. BigBird did not squash my thoughts, and had spoken with no implied negativity. Rather, he was the master of the reality check…"First you need to own one". Such bring me down to earth nonsense fettered my enthusiasm momentarily, but I bird rebounded quickly. The unspoken but predetermined understanding was that all monies for such a possibility would be self-generated by me my lonesome, without any financial support from my father whatso-no-way-ever.

When eleven, I saved what I thought was enough money to buy a dirtbike but my father said *no, no dirtbikes none*. I was no way not allowed to buy a dirtbike, not even with my own damn money.

Dumbfounded, dreams decimated, aspirations flattened, threadbare and reason to rise scrupulously extracted from my nucleus, uh yeah…all thus-then maintained resentment for my father turned quickly into straight-up angered hatred.

Backless

My world big or small is as I make it

Completeness, contentment fleeting, I'll take it

Mountain meadows upturning my frown

Kitchen tables, holding me down

Scars, addictions, and battered love's poison

I'm here alive now, I suppose for a reason

Roundness pushes me off my axis

This colossal bundle I carry, leaves me backless.

Three

~

Fallen

Felled, by the Most Vicious Inescapable Enemy

Chapter Three, Fallen ~

A tree, a tree, she the tree…existing long before I was born, surviving me by most likely a century or more.

When I lived with and upon her land she greeted me, she welcomed me, she drew me in. She offered herself flagrantly without judgment, without restriction. She called and she called and she called for me, both when close and far-far away, she tempts me still awhile forevermore.

Whisk-whisk sway-sway play-play…I hear her, I hear her summons, I hear her song inviting me.

I yearn to run to her, if for a brisk fall moment…I desire to hug her, if for a short springtime minute…I appeal to lay upon her branches, if for only a survived summertime hour.

I was not yet understanding her voice, her song, and without anything better to do, I found myself often sitting upon her massive bruting limbs…sitting, just sitting. In a strange way or so I dare propose, she the tree was a welcoming almost magnetic refuge, a place open to me under any skies, despite the stormed fury all around.

Bizarrely weird to realize now decades later, but she the tree was one of my first mothers, providing genuine kind and protective nature awhile her nurture. I had much a nothing sheltering me in my youth, not much a nothing by my measure, nothing so forceful and stout I might dare avoid or destroy, nothing, no, not even myself.

My fear fright and rage ran wild for several years before we moved to Whitney Avenue, although barely old enough to recognize its nametag, and then, pardon the echo…I clearly remember only one thing the first day we arrived at the new to us hopeful no-monster house, she the tree.

I do not remember my bedroom at Whitney, still…no clue. I barely remember the kitchen awhile truthfully, probably the photographic memory because of snapshots still existing, that of our father-led brood in the cooking room. I remember the living room area on our main second floor where we regularly watched our mother out the windows argue with police, before her taken or shooed away. I remember the outside black metal staircase, I remember the yard, the basement, the most always closed stand-alone garage, but…well, all I remember about move-in day is her, just her, she the tree.

I saw her there.

I heard her refrain.

She called me over immediately.

She wanted to tell me something.

She wanted to play.

She wanted a hug…me too, I wanted a hug, I wanted a hug too.

She grabbed me, I grabbed her back.

She gave me a kiss.

She held me, I held her back…she holds me still.

I have never seen her somehow or another until now, decades from when she first loved me in these ways. Back before in such approach, I love her in more ways still, our shared comforting connection…she be my first and only front yard tree.

Weird to connect the dots of these sappy surface but true meanings in the depths of my head and heart, hence I declare this dictum downright religious. That Whitney tree, she grabbed my hand awhile my full attention from day one and produces these here tears upon my cheeks now…such beauty, such poise, such attractiveness, she melts me.

She drew me in…hers much the stationary safety I felt in my youth, least for my first twelve years, she the tree. Yes of course, here and there sprang humanoids around but they came and went, in and out and undulating about within the confines of my functional world.

The only honest hint of operational soundness I felt was when upon her jagged skin her bark, only when playing upon her, only when sitting with her, only when standing nearby…yes a fricking tree.

Only here now and wondering how do I recognize the comforting love I longed for, hah, I nonhesitantly admit such frailty…I mindlessly expose that I found such power love and grace within my silly front yard tree, because zero inception existed elsewhere for such enchantment, such sorcery.

Coming 'round to the now…with the assistance of deep insightful diction from my dear gal pal Friendwords The Ferocious Lucy Fucking Brown, I recognize my life and all our lives exist alike and in the shadow of a tree. I adopted Lucy's reference to us akin a tree, and now hold my image soundly as the associated *Tree of Life* descriptors. The deep-rooted loving embrace I experienced decades ago at Whitney Avenue in she my tree now comes full circle. Full circle to when a few years ago with my pal Lucy Fucking Brown, I asked her how does she envision this her life rebuilding process as we worked on it together and she mentioned, "Let's start with the roots." The Ferocious Lucy's wicked-wise foundational assimilation blew me over then, as it does still today…*sigh*, humbled I am, teary-eyed, and thankful for such wondrous people in my life.

She my tree I felt blessed inward our connection…something so big, so strong, something not existing nor capable of threatening or hurting me. Guess if falling from her ever, breaking my arm or cracking my head I could say different, but fall I did not from her perch, me never slipping from her arms, she did not let go of me nor did I want her to…please-please tree release me not, never ever never, please tree just hold me close.

Hanging out in her our big front yard tree one afternoon, two neighborhood girls approached when I was thirteen…hum, perhaps quite possibly maybe I was actually twelve now that I glare intently at the timeline, not that it matters anyway oh well whatever no bother but, um, well…the Pimlico 'hood girls said, "Here, try this".

I thought it was a smushed-up cigarette.

Marijuana was absolutely *to a T*, the gateway trap door to all other drugs lay waiting for me, and it did no way not take long. From the minute marijuana and I went on our first date, it was hyper apparent weed and I would be an item for a long time. Grabbing ahold and forcing me to the ground under its weight of comfort escape control, neither did I want my new sweetheart pot to let go of me. No not none authority at home nor school held me accountable, so I was off 'n about on a perpetual free reign exploration. Considerations for a life of addiction was not a conscious maneuver, but because perhaps the void amid my head and heart, multi voids factually, my drug use beanstalked fast.

A couple weeks beyond while buying some pot the guy said, "Here, try this." I asked him what this stuff is called and he said "Speed." I asked what this stuff does and he said, "Makes you feel good", which was the only sales pitch I needed…sold. So therefore and then my relationship with amphetamines began, aka uppers, aka stimulants. After fully embracing pot and speed, I tried everything offered or put in front of me going forward, everything. Because and since I liked the stuff so much, and by this time hating all adults so much and resenting my father so much more, I figured why not…*why not*, I had nothing to lose. I was tired, I was so damn tired of the running and cringing and hiding, aka being frightfully and physically chased by my mother plus evading all the gosh darn yelling, so why not…now I could slow, now I could rest, least a while, *so why not?* Pot and speed made things better in my head and heart, so why the frick not? If these things felt good, and right, and better, and more-more is out there, then some of the other yet undiscovered stuff might even be better than pot and speed, so why not?

I anxiously awaited the additional discoveries.

Hallucinogenic mushrooms came next, and in rapid procession running to join the party was thy 'shroomers three sibling chemical LSD's. I tripped often, amongst and in between the other drugs I feverishly consumed. Although the acid trips were somewhat entertaining, it was not my favorite thing to do because of not always in control what amixed inside my brain. I ran to the woods, or bopped afoot the tall office buildings, or rolled about the streets doing drug deals when tripping. Once overboard acid trips began wrecking the day, *oh well*…I learned to layer other substances on top, then chemically exceeding the bad parts of the trip, sometimes anyway, and bringing the journey back 'round to the good. The downer pills aka painkillers then slinked into my world, followed in short order by the cocaine. Money for such feel-good luxuries appeared from my working jobs, from cash I could steal or swindle, or came from the drugs them lovely selves as I purchased larger quantities and sold some excess, me helping myself to regenerate more of my personal consumption supply.

Rather thought provoking was the true-true executive summary, it made no reasonable sense to just consume without also selling the stuff, meaning it made zero sense *not* to deal the shit, no…not…none.

Once within the come-come-conducive crowd, many drugs were openly shared, often in ridiculously giving ways. If together with friends and someone had a $30 bud of weed, everyone was welcome to partake in the puff-puff. If someone arrived holding a $350 eight ball of cocaine, most times others nearestby were welcomed to take a seat afront the lay-down mirror. If someone pulled out a $50 bag of assorted down-downer barbiturate or up-up-upper speed pills, everyone was welcome to stick their hand in and grab some. Most dealers introducing me to a new strain of street poison gifted free samples, while the togetherness and community supper mentality was ridiculously welcoming and, duh…intoxicating. Yes of course, like are you kidding me or what, not everyone shared. Not everyone possessed such positive preoccupation. Not everyone was honest, fair, kind, or even non-threatening. Some people held knives and used them, some carried guns and used them. Some stole, some cheated, some robbed, some maimed, some killed thoughtlessly, expressly for drugs hence the added pack-'em-full pocket money.

My quest for more-more-more mind numbing substances at times was frighteningly precarious, to say at minimum. I walked into neighborhoods, houses, rooms, basements, alleys, and got into cars where I did no-way not belong. I entered places and spaces where I knew no one, where I was the only person sporting my skin tone for blocks, maybe a mile, but frick to the no that ain't the goddamn point, merely speaking to my drug-fueled walk-in-anywhere bird brain brashness. Small-man circumspectly I waltzed in where everyone in the room knew without question I had hundreds or thousands of dollars cash in my pockets, and no fucking way this white boy was packin' a piece or would be bold enough to use it…no way, not here, so they knew I was the prey that day. Let me be crystal-crystal-as-fucking-clear-ice-100 here…this is not a fricking white or black thing, no fucking way forget it. I got relatively ripped off more times by whitey people than cousins of color. I love us all total truth 100…all sisters, all brothers, love us all, us all as one, one blood one, one Garden of Eden Mother one, one Bob's Your Uncle evolutionary spark one, fucking one all one, one…love…one, fucking period.

For about six years, Mark, Danny and I were inseparable, well, that is until drugs entered my life, then the pursuit and travel necessity of substance deals pulled me away from the neighborhood, and I began to lose touch with my two next-door pals.

Unseen and unknown to me at the time but intrinsically, I was trying to escape the everyday all-day wobbliness.

Scrambling to free the familia frights, I tempted my own existence. Although drugs much yanked both feet out from under, they more so blanketed me with a warmth and soundness I had never known. *So oh well whatever, bring-bring-bring it*…therewithin I was, operating the chanced drug danger game and no end in sight.

Running Down Roger Ray's Rage

My father enjoyed a robust workshop but his tools existed for his woodworking pleasure alone. Maybe if embracing Mother Earth's yield of tree products and not just my preferred tooling and fooling with metal, BigBird's stonewalled position would have changed, or, well, workably not. For all I might wonder he used woodworking as periods of alone and away from us kids time, and would have forbid me to participate anyway, impossible to say. Even trying to borrow a screwdriver, I got yelled at and sent off. When attempting to minorly tinker anywhere in the basement, his shouts chastised me for being where I did not belong. As it may have happened I was an irresponsible punk who could have broken his tools or hurt myself, but generally I felt entirely incapable of doing anything right. Although somedays tinkering in my father's shop is all I attempted to desire, and preferably alongside the masterful woodworking big bird himselfdom, such practice with or without my pop Ray Norman around was entirely outlawed.

Once paroled from the Gladys & Thurman Detroit Youth Reformatory late into my fifth year, and after BigBird blew the monster house coop for good with us his brood underwing, I was angry as hell, hum, but why? Perhaps pissed because of the dinner table nonsense in Detroit, feasibly fuming over letting our sentence run long at grandparental prison camp with no opportunity for appeal, maybe mad concerning the general yet still misunderstood situation surrounding my mother, maybe my ire-rage sprouted organically, maybe innocently plain scared and lonely, IDK, but I had a real temper.

Once approaching my teens I stopped building model cars. Each toy hotrod was heavily modified from stock, yet most often the piece of plastic art never survived my short-fused hammerfist...hah, only then it's display case was the inside of the tall kitchen trashcan. Without the blow-off opportunity of model cars, I had nothing left to smash. Requiring a readily available Roger Ray relief valve, hum, think-think-think...well, I had no one to bully except maybe my youngest sister Christy which regrettably occurred from time to time, and I was way too much of a wimp to mess with anyone else.

I never discovered or imagined the factor of self-harm cutting...contrarily today I might not have arms left to clack with.

I felt far too unsettled to shelter for long inside, meh...elsewise plausibly there I might lay demobilized from the world, squirreled away and hiding within a deep dark basement crevasse. My thoughts concerning the back-when-madness matter rumble around inside me feeling weirdly awkward, well, misaligned even, that is when digging in directly to explore my era-correct emotional exasperation. Such idealized conceptions and related truthful disclosures are an interesting journey no doubt, and frankly not ones I much considered before, not before you asked your wicked smart question my beautiful Birdy.

Well, let us see...yes for certain I was still mad as hell at 12 years old. Honestly it appears I released my anger through the only found channel, the drugs themselves then became my weapon, unleashing their heavy handed self-abusive blows, me mindlessly discharging my outrage into the swirling disorderliness of my internal drug storm.

Lower Rung

From the beginning of my memories, I felt exposed. I thought myself no-way not allowed but omitted, me outside the class of inclusion for every worthy contact point possibly interesting me. Held behind presumed acceptable boundaries, I thought myself barely of form but rather, guilty…guilty of occupying valuable terra firma real estate.

How was I allowed to stay? Seems I should not have been.

My literal gaze dropped, awhile my gate slowed, *ah fuck it*…I ran from my motherly fears and fatherly aversions not as much, I withered, I unbloomed, I nestled close to my drugs. Other's eyes I did not meet or greet, none, they noticed me not, oh well whatever who the fuck cares nobody…a speck of insignificance by definition and design that was me.

But then, oh wow hold up, but then…Miss Freed factually shocked me. I thought she was withholding some sort of hurtful agenda. It was like so weird, she refused to look away…her stare tractor beam locked upon my corneas. Although I glanced towards the door thus outside windows often, trying to shake her over-obvious attentiveness from me, I couldn't. Never meeting this lady before, I straight-up began to sweat, feeling beads of nervousness roll down the small of my back, just before they hit the waistband of my Levi's or until I hunched forward and my t-shirt collected them.

Minutes earlier with some sort of scolding disapproved tone, I was yanked out of seventh grade English class by one of the do-as-your-told-or-else manly office staff…*bring your things young man*…then escorted down the hall like parading for the gallows. I completely tuned out after instructed to *walk this way, we are going to talk to someone*…oh fricking hell whatever which to me meant more punishment. I thought soon to be tossed out of school, *I'm getting suspended again, maybe expelled*, my self-mumbling then continued…*oh well who fucking cares anyway not at all me*. I held only a faint flippant care in the fucking world about much of anything, except my drugs.

As Mister Executioner led the way my thoughts fled the building, pre-planning a couple drug deals for early afternoon, or quick as I can get the fuck out of here, can't happen soon enough far as I was concerned. Literally I shook my head, trying to clear the confusion fog and reorient…where are we for God's sake going? Huh what the…this ain't the principal's lair, jeez, we were nowhere near the office, what the hell? The surprise location for such soon upcoming-to-Jesus academia lashing was a weird one, not even a classroom, hah, more of a broom closet.

For like fifteen confused minutes I could not for the life of me understand what the hell this Freed lady wanted, but one thing beamed through crystal in that tiny dark room, and it was extremely unsettling…she would not look away, dang it, I could not shake her. An offbeat foreign sensation came back to visit, something quite frankly I had abandoned over eight years past, the creep of hope.

Well then and gosh dang no…Miss Freed still did not look away, wow, she was not fucking with me after all. Several months clocked by until her eyes finally convinced me, for once in my life thus-then far, someone saw me.

My breakout creative writing class with Miss Freed was engaging and for the first time I had reason to stay in middle school, instead of cut out after homeroom in favor of the drugs. Maybe, maybe there really was something to this lady. Maybe there was something to her, and oh wow wait a minute, does that mean…does that mean maybe there was actually something to *me*? I fought the notion, but after some days it gained slight dominance over my doubt. Why does she care? She seems to want very little from me. Well, maybe, dang…maybe I am worth being seen. But how on this earth could that factually be true? My mind wadded up. Might it possibly be that maybe I am worth one fractional shit instead of none…well, I struggled to even try to believe it.

Bizarrely, the same week I met my new creative writing teacher Miss Freed, I looked up through my PAB long hair to notice my woodshop teacher Mister Thomas was locked onto my eyes too, oh motherfucker…I turned to hide my tears. What the hell is happening? Where are these people coming from, these adults asking me questions then legitimately waiting for me to answer? So weird. First I had a teacher who really noticed me, who saw me, then I had two. Well, maybe…I sheepishly poke-jabbed my finger against temple with the thought, and it was just a slight maybe…maybe not *all* adults sucked. These two teachers sure didn't suck. Months went on and my maybes tried graduating to hope. Hope, hoping I could like keep this mystical thing going, although I arm wrestled the foolish notion…like for how long will Miss Freed pay attention to me like I was not less than nothin'?

Like for how long could I real-really hold onto a friendship with Mister Thomas and frankly, dang it all…I for all that is like true in this world wanted more from him than I could ask. Big bold and tender Mister Thomas seemed the person I needed in my life, but more than needed, I wanted, I really-really wanted. I wondered, hum, does he…does he have room at home in his house for me? I won't take up much space, I won't eat much I promise, I won't be much of an asshole as I am at home to my biological father, I'll try to listen, I'll really try, please just keep showing me that you care Mister Thomas, please. Yes I'd miss Beth but I could see her at school, it wouldn't be so bad.

Wow, my brain began to splay…maybe, just maybe.

But then, but then and I'm such a fucking idiot, what was I thinking?

Hope…*hope*…are you fucking kidding me, hah, false hope more like.

Fuck this, what a joke.

The first domino to fall was Ms. Freed, she turned on me. I further pulled back from school after that, and barely saw Mr. Thomas for the remainder of seventh grade. The following eighth grade school year I did not have woodshop, so the short yet revered connection with my make believe false father was then lost too. Oh well what the fricking hell ever…back to my old loser-loser lame-ass loser self while factually, the dismantled hopeful maybes made for now even a lower status. Lower, like sliding down the personal pride ladder and wishing I never gave myself any damn false expectations to begin with, aka Fuck all the Damn Adults, aka fuck this entirely fucking shitty fucking life.

Nothin' But Shortcuts

Once booted from creative writing class and thrown back into gen pop of eight-grade English, I entirely withdrew from the unsavory subject. When I *was* there, which was becoming increasingly rare, I literally slept through the period, my head flagrantly laid atop my arms on the desk. At first, domestic language teacher lady was annoyed, but she slowly began to just leave me the frick alone. Once in a while she'd repeat then yell my name and knock on the desk to wake me up, her then quizzing me with some stupid *pick-out-the-noun-in-this-sentence* mystery question. Haha, the joke-joke was on her, I soon became the laughingstock of my peers, me unable to find the person place or thing because I lacked the knowing. Teacher lady resented the damn disruption and she just left me to my bird naps after that.

Amusingly, I held some sort of ignorant intrigue with Geometry, seemed the topic was somewhat mechanical. I enjoyed fixing my bought-with-own-damn-money bicycle and lawn mower, hence I held some slight interest with this new-fangled-to-me math class. Sadly, Geometry began to inflict more damage than joy, I just didn't fricking get it. Despite trying to follow along when in attendance, I had no flipping idea how it at all worked. My teacher seemed to care less than none about me or the damn persistent red marks on my homework hand-in's, and oh well what the hell's damnation ever. I failed every assignment, well, until that is I grew so fed up I ceased all after-school work attempts with vigor. One day walking home, after screaming skyward out loud *I'm so fucking stupid*, I entirely gave up on the once intriguing math subject. Throughout all my legitimately dysfunctional school years, Geometry and middle school English were the only classes I verifiably failed, thus requiring me to attend remedial summer school.

Stupidly, Baltimore City truant officers were overly engaged with us punk ass bitch summer school students. During the normal school year, no one seemed to give a single-solo fucking fuck if I showed up or not, but for the first week of lackey summer term, that shit was like a prison sentence. The summer makeup classes only took a couple of hours each day, so I planned to just serve my time…attending all five days so to avoid getting roughed up by the wannabe academia cops.

Throughout school thus-then far, Geometry was the only class I wanted to learn about, but sadly, it seemed my brain just didn't work along those problem solving mathematical lines. Defeated, I committed to just camp out in summer school and hide, sitting in the back of the classroom and avoiding weird new math teacher dude at all costs. For fuck's sake and it was like the second or third day…we were in the midst of an in-class work silently by ourselves session. Some kids scribed feverishly on their front-and-back worksheets like it was a fricking race, while us others gazed lazily off into space. Hah, me I flagrantly pushed the dumb-ass foreign-language-math-assignment paper and pencil out of my way then opened the motorcycle magazine I brought with me. Dang, I never saw the dude coming…he slid the sheet back into the middle of my wooden work surface and just started talking, "So how would you begin to start solving this first one Roger?". Besides startling me that he even knew my fricking name, obnoxiously, he also placed the #2 pencil back into my right hand, then awaited my reply. *Oh what the fuck bro*, or so I thought…*just leave me the hell alone*, but he didn't budge except to hold his ground.

Ok jeez whatever, I almost mouthed out loud then continued to mentally ramble…*let's get this stupid shit over with.* Still holding my mag, while glaring straight ahead with contempt, begrudgingly I opened my mouth, not giving a fuck how my response would be perceived, "I have no idea dude". My blurt-out was delivered with slight disgust, disgust in myself that Geometry had gotten the best of me all year, and now this disgrace was scheduled to plod on for another eight fricking weeks.

Bracing for the guy to slap me up the backside of my head, I continued my roll cockily. Planning to only take a slight break from my moto mag review, I closed the monthly and laid it in my lap. Sans all clue I started scribbling a jumbled rat's nest with my damn pencil inside the left page margin, this my only response to the many puzzle-by-number equations laid afront of me. Probably sensing my disgust, Mister Way-Smarter-Than-I'll-Ever-Be remedial math dude kneeled down next to me, right next to me actually, his knees planted solidly on the skanky public schoolhouse floor, and his shoulder literally brushing up against my t-shirt side ribs.

Dude, really, you're touching me bro, what's up…oops, my pent-up internal weirdness fuck-the-adults factor almost said that shit out loud.

He tried to help me but I flustered, "I don't know" was my somewhat repetitive out-loud ramble then continued…"I really don't know, I don't know how to do it, I just don't get it". My tone and volume approached some sort of pathetic pupil argumentative snapback position, and several classmates looked up awhile let out their slight gasps, probably expecting teacher man to scold me as did I.

Without missing a beat, he kneeled tall and told everyone to go back to work. Then, weird, creeper dude moved in closer, almost whispering in my ear…*Just try it Roger, come on let's do it together, you can do this I know you can.* Oh for fuck's sake, I turned away…fuck, fuck, fuck…a tear rolled swiftly down my right cheek. I didn't think he saw me crying, but probably. Why the hell does this dude even fricking care, cannot he see I'm straight-up fucking brain dead stupid?

My emotional cauldron bubbled, I was mad at him for taunting me but more so, angry as hell with my own dumb-ass fucking self. Wiping my second and third tears away with my pencil hand again I said, "Dude, I…have…no…i…dea."

Teased Allowances

My pursuit of big-ass cool thing motorcycle racer dreams did not cease or soften oh no, I was determined…me bugging the shit out of my father whenever I was home. After two years of incessant nagging, after already doing drugs but still had *some* money left, my father agreed to go look at dirtbikes with me. I feared he was screwing with me, but ran full-force forward when BigBird was willing to entertain the idea. Unfortunately for me, much of my previously saved dirtbike money went towards drugs already.

      Chapter THREE

Although desiring a motorized two-wheeler greatly, factually greater than continued breaths themselves, I thought my father would continue to disallow it…I slackened my moto-saving purse strings. No longer did my fiscal means allow for a new unit purchase, so I searched for used opportunities. My neighborhood friend Ryan Gniazdowski had a worn dirtbike for sale and although I wanted to buy it unseen, my father required we have it inspected by his favorite auto mechanic. I was jumping for joy in anticipation, thinking the bike would be mine immediately, but my father held alternative plans. It would be another two flipping weeks before we could even see the bike.

We booked an appointment with my father's mechanic well as arranged the inspection with my pal Ryan. Graciously, BigBird purchased special brackets to fit onto the rear bumper of his boat-sized station wagon so we could transport the dirtbike. With the motorcycle wheel cradles securely affixed, Ryan allowed us to take the bike and have it checked out. After an acceptable bill of health, I handed Ryan $200 cash and the Yamaha YZ125C dirtbike was mine…oh my God I could not believe I finally owned a dirtbike, could…not…believe it. Although attempting to go riding straight away, there were more gosh darn delays. I was not allowed to ride without a helmet, I had to purchase my own brand-new red steel fuel can and also the required mix-in oil that goes into the gasoline, and I had to find some heavy duty boots. Another week ticked by and then for Pete's sake finally, I set off on my first ride.

Keeping the engine off, I pushed the moto for a mile toward Mount Washington, nervous to break the law by riding my unregistered and unlicensed off-road vehicle on the street. For a handful of rides I followed the same routine…push the bike to the railroad tracks then take off to the north on the adjacent gravel access road. Numerous options of riding areas existed, trails where other dirtbike guys pre-established makeshift practice courses in the woods. I became increasingly bold, rolling the bike fast as I could, then jump on sidesaddle and coast towards the tracks, then eventually, ah screw it, starting the engine and riding straight from the house. Not too many cops crept around…I rode on the street slow and quiet as I could, so not to draw undue attention to myself or piss off residents. Mostly I wanted to avoid the cops, thinking they would impound my bike and I doubted my monetary means to get it back. Eluding cops is never a good idea by my measure, but I did it when I had to. The gamble were the risks taken to get away quickly once the pursuit began, knowing backup would be called.

Certain I wouldn't have much chance to escape the helicopter, once chased I rode stupidly fast and my knobby tires were ridiculously unsafe to speed around on the pavement.

Thankfully I never crashed during the Baltimore City copper dirtbike squad-car pursuits, nor got captured. The moto rides, all of them, were grand adventures. The terrain and conditions provided increased challenges every ride, and most always beyond my ability. I made some chanced maneuvers but mostly remained calculated and safe. I knew what I did not know, I knew what I was not capable, and I knew the margin of error to get hurt was slim.

I learned to work on the bike by experimentation…modifying the carburetor, changing tires 'n tubes, replacing the chain and sprockets, and adjusting the suspension. My draw towards competition was heavily magnetic, exactly as I admired for years by this time. My one-path attraction was racing, period, but my father did not clearly understand my intended trajectory. After my first few rides, I already owned proper motocross boots, pants, pads, jersey, gloves, goggles, kidney belt, and I planned for my first race. The next conscious mention of racing was made with a matter of fact awhile assumed tone, but I was handed a hard *NO*. Enraged, I demanded to know why I was not allowed to race. The reply was quick and simple, arriving in legacy language of parental humanoids, "Because I said so", end of conversation.

Relentless with my intent to compete, I attempted supplemental activities to perhaps fall in good graces with my father, like sometimes doing what I was told or requested, or *like I won't even cut school this week at all I promise*, well, sometimes. Becoming clear were BigBird's background facts…one of my father's best friends was crippled in a street bike motorcycle accident. BigBird told me at one point he already did me *a huge favor* letting me own a bike to begin with but *no, racing was too dangerous…no way.*

Months later my father's answer to attend the licensed motocross track race sessions was still, *no*. Visibly he became tired of my pointless pursuit. I grew bitter, outwardly angry while internally rage filled and downright resentful. I *needed* to race, I really-really needed to, to me this fact chord was strikingly sound. Although sure yeah whatever, just riding the bike was fun, but no, truthfully the riding all lent itself towards racing. If I couldn't race, I was missing the escape and elevation I so desperately sought.

I wanted to stand face-to-face against a contest tougher than me, something challenging me beyond all known limits. I desired to get away and stay away from my shitty existence while pursuing something brand new and exciting, perhaps then able to rest with the satisfaction I did something, that I accomplished something on my own, not some-thing others demanded of me, but something for myself.

Cutter

Contemplating school comprehensively…my classmates, moreover the group setting intimidated me. Teachers or more accurately Fuck The Adults, they threatened me. Hum, well…being behind walls actually harmed me, quite 'litrilly I felt strangled by the closed windows and doors. Oh wow, this is new, holy fuckballs…I feared remaining stationary in class much because I perceived myself at great risk indoors, oh hell's bells I never realized that before. School seemed unsteady, unsafe, like I was trapped, held captive with arms behind my back at risk, especially after what happened to my sis Laura. I was devoid of faith in the truth of adult's words, fucking all of them, intrinsically my position concerning grownups founded on my arduous aversion to yelling and unfairness.

Although not faced or struck with much direct conflict at school, I was horribly unnerved and itching to remain nimble on my feet and moving. Shortly after starting to exercise this mobility, however truant, I gained the preferred taste for my school avoidance routine. Throughout elementary school grades 1 through 5, I recall school life being easier, or least not so hurried or demanding. My two different elementary schools were smaller, quieter, and our classes stuck together across all lessons. The peer relationships were snugger, more genuine perhaps, and certainly for me, less threatening. My propensity for cutting absolutely intensified once forced to manage additional teachers, classmates, and complex course schedules. Also regarding middle school grades 6 through 8, once the academic requirements heightened, I quickly fell behind by default of my commonplace nonappearances.

Snowballing then was my favored irreverence for taught lesson plans, thus missing the chance for assimilated learnings.

The more school I missed, the less concern I held regarding the damn matter. Concurrently, my interest to somedays even show up and attempt then became mostly but forever decimated. Although I knew not the oath of case, least partially as it appeared to me at the time, my father did not seem bothered by the school I was missing. Certainly the dynamic of only one parent around created a general freedom and independence for me, heightened by the truth BigBird was busy in his personal life besides his fulltime weekday job. I avoided being home because of my general unsettledness and now I clearly see the same wobbliness existed for me at school. Maybe it's no wonder once finding drugs I dove into the substance abuse cesspool head first.

Deep Hazards

I never occupied real estate as a tenant in someone else's brain before. Mostly I dare to imagine what other people are considering in their upper story. Now intentionally pausing slightly, and trying to think-think-think myself, but yes, fairly certain I am about to see someone die in 5 seconds…, 4…, 3…, 2.

The Baltimore summer heat was scorching this day, no real breeze to speak of, and not a single cloud within sight. Without relief from wind or clouds, the best place many of us punk teenagers could imagine for some physical refreshment was in the water. The cleanest water around our neck of the woods in northwest Baltimore City, apart a proper swimming pool, was Lake Roland. Swimming pools were not an option because no pools existed in the yard of anyone I knew, our families had no money for such extravagance. There were private club pools here and there but it was policy, yup…*No Punks Allowed.*

Located within Baltimore County and barely over the city line was Robert E Lee Park, owned by Baltimore City Parks and Recreation. Inside the 500-acre Robert E Lee Park sat the 100-acre Lake Roland, an old city drinking water reservoir. Lake Roland is rather serene, with a lush charming tree cover on its shore, but with a sometimes-funky odor.

Additionally some dead fish floating about here and there but no buildup of algae and otherwise, not the worst place in Baltimore to dunk yourself into on a hot and humid summer afternoon. A 120-foot-high dam sits at the south end of Lake Roland. The stream below the dam is popular for fishing, especially after Maryland Department of Natural Resources stocks the mini river with trout. Almost a mile away from the dam to the north is a railroad trestle bridge crossing the lake, sectioning the lake with two-thirds of the aquatic acreage resting north of the railroad bridge trestle and one-third of the lake residing south of the trestle. To reach the trestle, we walk on wooded trails and navigate the loose bed of rocks alongside the railroad tracks, making the iconic location inaccessible by automobile and a decent walk from the closest road or parking lot.

Standing atop the trestle this warm summer day, I challenged my commitment to exist responsibly within truthful reality, or not. My glare looked down on the water to the cryptic lair of teenage folklore…the bloody shallow abyss. For years I heard of the unknown concealment…an underwater graveyard entombing an old railroad car and other dangerous construction debris resting just below the surface. Several times before this day, I looked intently into the water off the trestle, trying to see something down there but had not yet caught a glimpse of anything dangerous lurking below.

The hazards, as I have been warned multiple times, will probably kill me if jumping into the lake from the trestle, and I was quick to heed those warnings.

Jimmy Pennington, who was also my older sister Laura's boyfriend, and Jimmy's friend Johnny Powell were about to jump into the water from the trestle. I was trying to brace myself for one or both of these guys to jump in and not come back out, ever. I never saw anyone jump into the lake from the trestle before, and respecting the adolescent mythology, I was certain this fact for good reason.

Experiencing another death right afront my face a couple-few weeks earlier, although bizarrely different, I was still rattled by the tragedy. So standing on the trestle watching Jimmy and Johnny about to jump into Lake Roland, was not something I thought I could adequately carry on my shoulders. My shoulders are the things I try to force away from my ears and pull back from my chin much as humanly-with-consciousness-on-top possible…trying to stand taller, keeping my head and eyes up, and facing the world with a little more intention, alertness, preparedness, and confidence I could collect otherwise, well, least at-times I tried to try. The burden of the death just weeks ago still weighed me down. I walked around with a pronounced emotionally distraught slump, figuratively and literally, being solely responsible for causing the tragic and horrific death about nine feet from where I stood at that earlier time.

Evidently, I was about to extinguish another life here at the trestle, in a hot second or three. I wanted to open my mouth and warn Jimmy and Johnny about the tales I heard for years…the deadly debris in the water barely under the lake surface. Up on the trestle as the presumed timeclock in my head counted down on a current but not-for-long human life, I was puzzled and thought this cannot be real. How can this be real?

                              Chapter THREE

Did I really do what I just did and now this guy is going to die because of me? Like the entire ordeal was a dream, a bad dream, well…another one of my nightmares actually. I was scared, confused, and I honestly began to doubt truthful reality itself. I had to think, and think fast. Feared being perceived a baby, I did not immediately speak up about the life-depriving hazards in the water.

Not that I wanted to be like these guys, both really bad-ass dudes, but I hoped for acceptance, respect, and maybe even protection by them sometime in the future. Jimmy and Johnny lived in Medfield, the neighborhood a few miles south from Lake Roland on Falls Road towards city center downtown Baltimore, and adjacent to Hampden where my dad's church sat. Medfield-Hampden was a blue-collar working community and the toughest white neighborhood I knew of. Innocently walking down the main street in Hampden, 36th Street, aka *The Avenue*…even walking down The Avenue was a huge risk for me. Being rather weak and vulnerable, I made sure to never walk down The Avenue alone. Although I knew not of a standing dispute between Medfield-Hampden and where we stood at the trestle in Mount Washington, but perhaps some bad blood existed.

Me not residing in Mount Washington proper myself, but I adopted this 'hood as my home base for some years. Mount Washington pushed up against the city boundary with Baltimore County and is a middle-class white neighborhood. Technically I lived in Pimlico, on the fringes of the Park Heights community. The part of Pimlico where I lived was a mixed middle-class neighborhood, then on the opposite side of the namesake horse race track, Pimlico-Park Heights was primarily a black middle-to-low-income community.

My earlier years found me gravitating towards Mount Washington and further north into Baltimore County. North is where I sometimes escaped, running off by my unsettled solo self for some coveted alone time amongst the woods and open spaces, fact-one…my brief interludes attempting to quiet the noise and flee the scurry. Later into my drug years I stayed shacked up indoors or running around for the purpose of doing deals, consuming and selling illegal substances as buyers or me myself scampered in and out of the houses. Purchasing larger quantities of drugs required my travel throughout the city and surrounding counties, heading off into all directions day and night.

These guys Jimmy and Johnny hailing from south on Falls Road and now outside their home turf, earlier strolled casually upon the trestle scene without a seeming care in the world. A bright idea clicked in my head to somehow help them or perform a valued service, something they could not accomplish on their own. Not trying to necessarily create a scenario and now they owe me something, but rather offer some slight assistance so we might enjoy some tit-for-tat returning of favors later.

Glaringly, although I am about to kill one or both of these guys, my intent was quite the opposite.

I did not get along with the toughest of tough guys in Mount Washington. As my frequent drug transactions with them grew increasingly risky, I thought certain something about to blow up. Constant mild threats got tossed my way by the Mount Washington crew and I knew it a matter of short time until they came after me, one way or another. The guys in Mount Washington were the only reliable source to buy quantities of downer pills. Many times I bought from them bagful's of pills, selling whatever I did not consume my bird brain self to friends or connections in other neighborhoods. If I could avoid doing business with the Mount Washington guys, I would have because they scared the fuck out of me, but alas…they were the pill source and pills were a critical item on my daily menu.

Further away in the opposite direction from Medfield was the Pikesville neighborhood in Baltimore County, primarily a mid-to-upper-class white Jewish neighborhood. I had a handful of very rough and tumble friends, insane actually, in Pikesville if I needed help, but mostly they were too far away to assist or protect me.

Mostly our bepunking hours concentrated within our home 'hoods unless going to fight somebody, so gaining some allies closer to home might prove important to me down the road. I possessed only limited trace amounts of cockiness, stoutness, and barely enough boldness to go most anywhere and meet with anyone if I could either quickly consume drugs, sell a healthy-sized batch of something, or walk out holding additional quantities of illegal substances myself.

My ability to effectively navigate the growing tough situations both in the neighborhood and also within my drug transactions was extremely limited and I knew it…I was a wimp.

Digging deep into my head and when not bleeding, deep into my emotionally thinking heart, some of my life experiences were on the examination table under the shade of my punk-ass-bitch thinking cap around this time. As chaotic pressures mounted around me I attempted to quiet the noise, struggling to sort out the cluttered disorder consuming every area of my life.

Same-same true at the moment, grappling with this shit on the trestle…sure a human life to soon lay out right in front of me easily as the last glass of milk spilled, quickly as the see-by candle's flame now lost…my stupefied sense and sensibility then cast blindly out upon the darkest of nights. Although having the chance to speak up and stop this horrific tragedy, it was not really my place and besides, I was radically afraid of showing my wimpiness. I began to freak but was mostly holding it in besides some nervous outward pacing around. Thinking intently about one of two options: one, speak up and my actions might save a life today but then *you're such a baby* will be my new moniker. Or two, don't be a murmuring whiny-whiner…shut up…don't show my fear, and let whatever happens happen.

Jimmy, Johnny, and another friend rolled up to the trestle about fifteen minutes earlier, with three of us other punks already on scene, myself included.

Obviously, I knew Jimmy but never before met Johnny or the additional amigo. The new-to-me guy Johnny wore long jeans while his two pals were wearing shorts. Jimmy and the third guy both with shorts on, climbed down the steep and well-worn dirt path from the trestle to the lake's edge, scampered over the rocks, and were in the water a few minutes after arriving. Seemed to me Johnny wanted to go in the water but had no shorts for swimming. An hour earlier when druggie-stumbling up to the trestle myself, I noticed a pair of still-wet and recently discarded cut-off jean shorts tossed in the bushes, way out of sight. I mentioned to Johnny he should try to wear the shorts from the bushes and directed him, which he thanked me for. Johnny came back a few minutes later still wearing his long jeans claiming it's fine, he did not need to go swimming today anyway.

A disgruntled Johnny seemed frustrated the shorts were too big, no way the makeshift swim trunks would stay around his waist once in the lake, he said. We stood atop the trestle slightly silent…Johnny seemed to stew on the fact he could not go in. We watched intently as Jimmy and the three other guys played around in the water. A solo wooden picnic table laid adrift way out in the northern part of the lake, almost 1,000 feet from where Johnny and I stood on the trestle. The properly afloat picnic table served as a play and safety spot in the deepish water. The four guys were having a blast, jumping off the tippy table and racing around the lake. Their whoops of joy and playful voices made the wait time there on the trestle with Johnny rather uncomfortable. Jimmy swam back to the trestle and urged Johnny to come get in. Johnny declined, claiming he had no shorts, didn't really want to go swimming today anyway thanks, then almost indifferently, Jimmy swam back to the floating picnic playground. I felt the need to assist, to contribute, to help Johnny go enjoy the restorative cool water with his friends.

I bought a new leather belt the day before at the mall, from a small independent craft booth manned by an entrepreneurial big biker-looking dude, and my one-day-old belt was sitting aside over there…protected, safe, dry, and with my long jeans as I stood in my wet fitted makeshift swim shorts, which I brought with me. A quick evaluating mental chat with myself and I offered up my brand new belt to Johnny so the guy could go enjoy time in the water with his buddies. Johnny declined, saying thank you but he did not want to ruin my belt. It was kind of a fancy clothing accessory for me…it still smelled new and everything, that new cowhide smell, made from heavy thick brown leather and hard to bend with a big industrial silver buckle, featuring some slight stamping and engraving customizing the belt. I did not spend much money on clothes and chose the investment of drugs instead. I never bought anything nice to wear and honestly, I struggled with the idea to give up the belt, but it seemed the right thing to do, at the time.

Johnny and I stood around awkwardly and chatted a while, swapping a few generic life shares…I then blurted it out, "Just use my belt, please". He left for the bushes where the publicly available loaner swim trunks awaited him. Walking back to the trestle holding the waistband of the baggy shorts in the scrunch of his hands to show me how big and loose they were, we both laughed and agreed, no way could they stay on by themselves. I grabbed my belt and handed it to him, to which he once more refused but said swiftly, "Are you sure?". Emphatically I urged Johnny to take my belt and go swim with his friends. Surely, I was earning points with the tough Medfield guys now.

Johnny took the belt, gave me a gracious thank you and yelled out, "Jimmy come back". Johnny wanted to swim race his friend. I was giddy, proud and felt almost semi-tough because I helped one of the bad-ass dudes and maybe, they might now think more of me. My sister's boyfriend Jimmy Pennington was forever nice but we never did anything together without Laura around, so now was my chance. I was happy to help Johnny and thrilled to do something nice for the bad-asses, hopefully something they remember when me myself one day needs the help.

A little while later Jimmy made it back to the trestle from the picnic table, scampered over the rocks at the near water's edge, clinging to the bushes alongside the trail as he precariously pulled himself up the steep and now slippery mud path, using his bare soaking feet as traction devices. Jimmy made his way onto the top shelf of the trestle, preparing to high-dive back into the water.

Oh shit...what had I done?

Jimmy and Johnny stood atop the trestle shoulder to shoulder, fixed to jump into the existence-ending waters and thinking they would race to the floating finish buoy. I was most definitely sure they would never reach the picnic table, and positive if they jumped into the water from the trestle, neither of them would ever surface again, alive. Johnny was about to jump into the lake and die with my belt on, and my sister's boyfriend Jimmy will never be heard from again. Shit, I really screwed this one up. These guys would no way be doing this if not for me and my stupid belt, alongside my fucking uncontrollable need to try and help everyone.

I was not, and still not, a good swimmer. Never involved in swim lessons beyond basic at-school try-to-stay-afloat instruction, I just never learned. Most of my classmates were scared to death of water so not to be the oddball, I somewhat fake-avoided the frightening water too, me standing frozen against the dry sidewalls of the pool building and alongside my peers, trying to fit in.

My only swim safety classes occurred during sixth and seventh grade...we would walk to nearby Northwestern High School like cattle going to slaughter, soon to be herded into the athletic department's deadly concrete vat of chlorine.

Barely able to tread water, I can sometimes float on my back if luck is with me. I do ok with a muted sidestroke swimming technique but that's about it. My older sister Laura Lee was a legit certified practicing lifeguard but I was too busy being a stupid fucking drug addict to worry about learning to swim proficiently. Accepting the honesty of my swimming limitations, I knew to be no help in the water and would quite possibly myself drown if trying to help save someone else. There on the trestle and although minutes earlier I enjoyed not having my big sister around, now I would give everything I have, and even give up ownership of my entire right fucking arm for the opposite to be true.

　　　　　　　　　　　Chapter THREE

I ran 'round the tracks desperately searching for something I could use to help rescue Jimmy or Johnny once they jumped in, like a piece of rope, or a big tree limb, like an organic life preserver that might happen to be lying around. I could not for pissing Pete's sake find anything resembling a life-saving device and while off looking, I heard Jimmy count down...5, 4, 3, 2...I distracted and paused too long to speak up, possibly saving their lives.

Three...two...*one.*

There they go, oh fucking hell...on the count of one, they both jumped.

More than jumped, they both *dove* into the water from atop the trestle.

Holy hell, that is it, they are dead, they are absolutely fricking dead, I killed them. Damn it, I fucking killed both of them, I am such a stupid fucking idiot. I watched intently as they plunged headfirst into the lake, both with good swimmer-diver form, after pushing off the trestle about 12 feet above the water. My chest was spasming while wracked with anxiety and fear, I started to have trouble breathing and I knew this shit was about to get much-much worse. Intently I watched their entry point...the water still rippling now bubbling from the major disruption after the tough boys jumped into the glass-calm lake. My eyes frozen open with horror, locked and eyeballing the exact spot where they went in, waiting for two big poufy plumes of blood to appear...their now-life-void bodies soon to rise up and bob around like floating styrofoam cooler lids, after smashing headfirst into the railroad car or heart-stopping construction debris below.

For twenty full seconds, there was nothing, and a full twenty seconds is a hell of a long time while watching someone pass from breathing to nothing but dead. Try counting to 20 out loud and see what I mean. Starting to panic and pacing around with hands interlocked atop my head, I almost gave up on the entire experience. Wanting to grab my dry clothes, sprint back to the parking lot, hopefully find a phone, I planned to ring 911, reporting two guys died right in front of my face, and come arrest me because it's my fault.

During the hellaciously long 20 seconds, I could not understand what happened. There was no blood, no more bubbles, no floating bodies...there was fucking nothing. Did they get stuck in some big deadly piece of something not incising their flesh, causing them to stop producing breath bubbles, something holding these two strong guys down from floating back up? Where the hell did they go? If impaled by the life-depriving debris below the water, why no blood or bubbles? What the fricking hell is going on?

The other three guys played around at the picnic table while totally oblivious that I just killed these two guys. *Poof*...fantastically, they both popped up and surfaced side by side after the excruciating 20 seconds. But Jimmy and Johnny popped up out of the water not near where they went in but almost 200 feet away, hardly quarter way to the picnic table but swimming like mad and racing for the floating finish line. Really? Like are you fricking kidding me or what, they are still alive...I barely believed what I saw.

A mountainous-sized emotional weight teetered atop my shoulders wanting to fall off but no, I could not process my new reality right away.

Gee whiz…I guess no railroad car or construction debris existed in the water after all. I may or may not have pissed my pants as I danced around atop the trestle in horror, after the bad-ass dudes dove in. The fact they were both alive presented to me as crazy. And being totally jealous, now being totally judgy, their swimming proficiency surprised me. Surprised I was, that the two guys made time alongside their toughness to learn to swim so well, so what the hell is my problem? Why did I not learn to swim better somewhere along the way in my life then-thus far? Ugh…anyway and onward, I attempted to relax my hyperventilation and start breathing normally again. My heartrate sky-sky-high, I pressed both hands against my chest, hoping to calm myself a little and hold steady, sensing my blood-pumping organ soon to explode from too much time in the atmospheric-anxiety red zone.

Breathing long deep breaths, I closed my eyes and smiled, embracing the soothing sounds like a springtime poem…listening to Jimmy and Johnny's hands slap the water as they raced away from me, thy graces sent to heaven the Medfield boys popped up alive.

Maybe all the cocaine I consumed this morning made me paranoid, or the big stinky bag of sweet bud in my over-there dry long jeans pocket made me nervous. Because if these guys had died, I might have been charged for the drugs I was carrying. I also feared if they died, I would be held responsible. Yeah sure, it is a stretch to say I would be hand-first responsible for their deaths but fuck-to-the-yes-100 factually if not for me, Johnny would not have gone in the water this day, no way-no how period fucking period. Also if not for me, Jimmy and Johnny would probably not have dove off the trestle. Even if the police did not make a link between me and their deaths, I would blame myself, their families and friends would certainly blame me, Laura would probably blame me and she would most def be heartbroken.

I tried to recenter, dropping my thoughts of grabbing my clothes in a hurry or running off to find a phone and call 911. Shedding a couple of grateful near-death tears, I sat down atop the trestle and let out a huge and literal sigh of relief, yelling and cheering for Jimmy. My screams of encouragement bellowed across the lake and the three guys at the picnic table joined in, "Go, go, go, come on!", they shouted. I wanted Jimmy to win because he was so damn cool, but I also wanted Johnny to win so he could praise me, acknowledging he would not have gone in the water this day if not for me and my brand-new leather belt. I cheered louder and louder, building strength from the proceeding terror of Johnny diving into zero-life waters with my belt on.

Holy hell I really could not believe they were both ok. Now I was not responsible for killing someone else this month. I wanted to leave straightaway because the stress really hurt me. I wanted to go home, wash off the lake water, smoke pot the rest of the day, and try to shed the emotional weight I was carrying…the emotional weight toppling upon me both from this scare at the trestle, and lingering still from the death I caused a few weeks earlier.

    Chapter THREE

The death I caused several weeks before was acutely hurtful to me, still, and radically bizarre, at the time. In a multitude of ways, the incident is hard for me to talk about, even now as I clack.

When walking to the bus stop for school, I was several blocks from home. The episode at the trestle occurred after school let out for the summer, so this earlier Roger Ray-causing death story happened near the end of the school year. I walked down the two-way divided section of Ken Oak Road in Pimlico, this divided lane soothingly tranquil…one lane on each side, a large grassy median between the blacktops. This divided portion of road is continuous and stretches least a quarter-mile, equal to three city blocks or so. Most the houses have garages out back and an alley exists behind the garages, so the divided street section is rather pristine. Only a few houses feature driveways out front on the street. The long stretch of mostly continuous concrete curb is elegantly majestic, with huge homes spaced far apart and ginormous trees overhead, shading the entire area.

Heading for the bus stop, when walking east on the right side of Ken Oak Road divided, I see a cute little black dog on the other side of the street, bouncing down the sidewalk happily in the opposite direction. The small adorable dog looked like a Lhasa Apso breed, cute curly hair with a couple of dangling swirls in its eyes, no markings and all black. The dog projected a fun and light personality, almost smug, even from across the street, like a worldly but humble college graduate who knew something the rest of us didn't. Feeling good to encounter such a joyful dog strolling by, our merry moods seemed to meet, right there on Ken Oak. My sunny disposition not at all in the slightest hurt by the fact I am totally stoned at the time…same-same as every other day. The cute pup danced its strut alone, no owner. I whistled and urged little cutie pie to come over and say hi. Pup-pup noticed me immediately and ran across the road to come visit, as requested.

Canine reference…our family owned a dog once who I missed dearly. Our Schultz the doggie he was near-fatally attacked by an unknown pack of animals one late in the night but recovered, then died a year or so later.

This was about to be one of the highlights of my week, playing with this cute little doggo on the sidewalk. I dropped my notebook and bent down to greet cutie-pup, who had a gleeful smile on his face and running fast across the street towards me, currently only about ten feet away from my welcoming hands. I was locked onto his exuberant gleam then almost out of nowhere and on my side of the road, an MTA bus came speeding by and caught the cute little smiling black dog right squarely under its wheel. The bus completely flattened the dog, instantly. There was nothing left except the lump in my throat and the hole in my heart because I just killed this cute little innocent dog.

Uh, oh God, oh God…horrifically shocked, I grabbed my notebook off the sidewalk and started walking away extremely fast, fearing the owner of the dog was nearby or watching from their house. There was nothing for me to do to help the dog, no, no…nothing, he was flattened and I had to leave, I was traumatized.

'Couple hundred feet down the road in the direction I was going was my bus stop. The bus did not pause or slow down when it flattened the cute smiling black dog but then the dog-killing machine stopped at the corner. This section of Ken Oak is mostly quiet from local car traffic but a rather busy route for the large Baltimore City Mass Transit Administration busses, aka MTA. Least five different bus routes must use this road and almost every three minutes, it seemed a large MTA bus was rolling by.

One of the neighborhood girls I knew sat on the bus, she saw what happened and came running back towards the little dead doggie. I heard her screaming hysterically soon as she exited the bus. She was on her way to school and certain to have books with her, but either left her stuff on the bus or dropped it at the corner right when she got off, because as she came flying past me in the opposite direction frantically crying, her arms were empty. It must have been sickening to be on the bus and watch the happy floppy-eared 'dorable doggie running, then feel the bump-bump as her bus hit and killed that cute little dog, but…to clarify, the bus did not kill the dog, I did.

My semi-catatonic and shameful bewilderment almost crippled me…I felt absolutely devastated and before reaching the bus stop, I considered my plan to crouch down behind a parked car then jump out, sacrificing myself to the next MTA speeding by as balanced retribution.

Dreadful dead dog digression done now.

Back to Jimmy and Johnny swimming happily across Lake Roland…perched atop the trestle I cheered louder and louder for Jimmy and Johnny as they raced for the bobbing wooden finish line. The three guys holding onto the floating picnic table further out in the lake heard my shouts and were now excitedly cheering too, but for barely a minute, and…well…and then, and then, oh fucking hell on earth damnit all…no more cheers.

No more words of encouragement came from me or my vicinity, only sickened silence as I watched in disbelief.

Something was wrong.
Johnny Powell stopped swimming.
Jimmy Pennington did not realize at first, but his pal Johnny was no longer racing. Jimmy was head-down in the water and pushing hard for the picnic table. Johnny started yelling but his screams were incoherent, Johnny was not yelling words.

Horrible…horrible…something was horribly wrong.

Jimmy stopped racing, paused, and treaded water for about eight seconds as he looked back and yelled at Johnny, "Come on, what's wrong, come on"…and then…oh motherfucker, and then…slightly after I saw *it*, Jimmy saw *it* too.

Standing there mortified atop the trestle, I was looking down and out across the lake. Once Jimmy, this awesome dude, once Jimmy saw *it*, he immediately swam back towards Johnny like an Olympic gold medalist with twice the force and fury he exhibited moments earlier racing towards the stupid fucking floating picnic table. Jimmy got to Johnny, but Johnny was frantic. Johnny was not yelling words, no…he was, Johnny was gasping for air. Johnny could not breathe, and he was freaking out. From the trestle where I was, to where Johnny stopped and where Jimmy was trying to save him, they were only about one-third of the way to the picnic table from the trestle, at best.

Johnny thrashed about violently, trying to frantically climb on top of Jimmy, Jimmy who was trying to calm Johnny down and hold him up. Johnny could no longer swim, Johnny was having some sort of breathing attack. Johnny was panicking and he pushed Jimmy under the water in his own effort to stay afloat. Johnny was…well, Johnny was…Johnny was now in the midst of drowning.

I could tell, Jimmy was exerting supreme force strength and patience keeping Johnny atop the water, I could tell, but Jimmy needed some help.

Feverishly, I searched again for something I could maybe throw into the water, something to help save Johnny…I found fucking nothing.

Jimmy yelled at the three guys to swim over and bring the picnic table. That waterlogged but properly floating picnic table must have weighed at least 200 pounds. The guys at the picnic table did not understand what was happening or what Jimmy was saying, so I repeated the request, screaming at the top of my lungs across the water…"BRING THE PICNIC TABLE OVER, HE'S DROWNING".

The three guys tried to push and pull the table as they swam, they tried for about 30 seconds, which again, is a long time under the circumstances. All three guys then abandoned the stone-heavy table and swam over to help save Johnny. It was total mayhem out there in the water.

Appearingly, least to me, Jimmy told the three guys to stay with Johnny and hold him up until Jimmy got back. Jimmy was going to get the picnic table himself while the three guys held up Johnny. Jimmy took off towards the picnic table and it was immediately apparent to me, none of the three guys with Johnny had the commitment to save him like Jimmy did. Johnny pushed each guy under the water least once in his frantic attempt to stay afloat. They then backed away and Johnny fell under the water, after losing strength to keep himself buoyant above the lake surface, and within the oxygen zone. Johnny popped back up, still frantic, gasping for air while choking on water, and totally thrashing about. One of the guys tried to help him but again, Johnny scrambled on top and pushed the helper under the water.

The three helper guys then backed up further, away from Johnny. Johnny went under for the second time, only to quickly resurface once more. None of the guys then moved forward or lent a helping hand to Johnny after that. The end seemed near for Johnny.

I feel absolutely fucking sick to my stomach remembering the moments after Johnny resurfaced the second time, I feel sick even now as I clack-type it out. Meanwhile, Jimmy was hundreds of feet away, trying to drag the picnic table over to Johnny, but he could not do it, the table was too damn heavy. I felt like a worthless piece of shit standing atop the trestle idiotically, just watching all this shit go down. I could not find anything to help, and I also knew my weakness in the water as a shitty swimmer might endanger a life, not help save one. Other than offering some shouts of instruction or encouragement, I did fricking nothing.

Jimmy abandoned efforts to tow the picnic table back over to Johnny. Jimmy started swimming back towards Johnny with what looked like all his might. Johnny was still atop the water as Jimmy raced towards his friend who was drowning. With an appearingly perfect swimmer technique, Jimmy was head-down in the water, racing towards Johnny. Jimmy was not heads-up, not at all looking around or communicating whatsoever, he was nothing but decisively hauling ass back to Johnny, not even turning his head to the side slightly to catch a breath, well…there seemed no time.

The three guys around Johnny were treading water, probably wanting to help but possibly realizing this a zero-potential situation not only for Johnny, but also for themselves. Jimmy sped back towards Johnny and the other three.

With every drop of horrific desperation, I kept saying to myself…stay up, stay up, please stay up, as I watched Johnny struggle to stay on the surface.

I knew no better, but Johnny had already been under the water twice and I could not imagine he had much more fight left in him. Jimmy was swimming fast, fast as he could, it was obvious as fuck. Jimmy was about 50 feet away from Johnny when my chant of *stay up, stay up,* went silent. I had hoped Johnny could keep himself afloat long enough for his friend Jimmy to get back to him. Maybe with Jimmy there instructing the other three guys, they could get Johnny back to shore safely. But then, and oh for God's sake no…Johnny went under again, for the third time. The three guys nearby inched a little closer to where Johnny once was atop the water, but they mostly stayed still. Johnny had been underwater for at least five seconds by the time Jimmy sped up to the scene where the others anxiously trod water. Frantically Jimmy shouted, "Where is he, where is he?". From where I stood, the three guys kind of mumbled a reply to Jimmy about Johnny's location then I fucking screamed…"HE WENT UNDER, HE'S UNDER THE WATER".

Jimmy dove underwater immediately and was down for at least one minute, aka a fuck of a long time. Jimmy surfaced, took two huge breaths, and immediately dove under again, staying below for about 30 seconds this time before coming back up, seemingly done with his pursuit, shaking his head in disbelief.

There was not much to say or do after that.

I felt hit in the chest with a fucking sledgehammer, gathering my belongings as the four guys slowly swam erect, making their way back to the trestle from where Johnny just died in the water. Jimmy was talking to the other guys and seemed pissed, but I could not hear what they were saying. I helped a guy or two make their way up the steep muddy path from the lake's edge, but then backed away as Jimmy approached land. Nobody was really saying anything at that point, it was extremely confusing and the frantic episode seemed to leave us all with an emotional hangover. I felt shame, embarrassment, and held the responsibility of Johnny's death in my hands entirely. Consumed with astronomical guilt and thinking these four guys should blame me, with a dose of mountainous regret, I shut down and withdrew, basically saying nothing to no one.

We were all on foot and shuffled our things silently, but then without a word spoken Jimmy took off like a shot running towards the parking lot, I assume to call for help. Although I wanted to offer sympathetic words about losing his friend, Jimmy already took off, he was long gone and besides, I doubt any appropriate language existed to gift Jimmy after I killed Johnny. I left soon as realizing nothing remained for me there. Instead of walking back to the modest parking lot, I sulked solo south on the loose and unsettled rock bed access road alongside the tracks toward home, about three miles away. After kicking rocks while the while nothing but head-down hurt, I slipped into the bushes and took off my makeshift swim trunks. I put my long pants back on but had to hold the waistband of my 29-wide 36-length Levi's jeans in the scrunch of my hand because of course…um, well…damn it…well, because Johnny was still wearing my belt.

Tears rolled heavily down both cheeks then I stopped, hunched over from emotional stomach cramps, dry heaving, puking up a small mouthful of water, just totally fucking sick about my recent stupidity and recklessness which resulted in a life being senselessly lost.

Briefly I thought how damn hard Jimmy tried to save Johnny and I felt horrible for Jimmy. Then I thought of Johnny's parents, his siblings if he had any, his probable girlfriend, his relatives, his friends, and the children Johnny Powell will never have. I thought of all the people who are going to be devastated because I pushed Johnny to take my belt and swim from the trestle this day. The magnitude of loss consumed me entirely…ridiculously exhausted, I lacked motivation of any kind, and did not know how to feel. I guess I would describe it as mentally blind, incredibly insignificant, incredibly sad, incredibly helpless, and incredibly disoriented. Lost, I was so lost in my head…I wanted to keep walking the tracks south into the bustling inner city train yard, fall down, and bird-cease to exist.

We all tried to save Johnny. We really fucking tried. We all tried our best to help but our best was not good enough, not good enough at all, by my measure. Oh this fucking life of mine, I'm such a fucking loser, fuck it, just fuck it all, and oh great how now not so fucking wonderful…approaching my exit path off the tracks to the uphill walk home, I hesitated. Does it end here for me now? Doesn't it, shouldn't it? It probably should, this should be it, this should be all of it.

Unreserved to thyself and plainspoken to a degree not previously clarified to even me, I then considered myself a misaligned and disallowed broken fucking lowlife worthless punk ass bitch piece of shit loser...go ahead, do what you want, do what you want to me I just don't fucking care anymore.

Oh fucking well and what the fuck ever, I looked down the tracks, then up the hill. Abusively, fuck it all...I began my hike uphill from the tracks to lie down another way, allowing the drugs to totally have their way with me. I thought myself a bad person, like I owed the world paybacks on an entirely unachievable level.

Fitting Out

The entire school dynamic became almost unmanageable because of my truancy. I wanted to belong, I wanted to fit in, I really did want to show or feel some sort of competency or aptitude either in subject social or sport but I didn't know how. Hum, I'd best describe it as wanting or needing praise or validation that I was ok, that I wasn't below average, that I was a legitimate component of the larger class or sport dynamic. Sadly I unexperienced fuck-squat of any such thing, I did not achieve even neutral or minimal levels of existence, I was each day down, I was each day on the out.

On some level I desired to become a skilled lacrosse player, the area's #1 sport, so I joined the JV team. Sporadically I attended the workouts but as some form of punishment for missing previous practices, I had to run extra laps each time. Regardless of retribution coming my way, I suited up anyhow, ran my damn laps, then participated in a few game simulations and drills. Because I relatively sucked at stick handling, and partly because my truancy record made me ineligible to play, I sat on the high school athletics bench during the few games I did grace with my part-time presence. I never played a single second in a lacrosse game, ever. Maybe the tension of trying to be part of the lacrosse team was more deflating defeating and degrading than uplifting, hah...like geometry. Maybe I was kidding myself even trying to be part of the team, while simultaneously engaged in a fight with that naughty little monkey, maybe. I would not have given up drugs, but who knows what might have happened if they let me practice and play regardless of my piss-poor attendance. My drug use increased to a condition of time incongruence, and the fuse was lit. I somewhat pondered indifferently while cringing...how long would this timebomb take to blow, how long could this shit go on?

Yours Truly…The National Statistic

Although in transit stoned sky high, such semi-euphoric states were not enough to keep me in school. Drugs played the role of big unruly monster cat for four years, capturing and torturing the small scared church mouse of my attempted educational efforts throughout middle and high schools. I consumed more and more drugs outside the building's walls before first bell, then the cat & mouse gameshow began in earnest. By the time I entered high school, I existed entirely within a overbaked marijuana snowglobe.

Throughout sophomore and during my brief junior year, I listened sans concern to the vice-principal explain with his sprinkling of scorn how I was a member of the prestigious *A-B List*. Such classification is comprised of mostly medically exempt students who because of horrific injuries or illness miss more than 25% of the school year, except for me the pathologically truant one. This heavy-handed disapproval was thrown at me with great contempt. For all I could reasonably understand, and perhaps it was a slight stretch, but the administrator looked to desire my abandonment of school in sophomore year. No counselors came forward, I am not sure we even had such resources at Baltimore Polytechnic Institute at the time.

I was suspended on multiple occasions in 10th grade because of truancy but once entering junior year, I was apparently citizen number one on the public-school-enemy shit list. For the first couple months of 11th grade I was out of school more than in, both from cutting and suspensions. Mostly because of wanting to avoid conflict with the number two school administrator, I skipped school even when I would have preferred to practice with the lacrosse team or attend mechanical drawing classes. The struggle with school administration then became a ridiculous fucking game.

BigBird was summoned for a meeting with my arch nemesis, the number two in line school boss. My father rarely offered me even slight the applied academic suggestion, but maybe I earned that irreverence shit from him honestly. Slouching deeper into my favorite Baltimore Polytechnic dire straits office chair, BigBird asked if I was sure I wanted to do this. I pondered my befuddlements for three seconds then flippantly shrugged and muttered, "I guess". Without missing a beat, Mister School VP on the other side of the desk happily obliged…"Since it's obvious Roger doesn't want to be here, we should complete the paperwork and be done with it". A nervous system string chord inside me instantly twanged…I snuck a peek sideways and noticed my father's head nod up and down in response, then BigBird's eyes hit the floor, and stayed there. I freely admit my heart sank as the pre-filled school removal paperwork speedily slid across the desk, landing right in front of me, with a pen. "Sign at the X…", the school vice principal said and continued, "…then give it to your father".

After struggling to make it out of 10th grade and giving up on my junior year almost before it began, I then left academic institutions behind me forever and good riddance whatever.

Falling

Too quick to shut down

And recover at all

I sit alone and wonder

If there's further to fall

My here and now hurts

The failures and yelling

Life's getting worse

The ending is telling.

Motherly Attack

Once my folding urban hunting knife with its shiny five-inch blade began traveling with me, well, however slight, I gained some certitude strength, both amid my sketch drug deals and concerning my mother. No of course I did not envision the need to pull my knife on the monster-mother. If that lady somehow did snare me within my own blind spot however, I was so damn mad at the world by then, well, hum, is this true…would I have fought her?

Well, let me be real for a sec…by that time I do not think she could have kept her hands on me for long, but if perchance she grabbed me by surprise, minimally I think I would have pushed her off me, even if I pushed her to the ground in process. If she had grabbed me with do-harm intent, I might not be of mind to look back and check on her as I walked away. I do not like those words as I clack them…the perhaps fantasized yet viable threat of advanced physical motherly contact, but there and here is my total truth.

Overall, possession of my knife the weapon allowed for increased emotional height and confidence when in my own shoes.

Funny I never lost track of that knife, probably because I held it so close for years…thumb on blade and about to flip. FYI Birdy, now the weapon resides in the garage, inside the middle upper junk drawer of my narrower red Snap-On rollcab top toolbox.

Teenage Therapy

The recall escapes me…I cannot remember the threat my father used to make me attend the weekly mental health meetings, so I won't make shit up. After the first few sessions, BigBird joined us for the last half of the three-way pow-wow trying to fix this punk ass bitch boy. But hah, I never opened up, we canceled the entire arrangement once it was obvious to all I was no-way not going to participate.

Once along into my drug years, while still residing inside monster house number two on Whitney Avenue, BigBird contracted a therapist after I presume he noticed a profound change in me. Problem number one in counseling was, my supreme defiance got us nowhere. Why so much my brick wall? Hard to say for sure, hum…without a doubt I echo-distrusted and disrespected all adults. Secondly, only jabber-generic inquiries were generated from her the therapy lady…questions she wanted to know, but not questions I was interested to participate in.

No words arose to challenge me, no inquiries about what scared me most, like what did I fear when looking forward, nope, naught nothing came up remotely relevant to me at all.

Nothing to stump me, nothing to stop me, nothing causing me to think or dig deep into any manner known or unknown.

More it was the so-says-me-at-the-time stupid shit like, "Why are you so angry?...Why are you mad at your father?...What went wrong at school?...", none of which I wanted to discuss nor desired to begin to sort out, neither in my head nor with her.

Although I am assuming judging and blaming, looking back I would say, well…she asked all the wrong questions, or least missed asking the right ones, then lost my respect.

Definitively I recall my first brain examination session. I was angry and defiant but attended anyway.

Mid-level down inside, I really did want to talk. I had some things to say, I desired some long-standing feeling sort-outs, you know, shit I had been holding onto for almost ten years by that time but boo-hoo so sad, so sad for me, my loss.

Therapist lady never caught me at the right moment. I judged her quickly and harshly, my loss. Her line of cross-examination flung upon me as blaming. Immediately, I stonewalled with my best defense…oh well, my loss. Not that I claim anything she said would have connected with me, because maybe not. Deeper down still, I was perhaps hoping for different questions…ok, like, different questions like what?

Hum.

Well, I guess, like…not sure but let me think a sec.

Maybe, maybe questions like this.

What do you think you lost of most value when your mother went away?

Is there something else that might replace or fill-in some of that loss from your mom?

What hurts the most in your life right now?

What could your father stop doing, so to help make your life less shitty, least for a while?

Yeah well…yeah maybe oh well whatever.

Maybe something more like that would have worked, maybe not, who the fuck knows, who the fuck cares.

Tripped

Once I would dream and reach for new heights

I've got the endurance but now not the mights

This life I've had, treated me well

I'd be psyched on the future, but then stumbled and fell.

Detached Attack

As a teenager I was tough, awhile frail.

A punk, alongside panic stricken.

Absconding, meanwhilst seeking my true core center igniter.

The paired operational bookends of human isotope variations that was me, PAB.

As an adolescent free-range wanderer, I semi-consciously attempted to remain out of harm's way when off on my own sauntering, acting out my best undesigned migrant of the local landscape. Much as I found the necessity to prevail in motion, so to maintain a duck and cover ease of escape from my monsters, sometimes that stupid-ass run off and hide angry bird shit just didn't fucking work.

Downright dejected but I don't remember the circumstances, I was head-down hurt, mid-day shuffling feet east along Glen Avenue on the farside boundary of Luckman Park, only a handful of blocks down from my home Pimlico 'hood. The park was barely ahead on my right, next block, and a couple blocks up on my left was the large area firehouse. The friendly festive firehouse was where my fellow local residents visited in winter, to slow-view the elaborate indoor model train garden.

Weird, this dude already drove past me twice in the last half-mile, and now he's pulling over to talk to me. *Can you please tell me where so and so street is?* I told him *go there then there* and he'll find it. I was elsewise annoyed, and frankly did not want to talk to any more humanoids rest-of-day if you please, aka head down hurt. I was outside killing time, delaying and avoiding a return home to the wobbliness. He said thank you while I kept walking, but dude seemed to want more from me, then sped off with somewhat frustrated disapproval. *Creepy*…this dude gave me the heebie-jeebies.

As he drove off, I watched him eyeball me intently through his rear-view mirror…oh fuck that noise. I ran across the street into the woods towards Cross Country Boulevard and away from the park. I was weirded out, I sensed something wrong, and I can mostly identify that badness appropriately…*shit, I think I need help, think I'm in trouble, real trouble, I need some help here please, real help.* I'll haul ass to the firehouse, they'll protect me I'm sure, they seem like good guys, maybe they can give me a ride home.

But no, oh jeez, slow down bird boy, wait up. I second-guessed myself and did not sprint for the safety of the large brick firehouse. I lingered in the woods for a minute no longer, then headed towards Cross Country. Mentally I readjusted my planned day's travel…I'm going to Pikesville. I'll walk to Greenspring Shopping Center and hangout there for a while with my stoner pals, so this creeper doesn't mess with me.

The toughest motherfucker I was close friends with in all of Baltimore was Pikesville-insane Adam Annenberg, and often Adam loitered at Greenspring. I greatly desired Adam to be on scene when I arrive, especially if this creep guy is pursuing me.

                           Chapter THREE

Adam and I held mutual admiration for each other but many times his emotional hair-trigger scared me, and I detoured spending any more minutes around him than I had to when he was in a mood. I'd been in a couple of large group gang-style fights with Adam and he was the most violent and damaging fighter on scene, every time. Adam was a lone wolf but legit ruffian, easily able to give my adversaries the Mount Washington tough guys a go, but Adam mostly remained in Pikesville, when not otherwise beating up those nemesis of his the neighboring Randallstown boys.

I convinced myself to be unrealistically imagining the creeper car guy's do-harm intent, so I softened my runaway stance. Stepping onto the sidewalk before sprinting to the other side of Cross Country Boulevard, with forceful intent I dropped my creeper fears and shook out my arms, relaxing my pre-tensioned shoulders. The traffic steady…I looked one way then the other, preparing to cross. Within barely a short-timed window to adequately reach where he requested to go, the guy's car pulled up right in front of me. I did not see him coming, it was unexpected and I startled.

Please-please-please…he sounded nice, seemed less intimidating this time, and acted more sincere. I felt slightly bad for him…*I can't find it, can you please show me?* I can't I said, I have somewhere to go I said…sorry, I said. He pleaded for me to help him…he really needs to find his sought place soon, he's late and doesn't know where he is, he's not from around here.

His older rust-colored Chevy sedan was pretty ratty. He was running Washington DC tags, I noticed that shit when he first sped off disgruntled. He pleaded then leaned over and flung open the passenger door invitingly, he begged for me to help him. Oh how bad could it get?

I chose to trust my fellow humanoid brother, however creepy, and I somewhat hesitantly got into his car. He was late twenties, maybe mid-thirties at most, wearing loose-fitting medium green nylon shorty shorts with a white edge band, no socks, flip-flop sandals, and a lightweight button-up short-sleeve barely draped across his shoulders, perhaps only the bottom two buttons buttoned maybe one, and the shirt wide-open up top, colored a very light, actually faint, pink rose.

He took off with me inside before I could even close the door, *oh shit*…in my deepest tough guy voice I directed him. Ugh, he seemed indifferent though, weirdly keeping his eyes on me as he drove. His small-talk voice grew soft but loud, almost seductive, and he drowned out my words. Readjusting my position, I sat tall in my seat. He was not listening to my route instructions, no not at all. He made a hard right U-turn at the firehouse and proceeded west up Glen Avenue, back past the park, towards outer Park Heights.

He was going the wrong way…he obviously held unknown-to-me plans, but then I knew.

But then I knew…but then I knew my initial instincts were correct, this is turning towards the bona fide bad, but quick.

My mind played through multiple rapid scenarios…how do I get out of here and how do I get away from this guy? A few friends lived nearby…Peter Slepinski, Wendy Coven, David Ankers, and sisters Jodi and Aileen Litofsky. Maybe if I jump out of this runaway hell ride before the guy picks up more speed, I can sprint to one of my friend's houses for sans-creep shelter.

Ok Birdy, you might want to look away or *la-la-la I cannot hear you* for a few seconds…*disturbing sexual yuck-yuck warning*…the guy scooched forward in his seat and his chin was almost touching the steering wheel. He opened his mouth to speak, and I prepared to jump.

His right hand rushed my crotch and landed on target…*Let me suck your dick,* he said sternly with some perverse inciteful tone…*NO, stop the car motherfucker* I shouted…I was more mad than scared, least for now, this guy is grabbing my junk, and he sped up. I let go of the door handle and slapped his rubbing hand off me quick as I could. *Please, I'll give you ten dollars,* he tried to negotiate…I screeched violently directly into his ear, *STOP THE FUCKING CAR.*

I pushed open the door against the heavy wind and he slowed greatly. I scrambled out of his trap, barely staying on my feet, sprinting back down Glen Avenue fast as possible and I aimed for the fire house. I heard my-side car door close but I don't know how he did it. He took off then stopped, I think he was turning around, I only perceive-heard this from behind as I ran.

Heading east down Glen, I ripped across the curb and into the same woods. Scrambling through the small forested area, I raced straight toward the firehouse…I dared not look back. The woods grew too thick and began to slow me down. I jumped back onto the sidewalk and briefly glanced around, I didn't see him, maybe he was down on Cross Country planning to cut me off. For the life of me I do not know why I ran right past the firehouse, well, that's a lie, yes I do.

Chapter THREE

I was far past Peter's house plus beyond David's and Wendy's too. Jodi and Aileen's place was one block past the firehouse, so I ran to the other side of Glen Avenue and up the hill towards my two gal pals.

Frantically I approached…both sisters were home and I busted inside.

Single momma Litofsky wasn't home, she was at work.

I asked them to call her please-please-please.

They said ok and did, but their momma couldn't leave.

She wouldn't be home for two hours they said, sorry.

The sisters tried to comfort-speak me but couldn't.

I remained for about 15 minutes then ran mid-block between houses all the way home. Once inside BigBird's nest I stayed put, consuming massive amounts of barbiturate pills alongside some weird frightened anger. I did not leave the house for another two days, somewhat scared but mostly narcotic immobilized.

I felt…I felt dirty, I felt very dirty, very dirty everywhere.

Not sure on this one but I think I told Beth what happened. For absolute certain-sure I never said a peep to my father, ever. This conversation seemed off limits concerning BigBird, I wasn't going to go there, no way and didn't.

For this one and only time in my entire life ever did I need a mother's comfort, and I rushed around to find it. Not for her to retaliate, not for her to gain details and call the police.

Rain

But where is the joy

Without first the pain

The things that we cling to

Despite all the rain

To have and to hold

It's stronger than stone

We live all together

But die all alone.

Four

~

Broken

Dancing the Thread-Thin Expanse Between Living and The Other Side

Chapter Four, Broken ~

I was struggling to get that darn bicycle wheel hub back together. My boss was constantly watching me with an overly critical and judgmental eye. If I did not get the hub back together correctly and soon, I feared he would yell at me.

He did not seem to be a nice man at all, and although I worked there for less than four months, I already heard him yell at most other employees. I desperately wanted to avoid his ridicule and especially, I did not want to get yelled at, I heard enough of that shit at home, for a long time.

I did not like anyone yelling at me. I humbly admit for the first time, I believe getting yelled at hurts me more than being physically attacked because, and especially back then, well, because…because I was emotionally fragile.

That particular bike wheel hub was way beyond complicated. The rear hub had multiple gears, but the gears were not located on the outside of the hub where you could see them. The gears were not at all like those many different mountainbikes with visible outside gears you my beautiful Birdy has owned. Rather, that hub had hidden gears that were located on the inside of the hub. These crazy little internal gears are called planetary gears. The collection of these hidden planetary gears interlock with each other and change position by your command, moving around inside the rear hub to alter the gearing you feel through your pedals. To change gears while you are riding a bike with these wonderous, but tedious-to-work-on internally geared rear hubs, you shift a small thumb lever on the handlebar. The thumb shift lever is connected back to the hub by a gears-controlling cable.

I was not proficient overhauling the internally geared multi-speed rear hubs yet. Mostly, my skills existed amid the traditional outside gears or the ever popular single-speed but internal pedal-backward-foot-brake bike hubs. I knew gobs more about the other hubs and gears because I taught myself to fix them by just doing it, over and over, figuring it out through repetitious but slightly altered experiments.

I was 17, working at a large and super-cool bike and ski shop in Baltimore called Princeton Sports. I really liked working there, fixing many different kinds of bikes and starting to work on some downhill skis.

I liked working at Princeton, except when I heard my boss Sonny yelling at one of our co-workers.

I began to wonder if I could quite possibly maybe stay off his I-am-going-to-yell-at-you-anytime-I-want list or if soon enough, I too would be the target of his throwing darts of belittling words.

The previous year I dropped out of high school and Princeton was my first fulltime job, my first bike shop job, and I did not want to screw it up. Possessing no other plan in life except learn as I go and stay far away from my father as possible without moving out, I also cradled a great love for the bicycle.

Wanting to reassemble the internally geared three-speed hub and fast, I was scrambling but I knew I could not skip a step. Sonny was randomly test riding some of my work and if I did it wrong, I felt like I would not only get yelled at for the first time by my first fulltime boss, but my over reaching idiotic teenage mind was convinced that I would also get fired today. Not knowing what the hell I was doing, I tried different configurations just trying to get the darn gear parts back inside the darn hub shell. But it was most certainly a crapshoot if the darn thing would function correctly anyway. I probably should have admitted earlier to Sonny I did not know how to fix those kinds of hubs, but he dropped the assignment on my bench and forcefully told me to fix it immediately, marching away with his normal I-am-the-highest-authority-in-the-land-and-ye-shall-not-question-me aura.

Later I received formal training on those exact rear hubs, those hubs previously puzzling me for months. In fact on that day though, I was having major trouble, and truth be clear, the stakes were high…extremely high. I did not want to billboard myself stupid in front of Sonny, definitely not here, and certainly not now. Already struggling with some slight regret and holding some moderate but mounting hopelessness, I tried to envision my future as a high school dropout, a long haired punk ass loser who didn't know fricking anything, and it was self-evident I was clearly addicted to drugs. Not yet labeling myself an addict or a junkie which would come a short time later, but at that time precisely, I already and manifestly sacrificed myself unconditionally to the drugs.

I abandoned my own power and free will of choice, giving myself entirely to the illegal street substances five years earlier and factually,

ok, well…now I bear some of my skeletons-in-closet emotional belly…but…um…well…I truly felt it had already been a full life for me.

Yup, a wary and full life for me so far for sure…clinging to the roller coaster of ridiculous life drama with my long gone but now back and multi-abusive mother, the violence out on the street around town, and my father's over worked and stressed out yelling at home…most all that nonsense simultaneously for the past thirteen years.

Weird to dissect it decades later, and somewhat painful to finally write it down or type it out for the first time of this here self-inquisitive life but on that day, well…working on that darn hub, I felt like my life was ratherish on the line. Thereupon fuck it all anyway, if it was my day, and it was going to be that darn hub that takes me down, then so be it.

Never previously admitting it to anyone, and I do not enjoy the self-analyzing bear-all review of this dark, painful, and hard to swallow personal truth after first discovering it in my thirties, but I recognize back then with Sonny…ugh, this really fucking hurts…well, I recognize that back then with Sonny…I was tired, I saw no other real way out for me, and I was moderately scared and lonely when at home, never wanting to go home because of the haunting perennial pain, no matter the house we moved to. The deep and scary birdhouse hurt was hatched before my memories began, and the troubling emotions were associated with home, wherever we lived. So, I tried to stay away from our house. Our house scared me, even as a semi-tough punk middle-aged teenager. Our house felt alive and unsteady, wobbly, dangerous, downright fucking evil.

The terror me and my three sisters felt was delivered from our mother's hand…our You-Were-Supposed-to-Love-Us-and-Protect-Us mother.

Although the darkness from my mother was chasing me, it had not yet caught me, but I was on the run from it, and tiring. My sisters were running too…oh hell, such fucking cuckoo shit, damn it, well *humph*, so anyway…but mostly, I was tired. If I got fired from Princeton, certain I would have given up on trying again at some other job, self-proclaiming I was a total failure, incapable of doing anything right, accepting the totality of my tiredness and residing within the comfortable, precarious, and probably short lived life as a cocaine and heroin addict in Baltimore.

The darn bike hub was fighting me hard, and coming into focus was the presumptive result I would walk away with the black eye from this senseless battle. *Oh shit*…I heard Sonny approaching as he talked loudly to one of his you-are-below-me servant employees. I exhaled a huffed-up chestfull of frustrated air, hopelessly gazing up at the ceiling in defeat mode…*oh fucking hell and back anyway*…my eyes searching the shop for a white flag I could wave. With Sonny approaching, I let go of the hub and the whole wheel dropped, only a few inches, the rimmed assembly then plopping onto my workbench with its reverberating metal twang. I pulled both hands up and stopped them halfway between my hips and ears, assuming the…*I surrender, please don't shoot me* position, and stepped back from my workstation one big step, with both feet.

I then lost all my strength, both physically and emotionally…dropped my arms, released my chin, closed my eyes, and waited for Sonny to come stomping around the corner from the sales floor.

We had four bike workstations and mine was the closest to the big wide opening out to the sales area. My servant station was immediately around the corner to the right as you walked into the shop, the same location where it sounded Sonny was traveling through right now. *Oh fuck it all anyway*…I stood there, I just stood there. For about six seconds I stayed still with hands up, which is actually a long time when you run the math. Literally I felt the hangman was coming for me, and I no-way could not run.

Chapter FOUR

Short time soon I believed to have the employment noose slip down around my idiotic teenage neck. I started to form the thoughts and mumble the words, barely under my breath…"Sonny, I really suck at this, I quit".

Quickly I shook my head in self-disapproval mode I did NOT want to quit, no not at all, but the stress overwhelmed me, figured I'm getting fired today anyway, so why not just leave now and keep him from straining his yelling voice, I will let him save that for somebody else, anybody else, just not me, fucking please, just not me.

Practice mumbling my resignation one-liner softly and gathering my most decisive I-am-done-here tone, I felt his inhabitance come around the corner into the shop. Looking down at the darn hub that was about to fricking end me, I was absolutely not going to look in Sonny's direction, although I saw him in my periphery. Hesitating slightly I sucked in one more breath of oh fuck it courage…I started to speak as he stepped onto my two-foot by five-foot rectangular grey anti-fatigue floor work mat, right under the soles of my mandatory-so-says-Sonny black leather work shoes.

After only blurting out the first two words of the last eight words I would ever use here while on the timeclock, "Sonny, I…", he spun around rapidly before even hearing or focusing on me, with that traditional Sonny vigorous body movement and as he yelled his customary, "*OK*", walking away half-whistling and drowning out my words.

The presence of his royal highness is requested to attend court at his thrown near the cash registers to help a princess with a broken string on her tennis racket, and she wants Sonny The Great to re-string it himself, right now.

Holy hell, that is weird…I just received a thirty-minute stay of execution as my hangman re-strings an oversize Prince tennis racket with its neon pink grip wrap. Ok, now my second chance on life…no I do not want to really quit this job, not in the slightest, and I am not going to let this darn bike hub punk me, I had to focus.

My two beloved seasoned co-worker senior mechanics Tommy and Wilbert were both away at our warehouse up the street, unloading a truckload of very big and very heavy boxed indoor exercise bikes by the hundreds. No one else could help me who was in the store right now. Although both those two guys who are now slinging 70-pound boxes know how to reassemble these hubs with their eyes closed, they would not be back for probably least an hour, so I had to figure this shit out on my own. Although I see now I should have run out the back door and up the street to have Wilbert or Tommy come help me, I dug into the idea I could sort things out myself, if I could just slow down and focus. I put a couple of these hubs successfully back together before, but did not have the reassembly process nailed down. If I could ignore all distractions and zero in on it, I felt confident I could get the darn hub back together correctly before Sonny was finished laying fresh string in the tennis racket.

Broken

None of us three mechanics had chairs at our bike workstations, and I was not sure why. Hum, I never considered sitting down before to do my work, mostly because the hectic pace in the workshop was so high that if I sat down, sure I would just pop up out of my seat 30 seconds later for something else. Ah, there it is…now I see, a chair would just be in the way. But if I had a chair and could sit down at my workbench, it would help me relax, help me focus, I could quickly rebuild the hub and optimistically, not get fired today. Quickly I borrowed a stool from the breakroom, located against the back wall of the building in the warehouse zone, further back from the workshop and farthest from the sales floor. No biggie about the stool, least six of them were shoved into that crappy little lunchnook, and I never saw more than three people in there at a time.

Sitting at my workbench intently reassembling the bike hub, blocking out all noises and distractions around me…*swoosh*…Sonny came out of nowhere and kicked the stool right out from underneath me, seemingly with rage and all his might. My boss Sonny was extremely, in truth violently, pissed off.

Not letting go of the bike wheel with said hub attached, I fell backward and barely caught myself before hitting the floor.

I strained my body in a weird twisting manner while falling, watchfully trying not to tumble into the long row of bikes nearby, sitting there propped up on their kickstands, bikes waiting to be repaired by me. Before I got my feet under and regained balance, Sonny was screaming, literally beyond his capacity of lungs. I held a scrupulous comprehension of that lung expenditure measurement, after listening to him yell at most everyone around me for the past four months.

"Do you see anyone ELSE around here sitting down? You do NOT sit down, and you NEVER take a stool out of the lunchroom ever again."

Despite my aforementioned scared and lonely state, I was collecting some slight self-confidence, pride and courage while working for Sonny, scratching at a slightly upward trajectory in my life. Hah…but in a hot second after my supporting stool was punted away, any life strength positivity I possessed two minutes ago, either surface-level or hidden inner light…well, it was immediately flushed from my very being. I was spiritlessly flattened, faster than using my thieving pliers to rip out entire car wheel valve stems thus deflating the tires immediately, not using a small stick to depress the little valve thing and anxiously wait for all the air to slowly hiss out of the wheels I was stealing.

Out and about in the world, I was not so pathetically on edge at that time of my life leading up to the famous stool incident with Sonny, despite some otherwise fragile descriptions I shared. It was years since I shed a tear about anything…hah, my outward appearance hardening. Mother Patricia had been fulltime gone from our lives for a full decade now, and although I was still extremely empathetic and protected all children everywhere, I was getting tougher, and I did not really have a choice in the matter.

For the previous three years before the stool punting exhibition by Sonny The Tyrannical, my skin had been growing thicker. I do not think I will share much of my encountered street violence within these here flaps, I cannot currently see the relevance outside of general morbid entertainment except to say, well…you my lovely Lauren know of my foundational intense aversion to handguns, but maybe not my entire *why*.

My firearm repugnance is the net summary after having seven or twelve too many aimed at my head…able to smell the distinct recently fired stinky but sweet gunpowder smoke permeating from the barrel, mere inches from my face, temple, or shoved into the hair on the back of my skull.

The back-of-head incidents were especially rattling to my nerves because for the rest of those few nights, I definitively recall walking around with one of the streets smells of death following me.

That being the smell of gun smoke in my hair from a handgun casually concealed in the waist of a pair of jeans by someone with no flipping respect for anyone or anything but money, a gun recently used to disperse murderous bullets at human life. So yeah, a hardening of my street-punk emotional skin was naturally occurring.

Sonny stormed off with his precious stool in hand, marching towards the shitty little lunchroom. Right then and there, I immediately felt a weird presence behind me.

For the first time in over a handful of years, I tasted a few rare pods of liquid salt in my mouth that had just rolled down my cheeks, originating from the inside corner of my eyes.

I remember still, right now, exactly how I felt the moment Sonny left the shop, as I stood there holding the darn wheel, tasting those tears, and right before I turned around to see who or what was behind me. I remember exactly how I felt at that very moment, *exactly*. And still, I am speechless to describe it. It was different than hurt, it was different than pain, it was different than fear, it was different than embarrassment, it was different than, well, most def 100…it was different than any other literal word I know. There is no word I ever heard of, or that I possess to adequately describe that moment, so I will not fake it and make shit up. Then with the flush of indescribable emotion that just melted me down, slowly I turned around to understand why I felt a presence behind me.

Masked Pain
Working my first fulltime job I was on edge, me not once relaxing when on the clock. Perhaps positive benefits resulted though, like living to learn acknowledge and accept the enduring challenge of strictness, what I would even judge as unfairness, while continuing to report to work the next day and the next. More the while I learned to hang in there and stick, despite the aforementioned tyrant-like boss hardship.

Ah, no, fricking no, that's bullshit bird boy, just bullshit. Oh crap, well, you are concisely correct…let us stay a minute and pull this one apart. When I peel back those shiny-shiny surface level *look at me I am totally awesome, I am strong and I am tough and I can do it* words, I admit to embracing the suck for all the wrong reasons.

Encased the notion…all the yelling or even hitting or cutting in the whole wide world wasn't going to hurt much as I hurt already so go ahead, or maybe it might hurt worse but who cares, go ahead, take your best shot…it is what I was accustom to, it is what I knew first, first in line and principally, it is the pain. I deserved it…I was a dropout druggie lowlife and this is how the world treats us lowlifes- like a doormat, like a non-figurative pin cushion, like a slightly-soiled throw-away paper towel, like a clean new disposable plastic fork but with one broken tine so trash the useless utensil that's me.

Rarely I was reflectively kind nor even neutral, I thought very little of myself. Occupying barely a speck of indifference on the fucking matter, I offered up this here inflated shell for sacrifice, giving freely this here bag of bones and skin to the world, go ahead, go ahead and poke your pins in my neck, wipe your feet on my back, wield your knives against my flesh, pound this torso with your clubs for the pleasureful and satisfying sounds of snapping ribs…go ahead I do not at all care, I just don't fucking care. I had done most things wrong in life so I had it coming, go ahead and punish me for my failures dysfunction and deficiencies.

I was the singular veritable one who finally drove my mother away, forever.
I caused multiple senseless deaths while my head was aimlessly stuck up my ass.
I hid from the operational world under the dark cloud cover of the drugs.
I was unable to withstand the simplistic public school system.
I lied and stole and cheated so go ahead and have your redemptive way with me.

Imprison me, chain me…beat me for fun, whip me burn me, kick me good.
Extinguish your cigarettes on my arms if you please or wish, zero fucks given.
Drag me to the water's edge, tie stones to my ankles, push me in, then walk off.
I won't fight I won't struggle I won't try to take you with me, let me drown.

I would rather someone hurt me than ignore me, least they see me, if even as a target, least they see me enough and care enough to throw their harsh words of stone at my face.

Yielded Promises
Thereafter smacking the wall of my intense motorcycle racer dream dead end, although barely thinking the effort worth it, I then switched my focus. One day at the magazine rack, my desire then adopted downhill skiing as its foster relation.

                          Chapter FOUR

Again a cover image snagged my eye and oddly, a new stream of consciousness arose gazing across mile after mile of Swiss peaks on the cover page, with an extreme downhill ski dude launching off a nearby cliff. The vastness of the Alps range, the sheer bewilderment and ruggedness of terrain grabbed me by the shoulders and shook me violently…incredible. *Come*, it said…*stay*, it said…*come stay long time.*

Although my initial target fascination was zooming down a groomed ski race course, blasting through the finish line timing light entirely depleted of breath, close to exerted-effort-pass-out, and my shoulders bruised and bleeding from banging the course gates the hell out of my way so to save thousands of seconds, aka a challenge tougher than me, the legacy beginnings of the alpine sport mesmerized me, the embellishment of nature…wow, just wow…the Swiss Alps. Hah… *fuck that noise*, I shook the fog from atop my face. Firstly, all that shit looks expensive, too damn expensive alongside my inclusive drug habit, never mind the fact I suck at all sports, then there's the truth I'll never travel fricking anywhere, more or less out of the country. The faint realities of actually one day landing on snow only existed on paper, within ski magazines.

Yet however, maybe to try…yes, to begin, to try and live within myself, betwixt a setting embracing me, amid a loving-me-environment, something pushing while lifting me, and perhaps…*scoff*…perhaps allowing some otherwise vacant innards to sprout, as it may be bloom, and perchance grow taller to tower over my shitty-ass current self. *Possible*…isn't it possible I thought, could not I just try to try for such heavenly alpine snowy meadows, if even near home?

Beth and I harassed the shit out of our father for years to take us skiing. BigBird promised time after time…*yes we will go, yes ok, we will go*, but he never took us anywhere near a damn ski hill, never. The longing and fake escapade of skiing with our father became a bad joke, borderline cruel actually, by my measure. Finally full of frustration, I gave up on BigBird contributing one single ounce of energy to help get Beth and I on the slopes. One too many again-delayed or broken ski promises from BigBird and I stopped asking…it was not going to happen, and never no way didn't.

One day when on the payroll clock at Princeton, I met and befriended a regular ski customer. The outgoing and friendly gentleman appeared as a prior athlete, still fit but least slightly past his prime.

He dressed smartly in outdoor chic attire, positioned somewhere between the realms of rodeo cowboy champion and hands-on millionaire owner of a construction company.

He donned fancy fitted jeans, muscle-filled flannel shirts, expensive but functional boots, and a meticulously-trimmed mountain man beard that matched his nickname to a T…*Wolfman*. Wolfman's real name was Roy Turner. I never called him Roy, I only called him Wolfman. Wolfman was probably mid-thirties, I was 17. After years of harassing BigBird, it only took Wolfman one week to fulfill my first realized life dream…one week, *one*. Wolfman handed out no false-promise business cards, *none*.

Wolfman did what he said. Wolfman did not have to promise, he walked his damn talk. Wolfman took us skiing. Yes oh sure I might have started skiing on my own later, but maybe not, impossible to know. I certainly have Wolfman to thank for getting me started on skis, without a doubt most def. Our first time, Wolfman drove me Beth and my next-door neighbor buddy Mark Weinreich to Pennsylvania, only an hour away for night skiing and Wolfman paid for everything. I fell down so many times that my blue jeans were soaking wet on the first run, and stayed that way the remainder of the night, soaked, but I cared less than none.

The ski experience was far better than I imagined it for all years prior, magnificent, just magnificent…I was hooked right away. That first night with Beth Mark and Wolfman, I became a skier. For a year I spent time with Wolfman, doing fun stuff or going somewhere exciting together. Wolfman sponsored Mark with his organized ice-hockey pursuit, and I believe Wolfman paid for everything. I enjoyed talking to him when he visited Princeton, Wolfman my faux-father hero.

I then discovered a previously-unknown perk when working at Princeton Sports. Not only did I enjoy free lift tickets to the local ski hills while also, the skis boots and poles were available to me on loan from work no charge. Soon enough, my two days off per week were utilized skiing. I was highly enthused to be on snow, even whilst high on drugs. Most days I flew solo, staying properly on the slopes and snug in my boots all day. Thanks much to Wolfman I also calmed and fit in a little more at work because now I was a skier, then sharing the passionate activity with my co-workers. Numerous ski trips were taken with work peers, both day trips and some overnight multi-day expeditions. My emotional stature began to bloom…I felt taller, I felt more sound, slightly filled-in, and least for some moments, the resounding shouts in my ears lessened. The overall experience was part-time magical for sure.

I saw semi-clearly through my reddened eyes…intrinsic dreaming can carry me somewhere sought, such realization propelling me more than ever before. Now this here my sometimes sunny but regardless get up and go opportunity…share my desires and when offered passage, go.

Ugly implied rumors began surfacing about Wolfman and, well…to state directly, it was mean hurtful shit. I never observed or experienced anything negative or scary myself with Wolfman, never. Neither did Mark or Beth nor anyone I knew personally. The gossip chatter popped up at Princeton, from people who knew Wolfman longer than I did but maybe they did not know him better than me, IDK. I was attempting to separate myself from free-range assumptions both public and private, so I tried to blow-off the Wolfman reports that frankly damaged my darn ears and stung my damn heart. This guy was my hero and I did not like people talking shit about him. I attempted not to entertain the negative hearsay, Wolfman gutter trash talk or otherwise. Me who for my entire life thus-then categorically hated all adults, aka *fuck the adults*, I loved Wolfman, *loved*…loved him like a father, like a brother, like a boundless exploratory adventure mentor-guide.

 Chapter FOUR

Now I am guilty AF passing along these rumors…I was told Wolfman volunteered with a Boy Scout troop. Evidently as I barely heard and intentionally did not clearly understand, the negative gossip originated from scouting interactions. I never tuned in and listened to the whole story, mostly because I did not want to believe anything of the sort. I detoured the negative reports about Wolfman best I could and rather, dealt only with the hand-first facts known and shown to me.

Wolfman, a supremely super awesome dude who went out of his way for me and my friends, spending his own money for us to have the time of our lives. Wolfman, the one who got me on snow when my father would or could not. Wolfman, leading me down my path to dreams realized, new opportunities and enhanced hope. Wolfman, the first adult stepping forward to aide me, guide me, push me, protect me, and not give up on me in ways most critical, by my measure. Wolfman, connecting me to both the brawn of nature's healing and the clairvoyance of a grand adventuring lifestyle.

Making it on snow would later prove to be a factual life-saving occurrence for me, and perhaps such opportunities would have never happened without Wolfman Roy Turner.

Perhaps such heart-sought adventurous life travels would have never become part of my factual DNA, without Wolfman Roy Turner. Perhaps and probably my breath would have been extinguished long before I ever met your momma, long before you were conceived, without Wolfman Roy Turner. Perhaps I would have never seen my 20th damn birthday, without Wolfman Roy Turner. I know not the proper clacked characters for you my precious to see, as I so accurately feel, how profoundly Wolfman bettered me. Pathetic by my measure are here now these chirps.

Wolfman absolutely without a doubt lit my world up at a time when I was clawing to find some light, any light.

Even though past my needy youthfulness, I enjoyed a calming and protective love in Wolfman's presence. He was so cool, so damn cool, so damn and supremely fricking cool.

Wolfman, helping lift me from my own dark emotional ashes…Wolfman, shining bright a new and correct path for me to journey…Wolfman, abruptly ending his own grand adventuring bad-ass life by way of reported suicide just as mine began…Wolfman, my setting sun, Wolfman, my shimmering star, Wolfman, my paragon.

The fuck-shock news hit me hard…my grand adventuring forefather Wolfman was found hanging from a tree in his back yard dead.

He Ate the Light

Feeling all I've felt before

Held down tight without touching, smashed face-first on the floor

Peaceful dreams in bed at night

Was supposed to make it right

Can't hide even in sleep

Wanting sans the seeing…wanting sans the creep

In the long run I try not to feel

Trying to forget doesn't make it less real

Wishing it would rain…wanting it one day ends

This brain be bleeding…not sure my broken heart mends

Choosing only the longest road

It be my journey, it be my load.

Hello Kitty Pillows

The girl's cheesy digital clock on her bedroom nightstand said 6:05, but hum, I could not determine the associated suffix…is it AM or PM? My comprehension of such basic life matters was caught in an unaccountable tailspin because while distracted, I lost track of the sun and moon. My moderately blurred vision and inability to observably focus fluttered wildly…I could not see the additional detail on the clock beyond the three large LED numbers. Attempting a held-inside game of elimination, trying to sort out such bewildering question, quickly I determined it a fruitless guessing game.

Squinting one eye closed and trying to focus on the electronic time-keeping machine, I puzzled thyself…when did I last go to sleep, a day ago, or two? Reopening my literal unseeing mind's eye, I squinted closed the other one hoping for alternative clarity…when was the last time I woke up, and what happened between then and now? I began to confuse myself and started to question much more than the darn clock. Wanting to ask girl alongside my shoulder what time it was but pathetically, I could not formulate the inquisition into proper sentence structure without being totally fricking rude. Because although we just spent a sizeable amount of time together atop her bed, I did not know her name, and how could I effectively initiate this line of questioning without addressing her directly, therefore existing on the spot as an inconsiderate dickhead?

Rather embarrassed to lack such basic information, both the inattentive void of time and the insensible unknowing of her name, I hesitated. Finally and without discord I blurted out, "Hey what time is it?". I joined her in looking at the clock and she said, "Six-o-six". Wanting to clarify, I volleyed back, "Morning or night?". She told me it was evening. Hum, I thought silently…did I lose one day of my life here, or two…, I was not at all sure. So, one added simplistic question for the girl on the bed next to me…"What day is it?". "Sunday…it's Sunday night", she replied simply, not even looking up but rather intently chop-chop-chopping our rock of cocaine on her fancy little mirror with its shimmering outer band of half-inch chromed steel frame.

I was slightly surprised she did not show any indications of thinking me either an asshole or possibly stone cold stupid, based on my rather obvious line of questioning. As we remained camped out in her room with blinds drawn and door closed, creeping closer and closer to the bottom of the sandwich sized Ziploc baggie previously half full of cocaine, I tried to gain my bearings, starting with the basic understanding of what time it was. I hoped my stupid quandaries would have run course by now, but hum, alas no, I could not help my dumb ass bird brain self, no, and well, I guess…one more perplexing inquiry because of my cockamamie time disorientation.

"Really, wow…Sunday night huh? When did we get here, Friday or Saturday?"…now certain this was my last question. Familiar girl with mystery name soundly grasped the six-inch-square mirror and purpose-built three-inch gold-toned metal snorting straw from me, and placed the reflective drug platform atop her squeezed-together knees.

Bending over into her own lap while smashing her left index finger against her left nostril and huffing all loose cocaine particles through the right side of her nose and up towards her brain she responded almost simultaneously, "Friday".

Doing her line then continuing briefly she said, "We got here Friday night, Saturday morning really, and yeah right, yesterday was kind of a blur". "Hah", I said quickly, not wanting to disrupt the dizzying flow of back and forth cocaine turns, "You're not kidding…I know we went out and got more coke but don't remember when that was, I know we ordered pizza, and didn't someone come over last night or today and buy some blow?" I then honked my line in turn and handed the mirror back to her. She eked out a simple, "Yeah…", but said nothing else. About two hours later all the cocaine was gone. It seemed pointless at this juncture to ask her name, so I kept my inconsiderate mouth shut.

Mystery girl and I paused there bedtop, both now beyond flat broke. Myself a bumbling hot mess, I started grabbing my stuff as she peeled back covers and climbed under. Apparently her fantasy danced around the unrealistic possibility she could soon fall asleep after the two of us blew through the weekend, consuming about ten grams of coke and collectively over $1,000 poorer. She with frailty pulled her comforter further overhead, then snuggled in and faced the wall. With tenderness I halfheartedly tucked her in as no name girl purposefully crushed some pillows. Candidly I wandered off, unceremoniously saying goodbye but surely she did not hear me, hah…I barely heard myself over all the ring-ring's shouting abusively between my ears. Then walking out, I locked the front door of her big fancy house nestled deep in the Baltimore County woods.

Almost 48 hours before, I was at a secondary drug supplier's house in Pikesville buying high quality Peruvian Pink cocaine, an eight ball, and sans-name girl walked in behind me. Oddly, only me and dealer were there before this girl showed up which was rare. Usually a handful of people hung around this popular place, especially on a Friday night. She was about the same age as me, 17, maybe a year younger or older but no more, driving her own car, then joining me and my dealer, we started snorting lines together from the dealer's pink stock of blow.

Dealer person got a phone call and had to run out *only for 20 minutes*, delivering some cocaine around the corner. They said we could stay here if we wanted while they were gone but I thought oh fuck to the no, no way…I'm not staying here and 'specially not on a Friday night. This was an active drug house and quite the cast of characters showed up, day and night. I wanted to avoid the probable confusion and uncomfortable interactions I would face with anxious would-be buyers banging on the door and calling on the house phone while shop boss was gone. This person trusted me and I absolutely trusted them, but I did not want to sit in their place when they weren't here, especially because a bunch of people were carrying guns these days. I would name the situation an escalating Baltimore drug market, and tempers were running high. Not to say at this time in Baltimore the drug trade was growing overall that I knew of, but within the communities and amongst the contacts I had, business was expanding.

 Chapter FOUR

Both the quantity of drugs in and out but also the breadth of scope with the variety of people we dealt with was growing, thus greater the risk. Not only the risk of getting robbed or someone overdosing in the house, but also the risk of getting busted. Tempers running high because coke was in short supply around this time and people were desperate. We saw new faces coming 'round because of the scarcity, hah, only to then have a large shipment of high quality shit hit the street, good stuff that demanded a premium price. So not only were unknown people desperate to score, but now since we had quantity of blow, some buyers were pissed our stuff was so expensive, hah…like we were ripping them off. Anyone who knew anything about coke, realized our price tag was worth it because the product was pink, aka good shit, and it was all rock, aka really good shit. When arriving in true chunky rock form, coke indicates its rather pure state. Only when in ground-up powder form could we cut the coke so by eliminating result, rocks cockily show off their potency.

I thought it only a short matter of time before some of us get arrested after an undercover narcotics officer, aka *narc*, tries to buy product from one of us. If even thinking to remain in my person's house this Friday night, my only consideration would be if they took all their supply with them but hah, most likely not. This house moved some quantity of product so most times, multiple ounces of cocaine remained on the shelf. A couple times before, this person asked me to *tend shop* while they ran out, me then serving as drug shop keeper, selling their supply to whomever showed up. I never liked tending shop, because so many strangers ran in from every direction to buy from me. Selling drugs to or buying from someone I did not know was an idiotic practice, and one I tried to avoid. With the high volume of transactions flying around, and trying to maintain a steady flow of supply and demand, sometimes the mystery sales or buys were unavoidable, by my measure. Lots of pot and sometimes acid ran through this house too, so assuming inventory existed and the stuff would remain when the boss was out, I said thanks but no, and I left when they left. I did not want to be responsible for anything possibly going wrong on my shopkeeper's watch.

Peer coke customer girl commented to me directly…she lived nearby and her parents were gone for a week, so we could go back to her house and finish what we started. Sounded like a good plan to me, but I had to drop off two separate packages of a gram each of pink on our way. I prearranged sale of two grams to two different people, and since supply was scarce, many of us were running around trying to satisfy our buyers. I paid $425 for the eight ball because of its high potency and because of scarcity at the time.

I was not yet shooting up but if I was, this quality pink was the strong stuff I might overdose from. Normally I would step on this stuff before I sold any, aka dilute it with foreign imitation powders, but one of my buyers was shooting, so I didn't want to mess up their shit. The other buyer would appreciate the quality and could afford a premium price. I paid about $120 per gram for my eight ball, selling one gram to the junkie for $150 and the second gram for $175 to the other well-to-do buyer person, which brought my cost of the remaining gram and a half down to about $65 per gram, a good little brief night of dealing that was originally destined only for consuming.

Around 1 AM Friday night we sat down on her darling poof bed, leaned against her *Hello Kitty* pillows in her cute rose colored bedroom with door closed, and started snorting lines together. She had a bag of pink too, more than the 1.5 grams I walked in with. Although non-knowing of her original intentions, we then ripped through almost 4 grams of coke. We barely spoke, until out of blow on Saturday. Hurriedly we left in my car, returning a short time later with a quarter bag of more Peruvian pink and $800 poorer, getting a deal on two eight balls, aka a total of seven more grams of coke, aka a quarter ounce.

Saturday night we finally ordered pizza after being starving for a while, and two slices of pizza is all I ate for 48 hours. At some point, I think it was Sunday daytime, maybe Saturday, one of her girlfriends came over and bought some blow from us then quickly left. I did not realize nor do I remember how much her girlfriend took or where the money went. I'm sure it was no more than a gram and I think we either lost the money or the other girl never actually paid us. Fast forward and all-all the premium pink-pink was gone, so I left to drive home to my father's house in Pimlico. Literally I had never met this girl before, I never knew her name, and I never saw her again. We spent two days barricaded in her bedroom but did not touch each other once, neither of us there for romance, just and only cocaine.

My in excess of $500 weekend blow bender was not planned, rather an impulse feeding my excessive desire to escape my fears and pains within the real world.

The pink Kitty incident was hard to recover from, financially. $500 amounted to over three weeks of bike shop pay for me at the time, but hah, I cared not for such concerns, because the overwhelming attraction to consume reigned supreme. Whenever finding the opportunity to snort coke, I took it, every avail-a-chance. Also was the nagging fact in my head I never learned her name but considering my condition of derelict heart and mind at the time, it's certainly no surprise, by my measure.

After ripping through more than ten grams of coke between the two of us, I for one was physically sick. Well, if we did give a gram away to her girlfriend, maybe our total was more like nine grams nose-absorbed, not ten. Regardless, I was sick not only because of the potency and volume consumed, but also from the stress and lack of sleep. Stress because like all other instances, the first line was the strongest rush, and I would spend sometimes 40 hours straight trying to duplicate or exceed that same damn high unsuccessfully, such buzz never to come my way, ever. The first session-line of the day was the most intense, even as volume increased and quality improved.

The only break mystery girl and I took besides re-upping our supply and chomping some pizza was the 15 minutes we spent together in her attached master teenage bathroom, as her nose poured a heavy flow of blood over her pearly white sink and shiny gold faucet. She admitted sometimes after heavy honking benders, her nostrils let loose with the red stuff. The nosebleed issue presented to me as beyond normal and quite scary.

      Chapter FOUR

I cautiously contemplated pulling out and leaving her house, before her nose bled again. Or maybe even worse, her body might reject additional quantities of the pink more severely, aka I was scared she might overdose. But no, her nasal bleeding finally stopped and we went straight back to the small horizontal knee mirror.

Standing outside myself and the scene awhile, dazed and bemused by the monetary and physical toll paid, I scowled at the truthful patheticness of selfdom when initiating such cocaine runs. Well, with precision I revealed to self-say…I lacked the operational controls to get out of that shit even if I wanted to, no fricking way bird boy, yeah right forget it, the allure was too great.

Later Sunday night after arriving home to my father's house although exhausted, I was unable to fall asleep for hours while my heartbeat pounded its drum so hard and fast I believed it would soon protrude from my skin. Attempting to come down by drinking a little water or chewing on some slight food, mostly I vomited back up what went down my throat, and then some. Although the general notion of smoking pot to calm my heartrate appeared as a reasonable idea, my stomach was in knots and I couldn't bring myself to even reach for the bong. I barely knew better but wanted to put the ordeal to bed, you know…flush or absorb some of the expensive pink amphetamine powder out of my way, so I could go crush some pillows of my own.

Each individual street drug wielded its own strain of vibrant poison against me. Typically within each substance family collective, shared characteristics became prevalent to me over time.

From my gained perspective and experience, pot generally categorizes as a depressant or downer, even times a mild hallucinogenic, but mostly pot got me up off my ass and moving. Excessive consumption of quality weed might produce an almost trippy experience, but irresponsibly would I dare claim such insight with certainty, because of my multi-concoction mixtures of adjacent drugs. The major considerations within my extended marijuana habit were mostly limited to the excessive expenditure of dollars, the occasional challenge of sourcing the rather expensive ground weed, and the at-time dynamics surrounding consumption of the then-illegal-everywhere ganja. The only real pot issue arose during sketchy dealings within the trade itself. Once offering myself to the clutch of the pot lifestyle, I discovered high quality potent exotics, selling for much as $25 per gram. Although mid-low-quality weeds sometimes presented themselves as available and more affordable options, mostly I avoided the low cost shit *dirt weed* because the risk of an ineffective high. Going price for mid-grade pot was $8 to $15 per gram. For my first eight years consuming, smoking began every day around 4:30 am after my sister knocked submissively at my bedroom door. My best friend little sister asked me the same pre-dawn question every day, "Roger, wanna do some bong hits?". We affectionately referred to the early AM smoking sessions as *wake and bakes*…waking up and baking our brain cells first thing. Never did I turn her down for a baking party before she took off for work. Mostly I had no choice because I owned the pot, owned the bong and also, I tried to do whatever Beth wanted to do.

After my sis left for work at Pimlico horse race track, I went back to sleep then smoked more by my lonesome when I awoke, and some more still before I set off to work myself. During work I snuck outside and smoked whenever I could and then after work, I smoked most the night's long before passing out asleep. Traditionally I consumed about a quarter ounce of pot per day myself, aka seven grams. The no-brainer benefit included the opportunity to also sell the stuff easily because of high demand all around me. For 13 years I consumed pot and for 10 of those years I sold pot most every day. Much of my pot dealing was selling grams or quarter ounces when trespassing on the Pikesville Senior High School parking lot before their bell rang, or around town throughout various neighborhoods. I also sold but less frequently, multiple ounces or partial pounds of pot to others intending to distribute smaller quantities themselves, but most my sales were to individuals for personal consumption.

The first speed family deliverable arrived to me in rather low dosage pharmaceutical capsule form, sold for a couple-few bucks per pill throughout all immediate neighborhoods. As you might be able to imagine, the results of speed pulled me up like consuming massive amounts of caffeine. When on speed, least for a time, the drug allowed me to basically feel no wrong. The era correct array of pharmaceutical uppers was vast, and because of intended medical usage, ingestion outcome of such illegals was highly reliable because of manufacturing controls. Layering pills and pot and acid and coke atop each other with great regularity for years, I learned how each drug affected me.

Although holding a supreme distaste for nutritional kitchen mushrooms otherwise, I began drinking magical mushroom tea at neighborhood parties before I was 14. Within weeks I was dropping solid form micro-dot alongside sibling windowpane acid chunks in my mouth, well as the minuscule paper tabs of LSD, all readily available around town. The hallucinogenic trips produced experiences akin to fantasized altered dream states, mostly neutral or positive, and then but rarely, time blocks of terror and fear. The uncontrolled nature of tripping resulted because of inconsistent manufacturing controls, and unknown beginning origins. Even alongside the ridiculous loss of brain and body function from the down-downer barbiturate pills, and the heart-stopping overdose power of the coke heroin and meth upcoming, I never felt so functionally out of control under the influence of those drugs compared to overly high on LSD. Yet, I continued to take acid well as occasional Mescaline and related cactus hallucinogens, for but a few of my thirteen active addict years.

Alcohol is referred to by our Native sisters and brothers as the *Devil's Water*, and some of the dirty word's origins mean *body eating spirit*. The word *ghoul* is also for goodness sake derived from alcohol. Old tales from the Mideast describe alcohol as an evil demon that eats human bodies. The Devil's Water destroys our liver, a non-negotiable critical stay-alive body organ, and more. Fundamentally I hated the taste of alcohol, so I somewhat opposed the Devil's Water booze. The downtown Baltimore *Hammerjacks* nightclub was a foundational wild happening in my back when. I never went to Hammerjacks alone, it was always a social event, and every time I left wasted, often unable to remember the drive home. All I ever drank at Hammerjacks were screwdrivers, aka vodka and orange juice.

Never beer, yuck…never whiskey or anything else, double yuck…just lots of drugs doused with vodka and OJ. Most every night on scene I walked outside the club to snort or smoke coke in the car, then went back in for more drinking. Quite often I brought pills inside with me and consumed my quaaludes or other barbiturates quick and easy as taking aspirin. Hammerjacks was a unique club, highly revered, and the culture of the place was certainly fitting to the times. The general theme was big poofy hair and loud-loud metal. There was a concert stage often featuring big national acts but the true allure was the normal every night vibe…heavy metal music cranked to max volume and pumped out through high quality speaker systems. The girls were dressed to the nines, and if any guys owned tight leather or form fitting nylon pants, like my Pikesville pal Jon Balk did, Hammerjacks was the perfect venue for such attire. *Hammers* was a two level building and within the expansive old warehouse featured about 20 different bars. Hammers was loud, wild, and exciting. Although most times I left Hammers falling down drunk and stoned, I now consider myself lucky I did not enjoy alcohol primordially. I doubt to have always made it home in one piece, if otherwise loving the Devil's Water. Hah…my existing track record of drug excessiveness stood aside a moderate miracle of survival as it was.

Somewhat because of self-blame concerning my later emotional stomp-out-quit at Sonny's bike shop, alongside the fact I might have just crucified a career I loved, aka the bicycle business, my drug use escalated heavily.

My making merry with the coke dope and meth became a literal game of Russian roulette, with mounting acceleration. I sprinkled powdered cocaine atop pot and smoked it for years before discovering crack. I both snorted and smoked dope, well as smoked meth, that is for the times such superior substances were available within my wandering circles. Coke when snorted or smoked was mostly a physically controllable adventure for me, but at times the emotional component of snorting coke borderlined death. Let me try to better explain. Cocaine does not produce a physical addiction to the point of body induced withdrawal, but the mental aspect of snorting coke is ridiculously powerful as described amongst my gal pal's Hello Kitty pillows, aka potential sans-life overdose fueled by emotional addiction, aka me unable to bird-stop.

  That night, oh boy here we go…that first night I smoked authentic crack, and whilst adrift in teenage wasteland wonderment mode I said out loud, "Wow, what's next?", my open mouth bird brashness inquiring what the paramount level of cocaine high might feel like, oops…the answer was readily available. In that cracked-up coke house was a box of previously innocent diabetic syringes, and then surprising even myself, I did not hesitate to shove a needle full of cocaine into the vein of my right upper forearm. Once I took that first shot, done deal, that's all it took, one shot, done…deal…done. On the spot and without controversy I knew for-fact-certain-100 that shooting was going to be my daily habit for a long-long time, quite possibly maybe forever, I absolutely fucking knew it as fact.

I held some sorta slight reserve for such upper level morgue medicines, but no way not for long. Darkness quickened in, death then popped up all around, and true ruination bled out from within me myself.

Feeling below-dookie-dirt shitty about myself, the needle high was too good to walk away from…yup, I stayed right there in that house up all night shooting, as would become most my entire life for the next few years.

Megatron Forces
The radical rush through my ever-wanting veins, the dump truck sized load of dopamine dropped into my idiotic brain, the lightning bolt shock of adrenaline launched into my gasping heart, the taste…oh that taste, the smell…ooh-ooh that smell, the taste and smell of my precious…the taste and smell of my precious cocaine I just injected into my arm.

These being the most familiar all-day everyday sensations I have been living with for well over a year. No joyful playtimes have occurred for a while now, not none…blackballed. No dinners out on the town, nope…disallowed. No visits to the nearby mountains or shimmering ocean, hum, duh, like are you kidding me no…abolished. Not even five minutes of sitting quietly outside on my dad's big ass front porch engulfed in a few moments of peaceful tranquility doing absolutely fricking nothing but watching squirrels scamper chatter and chase each other about, hah, revoked…not gonna happen. There was none of that and actually much less of what could be much more, well…but I cared not, not for a singular one of the other arguably enjoyable sunny life moments, zero, and same-same was the case for quite some time.

Six birthdays whisked by before I even realized to look up through my punk ass long hair and notice what the frick was happening, but who the hell cares anyway whatever no better.

I was living a shitty pathetic life as a teenage junkie and low level drug dealer in Baltimore, aka *Charm City*. Baltimore is still, per capita, the heroin overdose capital of the world whatever who cares just sayin'.

But on that day in my pathetic lowlife loser life, at that time in my drug supplier's house, I took things too far, it was too much. The shot of cocaine I just boosted into my arm was too strong, too-too strong, and I was going down. The ratio of tap water mixed with my precious cocaine had not diluted the drug enough for safe I.V. consumption. Or maybe the strength of the blow much stronger than I was used to, at the time. Perhaps still…there was some other drug, a dark drug, a bad drug, a dirty drug, mixed in with my precious, mixed in with my coke. Regardless, before I could even pull the needle back out of my arm, my eyelids were slammed shut with Megatron Force and 101% of my bodyweight inertia rolled back in my head.

Not knowing what happened after that, I…I awoke maybe ten minutes later, in the same room where for the last 35 hours or so, I was doing the same stupid fucked-up shit currently trying to kill me.

Chapter FOUR

And now getting slapped across my left cheek really, really, really hard with rapid disbursement of freezing cold contents from a large commercial spray bottle of water straight into my eyes and almost deafening screams, "Roger wake up, come on dude, wake up, come on Roger, Roger…Roger!".

This being the same death-trap-style room where I practically lived at my dealer's house, incessantly chopping up coke with a single sided razor blade upon a small broken mirror. Initially in my junkie career, I used a new needle every shot I took. The needles not being ones I paid for so once called out, I used the same basic needle all the time. Yes, and when the janky junkie tools were scarce, we shared. Only when badly bending or breaking the needle's tip could I get a new one. My veins were pleasantly robust and pronounced during the first few months of my everyday Whack-a-Mole game using the pathetically precarious poky instrument. Still and all, once tired of being persistently pummeled and playing part as pin cushion for twenty hours or more a day, my veins retreated. My veins ran away and hid far below the surface as they could squirrel away to out of sight, frightful fearful and frantic to avoid the certain abuse of the thin gauge low dose needle.

Bending and breaking needles resulted from my frustration and absolute need to tap into my awaiting circulatory system.

You my darling daughter may not realize that the injection of cocaine, heroin, methamphetamine and associated I-am-an-idiot consumed street drugs occurs into veins, not muscles.

Most prominent are the veins found on the interior of our forearms, while also smaller human plumbing offers up sacrificially in our hands, feet, and neck. Opposite the spectrum of street drugs or pain shots are the injections of immunizations, steroids and other non-death authorized medicines occurring when depositing the ouchie-oochie little poker sticks into muscles, not veins. The two intended injection destinations are no-way-not interchangeable. Traditionally, because bruising often occurs with the endorsed immunization and related *muscle shots*, preferably a large soft tissue area is targeted because the bigger stronger muscles can carry more abuse. The common muscles used for these other less-dummy people injections are the outside of the moderately-sized upper arm bicep, the frontside upper half of the large leg quadricep, and the big bad ass muscle we sit on, our gluteus maximus, the largest muscle in the humanoid body.

Digging for veins, sometimes my needle would bend. A few many times too often, once desperate and frustrated with the pre-abused pokers, the fragile bent needle tip would break. Horrifically advanced still, other times after pulling a small draw of blood into my drug solution injection container, the indication I properly resided in a vein, immediately I'd hit the plunger, thus slamming the entire contents into my arm and a smallish percentage of time only to feel none of the craved-for big-dummy positive effects at all, which is otherwise instantaneous.

Rather then my mortified experience…the dreaded immediate bruising and many times an immediate hematoma, usually an immediate headache, and certainly immediate rage because I just unceremoniously and mistakenly dumped expensive drugs into muscles, which was doing absolutely zip-zero nothing for me. After my veins retreated, the struggle intensified and by time I found one but not on purpose, I would move ever so slightly and accidentally slip out of the vein, thus missing the coveted cash depository shot. If you perchance notice internal forearm and back of hand scars infections and bruising, many times the attached poor soul is stuck in one of their own dead end life emptiness games, chasing veins. Not a pretty picture for your precious bird brain my dear darling daughter but total truth…bloody needle paragraphs now over.

Side note not digression, the following relates directly. Tragically in 2020 the world lost a quirky but hyper talented and beloved singer songwriter due to complications from COVID-19, the masterful Mister John Prine. The depth and talent of John Prine as one of the greatest artists to date is still unrealized, so says me big dummy junkie stupid head. Famously, John Prine wrote recorded and performed a shockingly accurate and deeply gut wrenching song, one of his best, the heartbreaking tune titled *Sam Stone.*

For me myself, I more accurately describe the song as disturbing, utterly disturbing…me once walking in Sam Stone's similar shoes.

The song's narrative is of Sam Stone, an American war veteran injured in battle who returned stateside to his kids and wife. Sam brought home his Purple Heart medal because of his injury inflicted by the enemy. Additionally, and now packed away deep within, Sam also carried home a new enemy, an addiction to his military prescribed down pain medicine, morphine. Drug addicted and broke, he got a job but Sam could not win the combative violence in his head nor over his addiction, aka the monkey on his back. Home life with the wife and kids went from bad to worse on every level, and Sam's family lost their house. The song closes with Sam Stone's American flag draped casket, the honored memorial practice for a deceased military person, and, um, well…Mister John Prine expertly claiming the tale *a sweet song played on a broken radio.*

I shed a tear every time hearing the melodic story of the crushing drug overdose death of Sam Stone the husband, Sam Stone the daddy. The hard hit in the song for big dummy stupid head me is the cold truth of addiction over all else as sung in the verse, *There's a hole in daddy's arm where all the money goes.*

So yeah anyway, hard to hit a vein precisely with a bent needle so I would grab a new poker. Or after getting moderately grossed out because of a bit-too-much splashed blood about, I trashed it and grabbed a new one. Same-same continued for over a year until I wore out the welcome at my main drug supplier's place, greedily consuming house needles before I faced another dreaded, *not today,* me then forced to turn around and leave the premises after purchasing my blow thy precious.

                              Chapter FOUR

Most times I debated, "Just one, please, can't I just come in for a minute, please…do I have to leave?," to which I got, "Uh, yeah dude, you need to leave, right now." Stumbling around town, I struggled to secure a consistent supply of the elusive new-in-package drug injection devices, not an easy exercise at the time. Some days needles presented themselves to me and especially during the coke focused period, I plowed through 20 or more needles before the sun rose on the following day. Me big dummy stupid head many times up all night, not sleeping or eating or drinking, just shooting more and more coke. At 17 years I sprouted up to 6'2" and although otherwise gangly, the junkie years drained me in multiple ways, yeah…I weighed no more than 145 pounds when shooting.

For me, the heroin shots were less frequent because this *down* drug took me in the wrong direction. The high of heroin is not actually a high at all, not like the *up* high of coke or methamphetamine anyway. Rather, the high of heroin, sidename dope, is actually a down-down-low, putting me into a heavily-sedated bumbling and mumbling state. The buzzing-in-my-brain low-on-dope timestamp sometimes lingered for hours, compared to the up-rush high of coke, only residing a mere few minutes, at best. The meth, aka crank, aka methamphetamine high is also an up-rush high, but the up of crank is different from the up of coke. The crank high also lasted many minutes, up to hours, accessorized with consequences.

The beastly high and physical ravaging of Crank is superior to all abused substances on the planet, but one.

Crank is a makes-you-absolutely-fucking-crazy, makes-your-skin-melt-off, and makes-your-teeth-fall-out high. I mostly shot coke because both the dope and the crank made me sick, and the withdrawal from dope and crank was horrible. The side effects of being sick from dope and crank were worth the intense high but for me and stupid as it sounds, I was often employed at the time so I mostly stuck with coke.

Not proud to say but displaying total truth, I shot up at work for well over a year, at my second bike shop job in Mount Washington and elsewhere, but, well…I tried like hell to minimize the vein banging time on the job, but it was hard to keep that shit paused for long, very fucking hard. On the clock, delicately I carried my junkie goods, aka the substances along with the tools, aka *the works*, into the bike shop bathroom or into the woods around the rear of the store to do the deed, before plopping back into work mode.

Coke's superpower is draining bank accounts, awhile elevating heart rates and sometimes stopping them cold with the diabolic tentacles of cardiac arrest. A primary dope addiction caused horrible withdrawals, aka *dope sick*, when I could not otherwise find the stuff or pay for it. Heroin, as it is dope the downer drug, slows our hearts sometimes to a ranking full stop. A primary crank aka meth addiction would also cause an equally horrible unwinding as heroin aka dope, but actually much-much worse.

I think the awaytime from crank, when I could not find it or lacked the money or hustle to get it, even the soft withdrawal period from fuck-meth-crank is one of the most horrific fricking things the human body is capable of experiencing.

The come down from meth-crank throws our brains into a tail spinning scrambled mess, and we possess no functional control over our bodies. The loss of effective brain control and the simultaneous loss of body movement is where the nickname for meth addicts comes from…*tweakers*. I speak of soft withdrawal because I was never a full-time committed meth head. I was thoughtful enough to know crank was evil, very fucking evil, concocted by The Devil himself, so says me big dummy stupidhead.

Working at bike shops during my junkiehood, I could not lose my job, or I believed I would die.

My strength and resolve amid self was near decimated and factually, I was looking for any opportunity to just be done, just be done with the running, just be done with it all. Only by way of the real bike shop jobs that came and went around that time did I keep a few coins of hope & possibility jingling around in my pockets.

Shooting-wise, I preferred the up high of coke, and not really the down low of dope anyway, well, ugh…sort of….so on some idiotic and ridiculously-responsible stupid head level, I chose to mostly stay away from a focused dope or crank addiction. Besides a bizarre dynamic I am not yet ready to reveal, dope withdrawal is physically uncontrollable and I was not going to subject my coworkers and customers to the hellish coming-off-the-down shitshows. And I knew better to think I could handle the tweaking at work when pausing my high on crank. Yes it was my super fucking dumb bird brain at work, playing the ROI, aka return on investment calculation of coke versus dope versus crank, but these, my truths.

The callousness of crank is different from all other substances but one, can you guess? Yup, of course you can my Birdy, because you 'litrilly roll your eyes at me whenever I go here and your momma even stating, *I don't think so*…yet yes for fact 100, crank aka meth is different from all substances but one, fucking alcohol. Alcohol and meth are twin sibling juxta-playmates, but alcohol is by far more superior and dominating, no lie, total…truth…one…fucking…hundred percent. Alcohol is technically a depressant. Abusing alcohol literally makes us fucking crazy, truthfully rewiring our brains to the negative. Unlike any other substance on the planet except methamphetamine aka crank, booze can make us psychotic. Besides, the liquor eats us up from the inside out, no lie. Knowing this shit firsthand after living it, tasting these demonic drugs and Devil's brews daily for years, I summarize to say alcohol is hands down the worst fucking drug available to humankind.

Booze is top dog worst drug because of the damage it does, its widely abused concealment, social bullying and easy breezy availability. Alcoholism kills and kills swiftly, shortening people's lives by almost 30 years and guess what my precious little Birdy? The numbers fucking prove it, legit, more people die from alcohol per year in the USA than meth heroin or any other single intended drug…over 100,000 lives lost to booze which is over 250 fucking people formerly alive per fucking day, stupid fucking cuckoo fucking debauchery fucking shit…soapbox mic drop. Bird brain drunk and drug addiction education side-trip digression now over, time to refocus.

Chapter FOUR

Back to the overdose room, taking the big or dirty shot of coke…*I was going down.*

Fairly sure I fell backward off my chair and laid on the floor, passed out until my friends stepped in to revive me. No ambulances were called, no doctors were summoned, and they did not dump my body at the closest hospital emergency room curb.

We never discussed what happened, hah…I just shook it off and kept shooting. My friends saved my life that day and later still, some slight strangers farther from home, also under overdose circumstances. Me and the needle played a stupid fucking game of tug-of-war with my beating heart for years, but it felt like decades of frantic Russian Roulette, shoving the loaded junkie gun in my mouth every waking hour…pulling the trigger over, and over, and over.

Hard to say what caused my first overdose. Reasonably, a strong batch of coke the culprit. Sometimes after a shipment pickup from New York and before we cut the coke, purity was high and the chance for overdose stupidly risky, compared to shooting stepped-on less-potent shit. As my tolerance grew, I increased the mixture of coke over water. The diabetes low-dose syringes only held a small amount of contents so if increasing the concentration of drug versus water, the shot really packs a punch. Thinking deeper and going sub-surface on the matter, intently pondering the truth of the situation at the time, here now a nervous blockage forms as I try to dissect what was going on with me behaviorally back then, and, well…but…ugh, my fingers now somewhat struggling to type…I guess I am not entirely prepared for the admission or share.

Well, guess I would say, um, oh boy thereupon fuck it all anyway here we go…my shooting grew progressively irresponsible in ridiculous suicide-type ways, and without much surprise, the overdoses resulted.

The specifics escape me, I do not remember how I prepared that shot, but, gosh fucking dang it, I am not sure why this is so darn hard to admit and…well, I began dropping all sorts of additional shit into my shots as time went on, aka ridiculously irresponsible.

Before the existence of heinous dirty drugs Fentanyl and Carfentanil, I ran proxy as death drug posterchild concocting my own lethal mix of poisoned potion dreaming to die, but not intending to do the deal myself directly. Often I crushed up pills without first identifying them and threw them into my spoon, adding the crumbled unknown tablets into the liquid mixture of the main coke, dope, or meth. The pills would have been either one of the multitudes of downer barbiturates lounging 'round or some form of amphetamines, or whatever else who cares not me. Sometimes still, I incautiously threw LSD atop my mix.

The add-in of acid might originate as the somewhat dissolvable solid *windowpane* form, like tiny brick sheets of sectioned cooking chocolate, appearing almost plastic like in texture and arriving in a variety of colors: blue, green, red or yellow. Sometimes the small doses of brick acid dissolved and mixed in with the rest of the solution. Maybe the acid would not break down, then remained abottom the spoon as discarded remnants, after the final coke mix got sucked up through the needle, atop a drop in filter. Often I placed a *tab* or two of LSD into my spoon for soaking before sucking up the final concoction, the tiny square paper tablets treated with the drug. Last-dance lastly, LSD also arrived in *micro dot* form, like little candied sugar droplets on paper, and the micro dot would partially dissolve in my coke spoon or if nestled in with dope, I cooked that shit, aka put a lighter under my spoon to melt down the contents, bringing the spoon-cauldron to a boil before my needle sucked up the witch's stew.

Experimenting with lots of different stuff, some of the shit capable of killing me on their own, and the potpourri mad scientist mystery mixture was certainly a larger idiotic gamble.

Much ado what the fuck ever, without question the needle will win, I collected such knowings deep within me, *this needle will defeat me for certain*, such words repeated in my head for months.

    My thoughts rambled 'round a while then muffled…who is so intent to kill me, some contemporary Jenghis Khan? Hah, the nano haze cleared quickly…the only murderer here will be me.

Thy Precious Baby Child
One of my main dealers was running out of town to pick up a shipment of resupply cocaine. They would be gone most of the day but still held current inventory. Likely because I was the primary loiterer here, a somewhat natural occurrence happened. I was asked to tend shop, charged with solo-selling as buyers presumably shuffle in and out of the house constantly. We estimated based on time of year and weather, I would not sell through the entire inventory, least it was highly unlikely. The concept seemed harmless enough, and I was honored with the entrustment of their commercial enterprise for an extended full day shift…me maybe on the dubious clock from 9 to 9. I was responsible for not only their inventory, but also their customers, their cash, and their house.

    A friend sat with me and having another person by my side provided some slight enhanced security, because of not knowing many the characters scurrying in and out, all with cash in hand and some with gun in belt. Like every day stretched across the last year or two whatever who the fuck cares like nobody not me, I allocated maximum daily funds for shooting. Because of the mini coke mountain in stock while tending said mercantile, I attempted temptation governance, warming up slowly with small controlled boosts. Otherwise punched out and apart from *Dealer on Duty*, I shot with reckless abandon but this day I aimed to maintain maximum responsibilities.

My committed process as shopkeeper was to avoid all in-spoon amplifications, like my random crushed up pills, drop-in LSD hits, and opposing speedball contents, aka mixing down heroin with up coke. No, today nothing but straight coke, least was my intent.

Buyers scampered in and out, and although some I never met before, I let the asinine gamble of selling blow to strangers roll along mindlessly. Some requiring to linger longer and snort or shoot before they left, and some running right back out the door immediately with purchase held incognito. Between the flurry of transactions, I began doing my own shots. In short order I burned through my fiscal means for the day.

It was fuzzy, I barely saw the micro second scare coming, and it was ugly, very ugly, very fucking ugly.

Dismally, I began to justify the indefensible…it's ok to do one more shot, it's ok to do another, and another. Before thinking it possible and without giving the situation enough semi-reasonable consideration, I burned through the shop's inventory…all of it.

Oh for fuck's sake, what had I done? I honestly did not notice as the hours clocked by, or realized seeing the stock near its bottom, well…until after it was gone. Panic flooded, I scrambled to think how I could spin this situation around. My dealer and I get along well, or so I believed, but maybe not *that* well. There were guns in this house and quite certain my dealer also packed least one pistol on their person, moment current. My brain-wracking was going nowhere productive and while panicking, the front door scarily opened, no knock, and no triple door unlock from my side of the wall like is necessary. The boss pulled their jingling keys from the door and gleefully looked my way…oh fuck me down to hell and back.

They strolled in with their billowing magic backpack and started emptying their pockets, well as going to offload their gun from an ankle holster, a pleasant upbeat look on their face, hah, maybe thrilled to see their crib still standing and not blown up or burned down.

I was true friends with them before I met the needle but now so deep into my junkie career, I was utterly unreliable.

Neither of us said hello and I couldn't locate a single appropriate word. I believe the look on my face told the story, and an immediate flush came over my dealer.

"How much did you sell?", they asked speedily with force. I struggled to speak.

"Well…", I began to answer while gathering my things because I needed to get the fuck out of there. "Well…all of it, kind of…", I said.

I tried to avoid eye contact from then on…I really, really had to get out of there. "What do you mean *kind of*?"…their snappy and overly-concerned comeback lingered heavily in the air.

With most things gathered I was over-inflated with shame gas, also frantic, awhile being strung out sky high. I wanted to puke and just might before reaching the door, feeling rumblings of upchuck a coming.

They walked over to their stash and saw the coke was gone. I watched them count the light stack of money in the transaction box then shot lightning bolts straight through me with a puzzled glare, both fists clenching what little cash laid abottom and hands outstretched to the sides like, *What the fuck Roger?*...but they did not say a word. In full flustered motion, frantically I fumbled towards the door, then not at all looking back. My friend shuffled off my heels a few mere inches behind, almost pushing me out of the way for the exit..."I know, I'm sorry, I did it all, I'll get you your money tomorrow, somehow"...my bare-all testimony pronounced with desperation, cringing with shoulders up to my ears for maybe bullets soon flying my way. I opened the front door but stopped, turning to them for a response before I walked out. Thankfully they still held just slight dollars in hand, not elsewise aiming their fancy black carry-on revolver my way.

"Uh, ok...tomorrow, I know you will, that's alright...are you ok?", their concern was genuine. I said *yeah, I think so.* "Are you sure you're ok?", now sounding fearful for me health wise, like maybe I should not actually leave a while but stay, and remain attending-scene monitored by them on rounds. My head shook up and down with patheticism...I walked out silently with friend person brushing hurriedly up against my back. The door closed and I heard dealer thy orderly lock up triple-tight from the opposing side. Once out from roof, friend person offered me a ride home but I declined, mad at myself while astronomically puzzled...I needed to think, I needed to figure this shit out...oh my God what the fuck did I just do? I said *no thanks I'll walk*, and they left.

Treading home shakily, and struggling to stay vertical, I behaved like a 'litral fall down drunk. My upper limbs were absolutely fucking killing me from the recently concluded contest. I felt dark red overspillage from the gaping holes get soaked up by my jacket as I rubbed my sore forearms...oh man, what a fricking bloody mess.

I halted several times dizzily, hands on knees, frantic depths of breath, trying to refocus and hopefully more clearly see the sidewalk cracks and curbs before restarting my attempted stumble along.

Amphetamine-poisoned, heartrate berserk, and while mind-a-racing, I struggled to imagine a resolution, oh fucking fuck...I just couldn't cipher one. Fuck more, unsure how much I even owed because not keeping track of what went down the pipes there towards the end. Frightfully irresponsible to rip through all I did, drowsily I puzzled the numbers...must've been $600 or more between what I shot, what we snorted together amid the bang, and the minimal boosts that thine security sidekick did on my dime. Well, no, screw that, hold up a sec...fucked-fact-100, they themselves could never do the deal, so I administered their friend come-along inoculations myself. I tended shop before both for this dealer and another, but stayed within the guardrails. Never ever nevermore did I want to tend shop while believably, I do not think this dealer will require or even allow my shopkeeping assistance in the future. Minimally, guess it could be said I cleaned the shelf of existing inventory to make room for more.

                              Chapter FOUR

Pulling together the only possible deal I could fabricate, the next day I rode my BMX bike several miles to the bank and emptied my savings account, all $200 of it. Hoping I could present a reasonable offer, I rode several miles back the other way to my dealer's house. Thankfully they accepted my proposal, but the price tag hefty, very fucking hefty. Taking a gram and a half package of blow with me, I then walked the fuck home. My hyper-fancy heart-prized Redline Proline II BMX bike was my pride and joy, a true work of glimmering chrome bike art, not even a year old since I finished building it. I did not race this bike, I sucked at BMX racing, yup, I was a total poser. I possessed the BMX passion that's for sure, more than $1,300 worth…craftily assembling the Redline over time using top-of-the-line new components, and building the wheels myself with choice select parts. None the sort fucking mattered any longer in the material world, I owed my dealer a fair stack of money that I did not have. I took drugs without arranging the deal beforehand, a maneuver in different circles which would have gotten me shot on the spot. I gave up the entirety of cash collected because that is what I owed them, cash. My bill outstanding was multitudes more than the two hundred dollars I possessed but reluctantly, they agreed to take my exquisite Redline on trade.

Dread consumed me entirely, and in a way I am not sure my diction will allow me to adequately communicate. Initially, I was not sure of the value they would find in my bike, although I would have honestly preferred to cut off a finger or three than give up my beloved Redline. They knew bikes, they knew me, and they knew this bike, they knew it well. After my multi year searching for perfect parts and my incessant bragging during assembly, my dealer knew this bike's history intimately. Literally shocked I was sacrificing my precious Redline, they asked several times if I was sure. My voice shaky but somewhat self-sacrificially stern, *yes I'm sure*. I had nothing else to put up against my debt except a finger or three, but a couple ounces of flesh and bone carried no financial weight in this house. Horrifically discomposed to burn through their stock without restraint, I walked the fuck away.

A modestly-inflated to generous credit was issued for the remaining value of the bike, a fair trade on the bank table but one I absolutely despised making. Decimated, I fricking left…I couldn't fucking believe it, my cherished Redline is gone. Since like eight years old I dreamed of owning that exact bike, 'litrilly lusting after it, it my alternative non-motorized off-road two-wheeler. Finally with a full-time bike shop job, I built the whip slowly and methodically over time, assembling the perfect parts I dreamed of for over a decade. For Christ's sake I spent more than a fucking year waiting for the exact wheel rims I desired, and another eight months searching for the specific extra-long chrome-plated tubular chromoly steel pedal crank arms, them fuckers like jewelry. Such maintained discipline, the carving out of drug dollars to make this dream a reality, well, the words escape me entirely, even to dabble within its aura, um, no…indescribable. I was mad, very mad, and very is but a token spirit for an unutterable inner hatred due to my runaway behavior. Steaming, I spun around looking to fucking break something.

Hah, and like duh, later in the day I went back twice for more coke. By mid-next day I burned through my remaining credit. Fuck, fuck, fuck…the Redline no longer belonged to me, *now* it's gone, it's *really* gone. Flat broke, no more Redline, and with the needle continuing to dominate, I sank.

Losing a possession I would have never let go of for any reason, 'suppose I set myself up for heartbreak by not imagining a divorce from the Redline was ever possible. Trying to then push past my fuming bike sorrow, I partially acknowledged to have mismanaged expectations, yes...any desires, functional possessions, and sunny days were canceled once I started shooting. Still, and maybe this better, I should've sold the Redline frame and all parts before assembly, so to save myself the heartbreak, hah, but maybe not...such notion akin the backward thinking of not wanting a dog because of the resulting lofty loss when they pass.

Potentially, the Redline incident could have been used as supporting testimony, presenting a motion to myself that now is time to move away from the needle once and for all...*see what my shithead self does while shooting, see, can I not see it, can I not fucking see it*? Hah, no, mostly the opposite occurred, I then self-punished. My sentence...self-ridicule, my sentence...enhanced irreverence of consumption because of the senseless sacrifice of my treasured bike.

It was just a silly bike, you might say. It was not a lot of money, you might say. To me it was more than a bike, it was a piece of me, it was my baby, it was my fucking child. Losing that bike cut me down, cut me down to the fucking ground, cut me down right 'bove the knees. Such fucked-up maneuver browbeat me listlessly, facing my own damn out of orderliness, such malignant disorderliness created by no one nor nothin' else except these goddamn hands, these goddamn piece of shit loser lowlife hands...oh this fucking life, oh this fucking allowance, this fucking allowance my fucking addiction.

This place, this place all new...this place my rock fucking bottom.

 Chapter FOUR

Disregard

Lethal undistinguishably-colored death cloud

He billows in with creeping atomic toxicity

Void of concern, shearing every lifeform with bitter and savage curiosity

Dastardly disregard for any existence

No thirst for blood but gluttonous consumption of incomprehensibility.

Spinning Disoriented Compass

The challenge while on the clock was great, both the struggle to stay in good graces with work bosses, awhile simultaneously manage the bullshit I suffered by my own hand. I teetered on the pinnacle of self-inflicted hopelessness, ah fuck it all who cares- nobody, unsure and mostly unconcerned for which way was which, often dangling over the edge of giving up on everything altogether. Unequivocally, I was a bloody hell hot mess in body, heart, and mind. Already distancing myself greatly from my father, I felt no safety comfort or support at home. I did not have any put together non drug using friends I admired, my-age grown-up or other-wise, not ones I thought to include anyway, so I knew myself on my own, for badder or worse. Yes sure I had some girlfriends in and out of my world for a while but my drug use was ballooning in damaging ways, which harmed everyone around me. The botched drug deals also withdrew lots, both by my own thieving hands well as similar rip off hands bats knives and guns laid upon me.

Although withholding some slight part-time desire to make something of myself, anything really, I was awhile mentally fragile because of the at-home chaos and attempted face forward without a high school diploma for fuck's sake.

I believed only a slight additional amount of negative pressure could have caused me to quit life, or least shatter the little positivity I possessed, leaving only then the pieces of me scattered across the floor of nothingness.

And then, and then oh wow…illogically, it was for-fact crazily absurd, into my 18th year or so, something happened, a piece of object machinery entered my life in a way I never knew such a thing could possibly impact me, never ever. On my mountainbike I ventured deep into the woods, then left to my own doing, then alone with my own thoughts. Also I was, exercising, and least for a while at times, away from drugs. With familiarity I took shit with me into the woods, mostly pot, but primarily when off on my new big-boy bike I acted with intention…my purpose to ride, escape, try to catch my emotional breath and maybe improve my cycling skills here and there however plausible.

Leapfrogging my withheld motorcycle racer aspirations, I showed up to compete on a two wheeler of the non-motorized variety, I showed up to race my mountainbike. Hah, what a fricking joke…fabricate-spying some slight possibility of self before factually attempting my first big boy bike race, once blundering in spectacular fashion, I squandered within the pool of patheticness, recognizing I sucked at this shit too. I fought an ensuing weakened battle against that motherfucker the drug needle, after laid out aghast at the end of lines, there whilst then proving without rebuttal that this lowlife loser self fricking sucks at all fucking earthly humanoid things, oh the fuck well, what the fuck ever. And yet, and yet…the part-time tranquil world I generated for myself on the bike was rather rapturous, so there had to be something more to this off-road two wheeler thing, had to, or so I self-taunted. I tried to rally, I rallied to try, I tried to get back on the mountainbike but couldn't, well, I should more accurately say I mostly *wouldn't* get back on the bike because of self-ridicule.

 Chapter FOUR

It was…it was my miserable choice to do, or do not.

With despondency and dedication I nothing but dunked downer pills and shot drugs all day, yes my mood and behavior akin both my Jekyll inside my Hyde…the fatalism melee practically unfuckingmanageable. Amid my up-down high a foggy creeping glimmer snuck into my periphery, a fifth-hearted dream about attempting another bike race one day, but well, hah, that is if an encore overdose didn't kill me first.

Granted Clear Path

A stressful restriction strongarmed my chest…my breathing belabored. An emotional dominance tug-of-war battle was on, and winning the challenge thus far was the searing anxiety currently clouding these eyes to outside sights, currently deafening these ears to outside sounds. The attempted endeavor of placidly lounging in the back seat of my friend's mother's car was futile, because of the pressure cooker distress building up steam inside me. While enroute to the grandest adventure of my life, I was simultaneously snarled in an entanglement of dread.

The heavy Baltimore beltway rush hour traffic was nothing new, but traveling in the opposite direction at this time of day was strange. Not creeping along to get home after a long day on the clock, but rather attempting to make it to the airport on time for an early-evening flight. Boarding my initiator flight in the afternoon added to my awkwardness, it all just seemed wronger than wrong. Despite only twenty miles door to door from my house, ludicrously the airport seemed to get farther away, not closer.

We inched 'round the beltway, the minutes rapidly ticked-ticked-ticked by, and my head hurtled towards total freak-out mode. First things first I thought, I must get control of my breathing. Closing my eyes, I silently practiced a few big long breaths. But the attempted breath control was not at all working, not in the slightest. The voices of fears and frights rambled round my upper story but no, I must quickly try to grasp control and soon present myself as calm, actually *innocent,* once we reach the airport. Gazing blindly out the car window, I approached the stressors from an objective however be it frantic perspective, running down the issues like studder-reading a presentation word for word from a flip chart.

Would I, would I be patted down and searched shortly after entering the airport?
Could I, could I gain safe haven in the bathroom before security laid hands on me?
What would I do, what would I do if I missed my flight?
If we reach the airport late, if late, how would I arrange to get on another plane?
What would happen to my gear if, if I, if I got arrested?

Mostly, I was anxious as fuck to dump all the cocaine I was carrying.

Only days after my 20th birthday, several glorious conditions deserving grand celebration offered themselves to me, while opposing factors caused me great worry. On the pleasing sunny side of the page, soon I would hopefully be skiing in the Swiss Alps, wow…today my first adventure out of the country, today my first trip to Europe.

Hence nothing but the repugnant reveals presided over the moment…perhaps not arriving to the airport in time to make my flight, I might overdose on airport property, I might get arrested attempting to transport controlled substances out of the country, hell I might not return home from this expedition at all.

Without exception I was unsure of the demands for immigration, customs control, and the general additional time required to check-in for an overseas plane trip. Now emotionally unhinging over the amplifying possibility of missing my flight to Luxembourg, oh hell why not, I strapped a bonus stressor upon my back…will I be able to fully utilize then discard the drug needles currently occupying my left front coat pocket?

I secured no earthly idea the difficulty involved rescheduling a missed international flight, and gave no thought to the people awaiting our arrival in the Benelux. Unfortunately as I quickly realized, I should have practiced forethought plans mapping this three ring circus I was attempting to orchestrate. Accepting the offer to go skiing and mountain climbing in the European Alps with my friend Ryan after dreaming of it for years seemed like a fantastical grand adventure. However, I failed to recognize the associated simultaneous complexities, mainly my current occupation as a full blown fucking junkie.

Supplementary to my mounting mental chaos, I recently visited the theatres and watched the movie *Midnight Express*, an insane tale about a young American locked up and sentenced to more than 30 years in a foreign prison for smuggling drugs on a plane, and the movie scared the shit out of me.

So between the open container of drugs located loosely on my person, and the bulk of drugs I planned to carry on the plane, my current state could be best described as fear-flooded.

Hah…only by way of a slight miracle were we on our way to the airport at all. A mere few days earlier, Ryan and I rushed from Baltimore to Washington, attempting to get our yet-to-be-secured passports. Thankfully the passport office was open on Saturdays, I assume catering to procrastination dummies like us. We screwed up and waited too long, then imposed to drive to DC and do whatever it takes so we don't ruin our chances to fly across the proverbial pond, aka Atlantic Ocean. We mailed away for our international travel booklets weeks ago, but once realizing they might take months to process, our only hope to fly overseas as planned was blast down to DC and get our credentials in-person. So on March 3rd, my big two-zero birthday, Ryan and I drove to our nation's capital, hoping not to get pulled over by Maryland State Troopers along the way. I feared a road-side stoppage because of course, duh…I was carrying drugs. The main route Interstate 95, between Baltimore and DC is a well-used highway for transporting drugs. When running to or from DC with contraband on board, I tried to use the less popular alternative route, highway 29, but today we were in a hurry.

    Chapter FOUR

Although the two cities are only forty miles apart, running up and down I-95 without incident is a crapshoot, and today was not a good day to get stopped and searched, no not at all.

I experienced a moderate level of paranoia during my life's time as a junkie, certainly a naturally occurring side effect of excessive cocaine consumption, but generally up until this time, I was intrinsically fearful of cops. Several times while properly existing in the presence of law and order, I was either unnecessarily hassled or arrested for random or rather invalid reasons. Mostly my tangles with police occurred, although I am assuming, because of emotional judgments against me…the unrelated circumstances like how I looked, how I talked, or the people I associated with.

The time standing and waiting for our passports in the packed government building was stressful enough, but only minutes prior, before exiting our car parked on the busy DC street out front, in broad daylight, I was shoving drug needles into my arms. Stumbling into the State Department building surrounded by armed government agents while strung-out on cocaine was not my idea of fun, but we eventually got the job done. Later that night Ryan and I arrived home safely from DC, with our passports securely in hand. Favorably, we did then later arrived to BWI airport with enough time to make our flight to western Europe. We were flying Iceland Air directly to the airline's namesake land of fire and ice for refueling, before then proceeding to Luxembourg.

But we never made it onto the damn plane that day.

Not pausing to consider possible consequences or alternatives, soon as Ryan's mom dropped us at BWI, with what I thought was a reasonable time cushion, and with my gear in tow, I immediately took off for the bathroom. Before bothering to check in for my flight, higher priorities entranced me.

The folded-up paper package containing a gram of cocaine in my left front coat pocket anticipated the bon voyage party too. No way was I willing to discard my coke in favor of time schedules, nor did I even consider it…the notion unreservedly inconceivable to me. Besides, I felt the need of parting gifts, a celebratory intravenous cocaine send-off before the dreaded two months apart from my precious babies, you know…apart from my darling drug needles. I remained for about thirty minutes locked inside one of the toilet stalls, shooting up the entire gram of high quality but pre-ground powder cocaine. Appropriately I only required one of the two needles I possessed…the second one supportively along for the ride, loitering on scene in case the need for a back-up implement was called for.

While dumping the coke into my arms fast as possible without overdosing, I was juggling a thing or three too many. All my gear sat in the bathroom almost abandoned, outside my pooper shack. The tall ski bag stood in the corner on the other side of my enclave, and my large overstuffed backpack half-leaned against the ski bag. I could see them under my stall but several times I paused as a pair of shoes approached my gear and hesitated. In a place like Baltimore, I had to keep a constant eye on my stuff, certainly a slight challenge while hiding in my semi-private shooting enclosure.

The mood inside the partitioned public toilet den was nerve wracking, with its ambient loud chaotic bustle and wide gaps between the stall walls and door panels. Constantly fearing someone can see me, I grew heavily distracted and fully anticipated Maryland state police to soon bang on my stall door…*open up, we know what you're doing in there, you're under arrest*….or so my daytime fright vision estimated. Frantically hurried while distracted I just kept shooting, and lost track of time. Our travel plans called for a couple months abroad, and fearful of carrying coke and needles on the plane with me, I was consuming all I could before we left.

Ridiculously, once finally emerging from the busy urban public restroom and discarding my drug needles in an airport trashcan, I missed my damn flight.

Ryan rejoined me and we scrambled feverishly to rebook our tickets to Europe, but ugh…we couldn't secure a reasonable plane departure until the following day out of New York, which by the way would require a hassle-filled Greyhound bus ride in the morning. So of course, the next order of business was, duh…get more coke. The thought of spending precious European travel adventure money on cocaine caused me slight hesitation, only slight, hah, no bother no better…I spent the rest of the evening at home shooting.

Stupidly in the middle of the night, I had to explain to my sister Laura over the phone, who now lived in Germany, and who was now standing in the Luxembourg airport not seeing us deplane as scheduled that…*oops, sorry*…we missed our flight and I forgot to call her. Laura was understandably pissed because of the wasted hour and a half drive from her apartment on Ramstein Air Force base. With an appropriately scolding tone, she instructed me to call her prior to boarding the plane or she will not make the drive again.

The timing of dirtbike neighbor Ryan's offer for me to join him on an international ski and climbing trip was stupidly ironic. I was severely fucked up at the time, definitely in the worst drug condition of my life, mad at myself over losing my Redline and failing on the mountainbike racecourse, this biddy barely hanging on by a spindly who-the-fuck-cares-anyway thread.

Grasping at the slight hope that positive change could await me in the Alps, I faced the illustrious mirror and tried to pull my loser-loser junkie lowlife-loser self together enough to get on a fricking plane.

I was granted clear path, I was gifted a chance…live out my dream of skiing in Europe or die by that motherfucker the needle, the choice mine alone entirely.

My Lost Story

My hands atop my head shelter me from nothing

My fingers across my face veil me from no one

My purpose hides craftily from even me

Lost warnings missed shielding me from today

Lost looking past the suffers, the bloodstains the stumbled tiers

Lost knowing what comfort will bring and when

This plot teeming threats nay promises, fronting nothing but nemesis

This one wants to see something else or nothing at all

This sinistrous stormy night oh lost are the stars, astray the poor moon, no allowance of hope.

Motherly Love

When amid the mountains I feel at home, emotionally, spiritually and physically. Only the hilly woods give me an indication of perhaps the touch of a mother's hand…the warmth, comfort, safety, and unconditional love that maybe a mothers love held. I can look into the mirror and get caught in thought, going deeper and deeper into self, mostly depart from harm befalling me. I can sit outside within the presence of inspiring nature, sinking into the beauty and peace of the many living things surrounding me, awhile magically, none of them there to hurt me. There is so much more I want to explain here, but, but there are no more words none, no not for that, for I know not, a mother's love.

Junkie's Paradise

I did not know what I did not know. I barely believed what I thought I did know. So, admittedly, I did not go looking for drugs and the discovery not so much a naturally occurring temptation spawned amid the stream bottom of a rough urban environment. Yeah sure, Baltimore is a tough place and drug infested but the allure for such life exit to fantasia was more so feeding the chaos within me. I could have kept walking past the drugs or left them behind once defined, least when minimally understanding the potential of their destruction. No one fucking forced me, no one pressured me, it was an initial so simple offer to which I could have easily fricking refused. I inquisitively experimented and quite literally, within five minutes of soaking up the seeping effects of comfort, calm, warmth, security and safety drugs provided, I was hooked-100. The protective shelter and caring comfort blanketed me in its own sick way, I echo-felt loved unlike I ever had, fucking ever. Finally, I found something right when most everything else in my life felt wrong.

Since my memories began I desired and sought coddling nurture,
hah…then I ran for eight years seeking safe haven.

With the marijuana active agent THC swaddling me underneath its burrito wrap, immediately I echo-gladly and soundly resided within its cover. Such nestling was not settling or running or napping soundly in mediocrity, no not at all. I believed I found my path, my new warm safe loving place in the world, albeit a clouded escape.

In case the extrapolation of this stupid fucked up shit whizzed by you, the downers were the first big noticeable drop off, the narcotic pills capable of slow stopping my heart feet-up but mostly sent this bird boy into a zombie like, almost asleep or brain dead walk about state. My yum-yum downers were from the old school barbiturate family, aka *barbies*, and of course I'm not a fucking pharmacist but by my proprietary desk reference, before the popularity of opioid pills were the barbiturates, my favorites being Tuinal's, Seconal's, Placidyl's, and the ultra-famous Quaalude's. Downer pills at the time originated directly out the back door of pharmacies so although life threatening, the makeup of each pill was consistently reliable. Once establishing a tolerance to the downers, I created a reliable baseline.

So if safely consuming three or four quaaludes at once, the next time I ate some, three or four *ludes* would affect me the same, long as I had not sacrificed my tolerance or layered too much other crap on top.

Still, the long way around remained…exploring the plethora of drugs easily and rather cheaply found on the streets of Baltimore. My repertoire continued, thy explorative consumption…lots of hashish, which was another drug I smoked in bongs and bowls, *hash* as it is called. Hash came in varieties and although similar to smoking pot, hash seemed to have varying effects. Hash was like a thick black or brown glue, very sticky and hard to work with. Onward then, my expansion of appended hallucinogenics caused varied states of euphoric mind bending…meaning, I observed extensions of color light and objects, well as viewed things to be present that were not really there. Peyote, Mescaline, and Bromomescaline which are powerful narcotics drawn from cactus in Mexico and the southwestern United States, or otherwise fabricated, were also parts of my trippy quiver, whenever available. When my regular cocaine sources dried up, I went anywhere necessary to score, most notably to Park Heights. In Park Heights, a couple full-length city blocks I utilized, hah, they legitimately operated as open air drug markets, remaining unclosed for business 24/7 year round, this my last resort to score coke dope or weed. Some shit was cheap and easy to find, some expensive and hard to find, some I liked, some not so much, some did great harm, and some were lusciously delicious, not just their effects.

Once introduced to cocaine, the blow became my far-far and away preferred drug, the one I put above all others. My affinity for coke was challenging first because it is so damn expensive…traditionally a gram of blow cost $100. Two people could easily snort a gram of coke in 30 minutes. Then, because the alluring drug is so powerful, it was time to get more, and more, and more. Shooting cocaine, I did not initially realize the gamble, or rather did not fucking care to even ponder the potential. When coke arrived I technically had no idea how good it was, until I did a shot. If doing a two-tenths shot, I would only get five shots out of a gram. Even with tolerance, a two-tenths shot of potent coke was often too much and put me on my ass. If the coke was stomped on, I could shoot much as three-tenths of a gram and not drop to the ground. Sure-sure to say each of the thousands of times I slammed the needle was a total gamble, literally a roulette roll of the chamber. Soon as I shot, I would start prepping the next. Once running through my purchased or fronted supply, it was time to get more, and more. Hard to say how much total cocaine I consumed in my lifetime, the cumulative between snorting smoking and shooting, but once shooting, most days were consumed with not much else. By my measure I claim the quantity to be a mountainous amount.

Concerning mine the maniacal meth, I smoked that shit on and off for a while, then began to shoot it too, but often mixed the devilish crank with dope to concoct an up/down *speedball* shot.

At times, many times, I tried to stray from the claw's reach of crank which wasn't hard because it not so much avail' within the rings I ran. And then really, the dope was the most dysfunctional component of all, but I'll save that lingering fucked-up legacy bullshit for later, maybe never. Well, fricking hold up a damn minute, fuck that, I cannot avoid this shit. Fucking fuck me…I am not being openly honest about the dope. There's something I'm holding back, well…because of never facing it before. Ah fuck it, let's go…factually-actually, dang, I, I…I loved dope, actually I loved dope more than coke, oh boy I think this is really gonna hurt.

The zinging euphoric rush of shooting dope is unbelievable and somewhat inarticulatable. Shooting dope is different than coke, still a buzzed rush and magical yet dope is more domineering and abusively pow-pow-powerful. Hence still, more than loving dope, I hated dope, fucking…hated…that…fucking…shit. I hated how dope crippled me 'n where it dragged me. Dope hauled me to the lowest floor of caged utter inaction, threw me in, locked the door thus annihilating all my options, held me in that depressive down-down dungeon, factually below the reach of shadow, actually beyond the end of day and night. Although such darkness was rather welcoming and desired at the time…*ouchie-oochie*…herewithin specifically-100, it was no-no no-way fucking not.

Defining to say I hated dope, well, *oh man here we go…when boxed in under such gloom-doom cover I could not function, I could not run, I could not adjust, no way, I could not escape by way of my own power, I was tacked to the floor, I was vulnerable and feared once trapped in such a down immovable place, well, I feared she would then come for me, find me, grab me, and hurt me…she being monster mother Patricia Lou.*

Oh holy hell fuckballs that feels weird to sort out cognitively for the first time, oh well fuck it whatever *ouch* who cares…enough of that stupid fucking shit for now.

Sometimes, I thought ambitiously and produced to-do ideas when on coke. The associated cocaine paranoia once consuming measurable quantity then boxed me in, but least I was able to be on my feet with coke, not stuck in a half catatonic state with drool dripping out both corners of my mouth like down-down on dope. When smoking and snorting dope I did not appreciate the defenselessness, although at times dope-only was available when coke was not. Truth be clear, none of my main dealers dealt in dope either, mainly coke. Mostly it was the trips to Park Heights to get the dope, or downtown east to get the meth.

The interesting-to-me dynamic of doing business in multiple communities was that when Mount Washington had pot and pills, maybe Pimlico and Pikesville were without. When Pikesville or nearby Randallstown had coke, maybe Mount Washington was dry. When Park Heights and adjacent Mondawmin had coke and dope, maybe Pikesville, Randallstown and Mount Washington were out looking for some. I bounced around and some days played the hero, bringing supply from one area to another.

                    Chapter FOUR

And then the must-mention, the integrative gamble of doing business…least half the bunch of times I got robbed, ridiculously, jeeze…surrounding us was a multitude of other people on scene, hah, but the guys holding handgun didn't at all care if they needed to fucking shoot me or not, depending on my cooperation. These guys seemed to not give one single shit, nor seem to have much to lose, like oh well whatever. Most times I could have been a cop for all they knew, but their actions displayed, meh…even if I were a cop they would not pause to fucking shoot me anyway who cares. So, whenever handgun came out, I tried to do what told, least appear to do as told, but sometimes held back, aka craftily concealed additional money or drugs on my person.

The buying, selling, fronting, and getting fronted from people more experienced than me in the business was everyday all-day relentless. Sometimes I lost money when I got ripped off, sometimes I was ripping people off, sometimes I swung fists and baseball bats, and sometimes I was the one getting a beating…the wildness being just part of the occupation. Almost from the start, nothing surprised me, not even seeing people overdose or stepping over pools of fresh blood on the ground. My first overdose recount was spelled out already best I know but retelling the second will remain mostly untold, well…kind of. Not because I fear sharing the second OD tale, no, not because I did something so horrible that I dread the reveal, no, mostly because I do not know all that happened. Regardless and admittedly, I was depressive-downward-distraught over not completing my first mountainbike race. Lower than low I sank, and uncaringly I threw around a blatant disregard for future heartbeats, or fucking not. Thinking I'd never amount to fucking zip-zero anything, shadow consumed me almost entirely.

Oh fricking hell I really don't want to unearth this, but I guess do I must, fuck oh well whatever…after a small heroin purchase inside a strange Park Heights house, in the company of people I really didn't know, I was forced to do a shot because the dope sellers suspected I was a cop. One shot turned into two but a bulk of memories after the third shot are missing. Birdy my precious, I'm…I'm sorry, I, I have a hard time talking about this. My dear baby bird, this piece of me and part of my past since it happened, I have tried to avoid thinking of it any more than I have to. Getting through these next few sentences or even paragraphs is going to hurt, and I, well…I am not looking forward to it. I'd rather not stir this one up but you my darling deserve to know, besides and soundly, you asked. I am partially embarrassed but more so and frankly, I still carry some unsettled horrors from the ordeal.

I do remember more than I am about to share but sorry, here and now, I can't, I just can't, but will share what I can. Ask me about the rest, if you have to.

The trouble began with my first shot. I did not want to shoot there, no fucking way, I wanted to take my shit and leave. But I could not leave, no way, I had no choice, I had to shoot, handgun said so. Not planning to bang on site I brought no works with me, so I had to use house works, aka a dirty dope spoon to cook the shit and fricking hell motherfucker…oh well whatever, a used needle to shoot the shit.

Early evening I had walked to Park Heights possessing keys, some slight excess cash and other insignificant shit in my pockets, all of which after a short while went bye-bye. Later the next day or the next after that, not sure which, I found myself at home in my jeans t-shirt and shoes, sans socks and missing something else baselayer-bottom. Also upon my return then missing was my jacket I previously wore. I was dirty once I arrived home, unhealthily dirty…dirty *everywhere*. I smelled like piss, plus some kind of bleach or cleaning solvent or hairspray or something, IDK. I might have blacked out, sure yes it's possible, never happened like that before, but possible. Strange marks and bruising existed on my body where they should not have been. There were splotches of sticky residue across my torso, hands, arms and knees. I had vein marks and sub-skin-surface muscle bruising on the back of both my mitts where I normally did not shoot, but maybe it was just a wild multi-day shooting blackout and the sticky residue was something like glue syrup honey or chewing gum, IDK. So yes therefore I am lying to say I overdosed a second time, because I do not know for fact, aka I was not there, *consciously*. For over a week afterward, I emotionally lingered at my primary and secondary coke dealer's houses more than normal, a little unsettled to venture out too much. I avoided Park Heights, Pimlico, and nearby dope-heavy Mondawmin for a while, preferring to be around only people I already knew. I felt weakened, like physically…my insides bothered me greatly for a couple weeks, like really bad tummy stuff.

The while, although organically distraught and weirded-out, I was so damn and ridiculously fucking tired…tired of the running, tired of the hustling, tired of the fear, tired of all that which laid down with me threateningly, swirling around inside my head every fricking night.

Not completely sold on the idea, or oriented towards any conscious direction at all, but I began to prepare to go one final step lower, just before Ryan pitched Europe my way.

Beyond Ballsy

I received a phone call at my father's house, *Hello*… it was a Tuesday. I did not recognize their voice although once self-identifying, *Hello, oh wow, like really, I mean hi*…I knew intimately who they were, a local drug seller, one of the infamous Mount Washington tough guys. Somewhat laughingly, although I part-time creeper-stalked this exact dude, I had never heard his voice before and he entirely surprised me, me unbelieving I was actually right now talking to him directly, wow…'litrilly an in-fact fantasy of mine. But anyway whatever, the ask, to buy a quarter pound of marijuana from me, aka four ounces.

Within an hour I tracked down a source, a rather disconnected source for me as it was, and would resell the quarter to tough guy. I called tough buyer back and verbalized the deal. We quibbled briefly about price, hah, although on some level I did not at all no fricking way want to do business with this dude, but had to. Totally assuming and judging, but I was somewhat surprised he agreed to my $1,200 quote, an estimate I thought would exist beyond his budget.

                    Chapter FOUR

Weed was scarce at the time and this batch of pot was quality bud, priced at $15 per gram but for a ¼ LB, I priced it at around $10, granting the bulk discount per quantity.

Strangely I must make an asterisk *technology note. Considering such outlandish detail somewhat inconceivable these days, but looking back, our family had one OG phone and the device was hardwired to the wall. Any drug deals I arranged over the phone were made by way of the household family communicator, located in the kitchen and directly adjacent to BigBird's bedroom.

Multitudes per day my father answered the ring-ring…it was for me, and when home I pre-arranged many deals over that phone.

Often buyers popped-in without first calling, hence a steady flow of people in and out the door, or hah…more accurately, in and out my second-floor bedroom window.

Ridiculously, tough guy quarter pound buyer and I went back and forth trying to agree on a day and time to do the deal. The weirdness surrounding the rodeo dance of rescheduling seemed odd to me. About five or six of these closely-associated guys all ran together and it struck me strange none of them could meet, once I was ready to make the handoff. During the comical back and forth, different dudes from the tough guy crew called me, them representing the group and speaking for the original leader of the pack, aka thy worshiped one. Seemingly, they were playing games with me. We finally nailed it down, I would meet the Mount Washington tough guys Thursday night and swap the quarter for cash.

Mid-day Thursday I picked up the four big bags of weed from the county dealer I knew slightly, but someone I rarely did business with, uh yeah, a guy I did not do biz with on no-way purpose. My source fronted me the four OZ's and based on the prearrangement with the tough Mount Washington crew, I promised to pay dealer dude mid-day Friday. Tough guys rescheduled again and now they wanted to meet Friday night. The newly scheduled Friday deal already messed me up. I called my dealer and said I couldn't pay until Friday night, a notification that was not well-received. Three things tugged at me. One, I did not want to piss off my dealer by delaying payment. He nor his big gun were the understanding types and certainly characters not to mess with. Two, I wanted to get the pot quarter out of my possession and out of my father's house. Holding onto such quantity even for several hours made me nervous, worried about getting ripped off or busted. Three, my suspicion grew rapidly that the Mount Washington guys were fucking with me, and finagling to burn me on the quarter. I was tempted to pull the plug and cancel the deal, telling them sorry, I couldn't get the stuff or I already sold it to someone else after one too many rescheduled meet-up's. I did not trust them. Numerous times before, these guys threatened me directly and although I wanted to believe we could do this deal cleanly, I suspected the opposite might turn out to be the case.

The tough Mount Washington guys carried a rare and ridiculous high stock of echo-echo…downer pills, not steadily available anywhere else. I already established several streams of down-pill sales to connections elsewhere.

Sum-sum-some of my connects consumed only downers not pot or coke, them purely popping pills. Pill profits were puny but because of my ability to supply a steady stream of the pleasure pellets to one crew in Pikesville, I was getting better supply and pricing on cocaine. Trying to maintain good sources for blow, I believed the need to maintain my supply chain of pills, so I reluctantly moved forward with the quarter sale to the city-residing tough guys.

The plans for Friday changed to Saturday and the for-gosh-darn-sake Saturday arrangement shifted to Sunday, hah…then they canceled. Rather fed up, I called back Sunday and gave them one final chance. The guys wanted to meet mid-day Tuesday but it was my day off and I already plotted to be out of town. I proposed we meet on Wednesday because I was going skiing the day before and they agreed, great, Wednesday it was. I said I'll see them Wednesday at lunchtime in front of the ice rink…if by chance something changed, I have to dump the pot elsewhere, I wasn't going to hold onto it any longer. *That's fine* they said, *have fun skiing on Tuesday*, they said, *we'll meet you at the rink on Wednesday noon*, they said.

I wanted to get this circus deal done and hopefully not get ripped off. By this point I was hiding from my dealer and ignoring his calls. I did not have the money to pay him and maybe I should have given the quarter pound back, but I didn't. I had to be careful where I went and who I talked to for the next few days because if crazy county dealer dude catches up with me, I'll probably get beat up, or worse. If these Mount Washington guys burn me, the financial toll would be a hard hit. My cost on the quarter was $900 and I had zero money in reserve for such a loss. If I couldn't pay my dealer, he would absolutely take it out on me physically, zero doubt concerning that presumption. There was no one I could borrow money from and I had nothing left to sell of value that could be moved quickly, nobody was interested in my mountainbike, they didn't understand its purpose…I might really get screwed on this one. I was also holding onto the deal because I wanted to make the $300 profit, I needed that damn money.

Looking down the road…in the end, the future outcome of this deal felt telling, like the net summary no way worth it.

Fuck…I was already over 48 hours late paying dealer and the fricking dude was calling my house multiple times a day, which made me extremely nervous. I had known several previous contacts that got killed for much less. My father was growing agitated too…*who is this guy calling our house late at night and what does he want*, BigBird asked me several times. I was concerned county dude might find out where I lived, and show up to collect come hell or high water. Thankfully I ran 'round avoiding him on Monday. I couldn't wait to get the frick out of town Tuesday and remain unreachable all day.

Concerned about my dealer's big fancy sidearm for-sure-soon gunning my way, I urged Pikesville skiing buddy Michael to please-please pick me up soon as possible on Tuesday. Without 'ncident, Michael Greenstein collected me in his hot-rodded-up Chevelle skimobile early Tuesday and we zoomed off for the southern Pennsylvania slopes.

          Chapter FOUR

Later the day around dinner time, we rolled back into Pimlico and turned onto my street. I was shuffling around inside Michael's jacked-up 'rod organizing my stuff, me preparing to unload. Briefly I glanced out the windshield and screamed "BACK UP-BACK UP-BACK UP-RIGHT NOW". Michael slammed on the brakes, threw it in reverse and we zoomed backward about a quarter block. Peeling wheels slightly around the corner and away from my house, I told Michael to take me to a nearby friend's place, unbeknownst to ski pal but it was in fact my main cocaine dealer. Frantically I fled for friendly coke dealer's house, leaving Michael awaiting in the car, *keep this fucker running* I quickly instructed, half-heartedly anticipating the po-po probably tailing us after peeling wheels away from copper-occupied birdhouse. As I ran for the blowhouse door, *shit, shit*…I rapidly processed if I soon had to flee this place, abandon residence at my father's house and just go on the run, running both from the law but mostly ducking my no-way non-understanding dealer's big bullets.

Four or five Baltimore City cop cars were parked directly in front of my house, I knew the trouble related to me, like how could it not be?

I asked to use the coke-casa phone but they were nervous about me even being there, after I said cops were parked all over the place in front of my dad's house. They made me promise not to speak detail on their phone but yes, it's ok if I call my father. BigBird picked up before the second ring, like almost anticipating it would be me the PAB calling. I barely said hello and he pronounced with supreme sternness, "Roger you need to come home RIGHT NOW". Oh fuck…I had no idea what happened but immediately I worried about the four ounces of expensive weed stashed in my room, never mind my amassed drug tools, especially all my cocaine gear and some slight stock. I asked him *what's going on* but BigBird just repeated himself with heightened gusto.

Tentatively I hung up, and aimed for the coke house door. My dealing friends wished me luck then forcefully notified that I not come back for a couple of days, minimally, no matter what, or they will pretend not to even know me. Michael asked what was going on but I kept him in the dark, Michael did not do drugs. I said to please just drive me back to BigBird's cop-flooded house.

With Michael's nasty big-block Chevy hotrod grumbling angrily out front, I unloaded my ski stuff as the cops began to shuffle from the house. Passing the City's Finest on the sidewalk, they glared at me accusingly, one officer almost snarling my way. Under my breath I snarled back multiple *fuck you's* as each copper walked by…fuck you, fuck you, fuck you, fuck you, and fuck you very not so much…*assholes*. By the time I walked up the porch with both arms full of ski equipment, the last cop to leave held the door open, hah…somewhat relieved, I spurted a short-baked *thanks* his way. Walking in, thank fuckness…I was entirely surprised none of them stuck around to put me in cuffs, uh yeah…I still had cuts and bruises on my wrists from my most recent tangled run-ins with local city and nearby county law officers.

The scene in the house was immediately surreal. The TV was off. None of my sisters were downstairs.

Some rustling sounds fell from the second floor but none of the audibles were normal, not normal for this house anyway. Honestly it was creepy as fuck. I walked cautiously through the living room, and turned left through the dining room. While slinking I noticed but barely, both rooms were askew. Large buffet-style cabinets existed in both the living and dining areas but hum, the drawers and cabinet doors were flung open, with various items littered on the floor below. Something was wrong. I could not understand yet what happened. Besides fearing the disappearance of the multiple bags of bud valued at almost a thousand bucks, I disturbed for my sister's safety…oh shit where are they, why are they not downstairs, are they for please God's sake ok?

BigBird greeted me in the kitchen. I tried to push past and get upstairs toot suite to check on my pot but strangely, BigBird stayed solidly stationary. Traditionally, well, like always, when I stepped close to his personal space, he backed away or stepped aside, but not this time. My father needed a word with me first. I didn't hear a single syllabled thing he said, I just wanted to see if my presumptive nightmare was true…fuck, is the quarter pound gone? During the chew-out I looked around disconnected, hoping his opposing physical stature softens soon so I can squeeze by but at the moment, he was blocking me entirely. *Ho-hum, ho-hum get on with it would you,* or so I non-bothered to myself while his speak continued. Briefly, casually, I looked left from the kitchen into my father's bedroom…*oh fuck, oh fuck no, oh my God,* I couldn't believe what I saw.

BigBird's room consisted of a sitting area directly off the kitchen and attached past his sitting-style office was a small bedroom. Fucking hell…his office den and bedroom shit was thrown about everywhere. My father's hundreds of books and decades of hand-scribed sermon papers were scattered across the den floor, and his clothes thrown all around his farther-away bedroom. Quickly I realized this was a break-in burglary.

With uncertainty I now proceed, not sure I can satisfactorily expound upon the supreme feeling of violation, the painting descriptive of eerie notions, yes, an uninvited dark human in the house ravaging through belongings, fondling personals…this sensation-horrible mostly existing beyond my diction.

Akin the devastation of a flood, a fire, a wrecked car-totaled, or an undesired abrupt end to a dreamlike romantic relationship, these losses are rather cataclysmic. Aside from an unfaithful romantic partner, I believe the unnerving of a break-in burglary is almost bad as it gets, relating to at-home life tragedies that is, outside the bounds of extreme illness death or horrific physical attacks like rape.

Fuck-factually I never observed my father more pissed at me, fricking ever. Not til a slight time later did I understand why. He was downright angry but honestly I was giving him or his emotions zip-zero no never mind. My full focus was on the quarter pound, *fuck me, fuck me…*hey what about…*outta my goddamn way dude…*I pushed past while faking a mouthed-off distraction, and ran upstairs.

          Chapter FOUR

Christy and Beth were both in their individual bedrooms with, uncommonly, their doors open, both of them sitting on the floor of their personal thrown-about disasters. I made visual contact with each as I whisked past. Christy held tears in her eyes still, while Beth's salty droplets danced down her cheeks, at the time. Laura occupied the third floor and although I couldn't see, I heard unsettled noises coming down her steps, Laura's attic bedroom up-step door existing right next to mine. I barely noticed while scooting up the inclined hall but my father was blazing hot on my heels the entire way. Once reaching my door, BigBird was standing a mere few inches behind, still scolding me with incomprehensible words that escaped the entirety of my concern.

My room was flipping trashed, like totally. I looked around intently, visually scanning the damage foot by foot as my eyes glared floor to ceiling. My big clear plexiglass Tokemaster bong was sitting squarely on my desk in its purposeful holder, still ready to go thank goodness because spilled bongwater would have just added insult to injury. About four posters from the ceiling were torn down and laid on the floor, while another ten or so ceiling arts remained up there, untouched. I tried to find the perhaps missing piece and comprehend if my nightmare was true, but I wasn't at all sure.

BigBird dragged my attention to the hundreds of assorted Ziploc baggies scattered across the floor, well as the multiple rolls of aluminum foil, both used for marijuana packaging. Not sure he knew the comprehensive functionality of the large *Ohaus* triple-beam weighing scale and the various coke dispensers, grinder, and related paraphernalia thrown about. I barely tuned in but my father said the cops offered to stay behind and arrest me once I got home. BigBird said he told them maybe, but then no thank you, not at this time. "The police know what all this stuff is and they would have been happy to lock you up purely because of the cocaine residue, but it was my decision, you better clean all of this up, you're grounded for two months, no one is allowed to visit, *blah blah blah…*" but I barely heard another word. I wanted him to leave me the frick alone beginning immediately, to see if the quarter pound was nothing but stolen.

Finally he left. I closed my door and kicked a bunch of baggies and various magazines aside so I didn't slip and fall. Precisely as I was about to check my stash area, Beth busted into my room which was weird, she always knocks. Not really up-front mad, but rather my best friend sis seemed extremely hurt, and confused. She asked, "Roger, what's going on?". I said just wait a minute. I closed the door behind her and moved closer towards my stash to check on the quarter.

Pathetically, I then had little to say in response to Beth's pronouncement, "You know they stole all of dad's cameras don't you?".

My father's primary passion even in front of woodworking was photography, and he had a decent collection of cameras, maybe five or six total. He until then still owned his first camera, an old look-down-from-the-top reflex box design from his high school days, and other cool old cameras he used to help pay his way through college by shooting weddings. Also in BigBird's assemblage was a then-modern-day Cannon high tech unit containing every feature and multiple lenses. Turning to Beth I asked, "*All* of them?".

My semi-somber question hurt, even coming out of my mouth. "Yes *ALL* of them", Beth replied speedily, using a heightened tone of re-centering accusatory frustration.

My Tum-Tum-Tumultuous Relationship With Handgun
"I don't fucking care, give me my fucking money", was my unsympathetic response to one of my semi-regular buyers who I fronted drugs to three weeks ago, after they then claimed to lack the owed-to-me funds. Still their stupid excuses continued even though they promised me, and promised me, and promised me they will have my money tomorrow, tomorrow, tomorrow, my face then only inches from their grill, I screamed my paraphrased words of pay up bitch.

Such interactions did not happen daily or even weekly but probably monthly, for a pretty solid ten years. My frustrated verbal assault delivered after their senseless claim of zero bucks aggravated me. I did not fucking care about their empty pockets and most likely they already sold the drugs and spent the money, or did the drugs themselves, and now want to fuck with me. It was simple business math, I gave them drugs and now they owe me money, I want my fucking money. This game went on and on and on…sometimes I never got paid, while at times I did the same damn thing to somebody else, avoiding and finally escaping their reach without making good on the debt I owed, before we both moved on and let it go.

Such was the risk management, inventory control, asset velocity, mortal defensibility, and cash flow turmoil elements of my lowlife piece-of-shit loser punk-ass-bitch drug-dealing life.

As it may well have been, the biggest challenge was the fact I simultaneously consumed the same drugs I sold, and sometimes a portion of each deliverable. The resulting corner I backed myself into created ridiculously dangerous scenarios. Often I cheated the weight of the package, portioning off a little bit for myself. With pot and hash and related substances, I many times sold *light bags,* aka underweight. Most people never weighed their purchases before digging in to consume, so I mostly got away with those rip-offs. There was no way to alter the material or cheat the count of the acid or pills, so I tried to upcharge per unit where I could. Concerning the coke, I either sold light packs, and-or stepped on it, me cutting the blow more than how it arrived. Certainly the height of such aggressiveness occurred during my time as a junkie, when sleep was minimal, financial upheaval compounded to its height, thoughts most scrambled, and my desperation to score more for personal consumption ran beyond measurability.

My most fucked-up deal ever began so simple, then escalated to a robbery, and worse. I sold excessively cut-up coke to a guy, Rodney, and for oh bloody fucking hell shit's sake I should have known better. This shit went down when I was shooting, so attempting to mince off much coke as I could for myself, I in fact ripped Rodney off. When plowing through a couple-few hundred dollars of coke and-or dope most days over years, barely could I keep from being greedy, even with Rodney. From day one I knew Rodney was not a guy I should be fucking with.

   Chapter FOUR

Honestly I do not know what the hell I was thinking stepping on Rodney's blow, duh, clearly I was not thinking at all. After scoring two grams from me and he didn't get high off the shit, Rodney came back at me, he came back at me hard. A plethora of thy dearest people to me could have been murdered the night Rodney came to collect his refund, plus interest. Rodney seemed to anticipate the way it might go down…cunningly, he premeditated a strategy with proper implements to assist in the smooth execution of his stomped-on coke refund strategy.

Across the span of my teenage wasteland druggie days 'n beyond, my emotions ran the full spread of pathetic biddy baby to full-blown fucking asshole holding a knife, stealing and cheating others out of everything I could get away with. Approaching my teen years I thought to be collecting a mild tough-guy self-image, but the first time I got punched in the face, it humbled me quickly. Luckily I didn't get knocked out nor did the guy break my nose, but I didn't feel so tough after that. The sensation was shocking and I wanted to cry, but couldn't. Seemingly he did not put his full effort into the punch landing squarely in the middle of my face or possibly, I saw it coming enough to pull back a little. Regardless, dude guy confidently took what he wanted from me as I stood there, startled and practically helpless. After the first nose punch, I carried a higher level of awareness, well, least I tried.

Between the ages of nine and twelve I got mugged a few-to-handful of times, once in broad daylight with a knife pushed up against my belly on one of the fricking busiest streets in Northwest Baltimore City, Reisterstown Road. I was walking home the long way after school one day, and the guy confined me on the 10-foot wide sidewalk, a few blocks before my upcoming turn left at Northern Parkway. He drew his blade and it stayed out for over four minutes, as hundreds of cars drove past by the way, thank you very little not so much. Sketch dude was anxious for me to quickly empty my pockets but he had plenty of time, not a single car stopped or slowed as I stood with my hands up above my head. Initially I did not fear getting sliced or incised but Sketchy grew super edgy. He became infuriated when the only item of real value I produced was a 9-volt battery still in wrapper, my earned frequent shopper gift I collected 30 minutes prior within the rewards program at the nearby RadioShack store. Even though emptying my pockets right there on the fricking sidewalk, sternly he insisted I still concealed money.

Enraged, he stepped forward with his knife against my t-shirt just as I stepped backward, demanding I "hand over the money".

Not sure I factually actually would have been stabbed if not simultaneously backing up, but it absolutely seemed like such was the case, at the time. He punched my hand away while grabbing the then re-gifted rewards battery and stormed off, casually strolling up Reisterstown Road towards the Plaza, still holding the knife by his side and sporting his who-the-fuck-cares nonchalant indifference. I walked home shaking my head while chuckling…I almost got stabbed over a damn 9-volt battery. Although for 15 years I carried my own damn knife, my main intent was not attack or harm, but defensive protection from the many times I tangled with guys much tougher than me.

After one too many attack losses, I sought out and bought a large folding hunting knife from an Army surplus store on Liberty Road in Randallstown, *Sunny's Surplus*. My weapon traveled with me everywhere, even school. Well, that is during the rare times I bothered with the damn place, the shut-up, sit-down and learn-something place. Not that I previously adopted the role as victim, but anticipating more shit to come and finally, I was sick and fricking tired of getting ripped off or beaten up. Although carrying my knife did something for me, rarely did I think to have the upper hand. Other guys were most always willing to go much further, risking everything during our physical tangles for seemingly fricking nothing, well…maybe to just release pent up anger or maintain their tough bully image. I stood outside of control amid most encounters, but I was already fricking in it, so while still lasting of breath, I chose to play along with my own flipping knife and just keep moving, best I could.

Physically, I was weak and unconfident. Emotionally I was frail, least compared to my general environment. Fights occurred here and there, threats were both given and received, and I weaseled my way out of physical confrontations best I could. Certainly I got into tangles I could not always get out of, and I just had to take the lumps coming to me. Once carrying my concealed folding blade, I tried to never pack it into the house of a person I did not know. Most times I stashed my dear companion in the bushes on my way in and collected it afterward. Too many fricking guns were around for me to even attempt possession of a non-handgun weapon inside drug houses, which of course would have made me an operable threat, however diffused.

Within my world of the Baltimore street-drug trade and after only about a year, when I was 13 or maybe 14, I grew closer with firearms, and I had no choice.

The first time I met handgun, I hated him immediately. I never faced a more intimidating adversary and bizarrely, an objective opponent specifically designed and constructed to kill me.

Although many of the drug-for-money exchanges occurred outdoors, maybe half of the outside guns were concealed so the threat not immediately visible, aka out of sight out of mind. I only picked up handgun once in my first thirty years of life and quite literally, it was one too many times…fuck-zero thanks. Generally, I tried to operate on the street and in transaction rooms where I knew people already. But anytime handgun is in the room, there are no rules, no safeguards whatsoever, and always I felt endangered, like literally placing my head under the guillotine soon as I walked through the door in their presence…handgun.

Echo-preferring to stay within known circles, at-times spotty availability had me strutting into sketchy places to score, even sketchy places close to home. I did not grow up or go to school amongst the tough guys in Mount Washington and although interacting with a few of them in a somewhat friendly but fake manner, I was always the outsider. The one Mount Washington guy freaking me out more than all others was a little older, Howie Transue. Howie was the guy who called my house to buy the quarter, and oh yeah also by the way, Howie was a tactically-trained elite forces *Army Ranger*.

　　　　　　　　　Chapter FOUR

Howie held a vouchered reputation as the craziest motherfucker in the neighborhood. Famously, Howie also rode dirt bikes, and constructed a practice course in the Mount Washington woods right off the railroad tracks that quite frankly was ridiculously hard to ride. Two hills on *Howie's Track* were stupid-hard, and though attempting, I never once made it up those hills on my dirt bike. And never had I thus-then spoken to Howie in person, except as you already know, *echo*…over the phone.

Watching Howie ride his track, I was verifiably entranced but hid to stay out of sight. Howie ripped around his hilly and heavily wooded course at three times the speed I ever could, and with my jaw laid upon the ground in awe, I watched him effortlessly fly up and down those crazy-ass hills. *Echo-echo*…I idolized dirt bikes, the sport, the imagined grit required to actually participate in the darn activity, and plainly put, I worshiped everything about these motorized off-road two-wheelers. Once I saw Howie ride, I trophied him a local professional racer, and I could stand there in the woods all day watching him blast around like a flawless Tasmanian Devil. I never saw Howie slip-up or make a mistake, ever. Weirdly, for all the admiration I embraced well as desire to connect, I otherwise stayed far away from Howie as I could, and I think my fear transparently projected through my weakened presence.

I really tried collecting the nerve to approach Howie…thinking about bringing cash with me, I'd offer to pay him monthly or weekly for moto race training. I knew the value worth it to carve off drug dollars for dreams-come-true coaching, and maybe I could even ride along with him to races, or I'd pay extra for that, because for God's-truth-certain my father would do nothing of the sort. I knew for absolute, one day, one day I would race dirt bikes…even part-time dreaming I could somehow make a living at it. Barely did I spy any slight path forward for myself, but maybe…maybe I'll be a pro motocross racer because frankly only otherwise possessing an elementary education.

I knew no other so savvy to help guide me, mentor me, and push me than the masterful Mister Howie Transue himself. Fucking hell, I scared too long to open my damn mouth, and any such relationship with Howie was then nothing but blotted out. In rather grand fashion, Howie Transue killed himself, surrounded by his Army garb and motocross gear tacked up on the wall. Seemingly it was a radical self tribute and fantastic send-off for the craziest motherfucker around, Howie hanging himself from the rafters of his Mount Washington Falls Road garage. Although hearsay, I was told directly by one of the second-tier tough guys in Mount Washington, a really decent dude actually, that yes, it was in fact Howie and his crew who burglarized BigBird's house.

Wrong-hand option-option…the physical confrontations continued, both within the drug transactions and also simply out and around town. I suppose if an academic, a bookworm, an athlete, or if I had a mother at home partially wrangling me, I would not have been out on the streets as much, but duh, none of that shit applied to me.

When I first shook hands with handgun, I was in the house of one of my dealers in Baltimore City, slightly north of downtown central.

My dealer's shiny-shiny large intimidating semi-automatic weapon sat there loaded, with a spare full clip next to it, on an end table in their main living space. When I arrived, four people were already in the room, two of whom I did not know, and no thank you yikes…I did not at all want to know these guys if you pretty please. I was totally judging, but the two unknown dudes were not the kind of guys I desired anywhere near my immediate circle.

The two unknown guys in vicinity of handgun were unlike anyone else I ever met in Baltimore. Maybe every few months, an out of town visiting stranger would appear on scene, accompanying someone I knew during one of our otherwise normal transactions. Traditionally, these visiting strangers were introduced to me or identified as *a friend*, and the conversation then avoided all reference to the out of towners, like we were playing a game that the tag along humans were invisible. Now and then the *friends* were said to hail from DC or Philly or Delaware, and for the most part, these people looked like the rest of us. The DC boys were usually a little rougher, wore their pants a little lower, wore more jewelry, but basically looked like us.

Not these two dudes in the vicinity of handgun though, no fricking way. They were similar in stature, and although seated, I estimated them both to be over 6'3", athletically stocky, physically fit, and chest muscles filling out their black mesh and plain white t-shirts, respectively. Black mesh shirt guy donned a perfectly-fitted leather motorcycle jacket, not the punk biker kind with a built-in belt, but more the short Euro-cool purpose-built street bike motorcycle designer jacket, you might know the kind, both functional and exotic. His hands were either dirty or had tattoos across his fingers and knuckles, maybe a mixture of both but no way was I going to look too closely.

White t-shirt guy sported a worn but neat jean jacket, and a properly prepared black leather vest over top, with several silver rings across both hands, and a manly bracelet or two. The rough and tumble dudes duo were well put together, both in physical stature and in dress. They wore strange pants I had never seen, slightly poofy but not cheesy, somewhat similar to military issue but with a nightclub flair. They both wore black leather boots I was not used to seeing around here. One set of boots had large silver buckles on them, and the other I couldn't really tell what was going on there.

I never saw these guys before and they were off-the-scale rough and tough. Their facial expressions stood as terminally aggressive and although presenting as slightly dirty, they both were extremely intimidating. Immediately I felt like these guys were sure to be packing guns on their person. Yes I was totally assuming and judging but it all lined up…they appeared as the kind of guys who have killed people before and wouldn't hesitate to fucking do it again, anytime anywhere.

My friend the dealer of the house introduced them both to me not by their names but presented the collective pair as…New York.

Oh fuck, I knew what that meant. Soon as the words got spoken, no longer did I need an explanation, fuck to the no did I need anything, nope…these guys were our cocaine connection up north.

                 Chapter FOUR

The backstory as prior told to me and at-time understood…these guys and their associated crew was the direct connection to the main cocaine supply. My local dealer rode trains to New York and picked up from these guys regularly. They must be on their way to somewhere, and I was immediately motivated to get the hell out of there soon as possible, hopefully without making anyone overly nervous.

I hoped not this time nor here because I was a regular, but sometimes in other houses where I didn't know the seller so well, I would be forced to do certain things to earn their trust, like boost a shot of coke or dope. Many times guns were brought out and laid on display soon as I sat down, surely as direct intimidation, a threat meant to say *don't try anything or I will fucking shoot you*. Sometimes I got frisked walking in the door but mostly it was the immediate presentation of handgun that straightened me up, their show of force sort-of threat, the subliminal but clearly understood ground rules…*this is my gun, I'll gladly shoot you so go ahead and give me a reason.*

I walked over to sit down inside my dealer's house…a big open and inviting soft cushy chair laid awaiting but I immediately swung around and changed directions, when I saw handgun positioned only inches away. Immediately I knew this was gonna suck when I saw the gun.

The big ready-to-kill gun with *New York* in the house was on the end table alongside cush chair, and oh fucking hell, it was the only unoccupied seat in the room.

Awkwardly, I performed a small confused dance, me circling around idiotically. The only option was to sit on the floor, a dumb move in front of this crowd. However intuitively, I knew for fact I had to sit in the damn chair. For me to sit on the floor would have identified me as a wimpy fucking baby. I knew I could not stand, fuck, I had to sit deathly close to handgun. To me, if I stood it would have been construed as a threatening maneuver, placing myself in a vertically higher stronger and dominant position, aka really-really fucking dumb. As I saw it, standing would have maintained my upper hand of accessibility to maneuver quickly over those sitting stationary. The last fucking thing I wanted to do was make an aggressive move against New York, so quick as I could, I sat in the goddam death nearby chair.

Juxtapositionally similar is the position I try to modern-day take when sitting down at a restaurant, the scenario your bro-bro and I review many times when we go out for tacos, that being…my back to the wall and facing the door or entryway, thus eagle-eye watching who or what comes in and out. Right before I parked it in the chair at my dealer's city house, I realized how much I fucked up. Soon as I sat, playfully, I was instructed to pick up the damn gun. I must have given off an aura of *um…hell no, I hate you and or I am scared of you* because of my burnout pirouette circling the room, aka my reluctance to sit adjacent to the human killing device. I respectfully declined to pick up and play with handgun. It was my dealer pushing me, but maybe they knew to make a show of this, so to prove me safe to our northern guests.

My eyes cautiously scanned the room and New York One looked anxious. His hands moved away from the chair armrests and he placed them high in his lap, near his waist. New York One then had controls spaced wide apart and close to on his hips as he could, while seated. Barely an introduction was made previously and although I claim not to have met him before, I did know this exact man as someone blanketed in trouble.

Fuck…I hated this crap but too late now, I'm into this shitshow up to my neck at the moment, no safety rope available to pull myself out of this pit of puke and quicksand. Instructions were repeated with additional sternness for me to pick up the gun. I did so only with my right hand, gripping the grip and moving my index finger nowhere near the damn encaged trigger. There could have been a gunfight right then if I did or said anything to make New York One or Two nervous, and NY character One appeared ready to go, prepared for a seated draw against me. I was there to buy an eight ball of coke, not play with fucking handguns. Although un-allowed to leave until I also shot up, supposedly proving to New York collective I wasn't a cop, I got the frick out of there fast as I could, happy to take a previous new in-now out of package needle with me.

With slight irony and great sadness, about a year later in the same house, an attempted late night while-they-were-sleeping robbery occurred. I was told a gunfight ensued, someone went to federal prison and tragically, a couple of lives were lost in the struggle…fricking handgun.

The most fucked-up deal I ever did escalating to a robbery and worse, involved flipping handgun. I echo-sold excessively cut-up coke to Rodney…my slight acquaintance awhile prior schoolmate Rodney strolled into my family's third Baltimore area house on one-way Ken Oak Road undivided that night, claiming he wanted to buy more coke and some pot from me. But, ah, hard no, in reality he was coming back at me with vengeance, demanding a refund, plus bonus percentage. After we emptied our pockets and my stash box into Rodney's one open palm that did not have a large semi-automatic handgun in it, I was thinking of ambushing him on the way out. There in my Ken Oak second floor bedroom, and for Rodney to escape, he had to walk down the interior steps to access the side exit door. No way I thought, no way he could walk down the steps backwards so I chawed on the idea of jumping this really hardcore dude.

Knowing Rodney would not fucking hesitate to shoot me, and although he would also probably no-way not leave any witnesses behind alive, I was sick and fucking tired of being taken advantage of. All my internal angst balled up, my fear, my anger, my self-hatred and fricking all of it…fuck it just fuck it, I prepped to thoroughly unload on Rodney once he was going down the steps. Out of all the people who pulled guns on me then-thus far, Rodney was different. Firstly, I knew him. Secondly, I knew for fact he lacked hesitation to fucking shoot me dead, he was 100, 100% that kind of guy. The empowerment knowing Rodney would shoot eliminated the variability, thus giving me an advantage because I knew exactly what I was in for. Well, as I speed-figured…since several friends, my three sisters and father were all in the house at the time, I thought there not a better time for me to once again, fight a guy with a gun, but maybe not why you might think.

                         Chapter FOUR

With my defensive mechanism at its peak highest performance level, this thus gave me massive protectiveness muscles to jump Rodney proper, or die trying.

Sim-sim-similarly a few years before, one night just as my working skates came off, I confronted then full-speed chased an armed guy right out the front fricking lobby ice rink doors 'cause he threatened to shoot *my* kids, waving his big gun in the noses of my darling little seven-year-old skater patron kiddos. No fucking way that stupid fucking shit is allowed, like are you fucking kidding me or what, fuck to the zero asshole, these are *MY* kids, let's go fuckface, *game on* motherfucker. Whole-wholeheartedly-100 prepared to die that night at the rink, fucking *ZERO* hesitation, I output every possible human effort, I did…not…fucking…care, me chasing prickface for like a mile, down and up through the skanky Jones Falls river then I finally caught him, gained control over his fucking 9mm handgun, and dragged him by his bitch bully jacket collar and arm, back into the hands of awaiting and rightfully so pissed-off Baltimore City Northern District cops.

Well then, oh fuck it…I said to self, sitting in my room sizing up Rodney, just fuck it- I was going for it. Uh, well and then no, immediately I abandoned all such thoughts. Rodney shoved the money and drugs he stole from us into his pocket then with his free hand, put his arm tightly in chokehold position around Mark's neck, aka my best guy friend next door neighbor Mark Weinreich. Rodney's gun was now pinned against Mark's temple and Rodney suggested I let him *walk out of here* or Mark will be *the first one killed*. Rodney knew Mark too, which made the situation deathly grave, aka Rodney gave zero fucks. My hands flew towards the ceiling in surrender mode and I told Rodney, "I'm not going to fucking do anything and neither will anyone else, get the fuck out of here and don't you dare hurt him", as Rodney dragged Mark backward toward the bedroom door. I kept my hands high while scanning the stage slightly. Two buddies glared at me with weird smirks, exactly like *come on Roger let's get this fucking dude* but I shook my head *NO* side to side softly. No, no, no fucking way I was gambling with Mark's life, so I let Rodney go.

Once allowing two sets of loosely cojoined footsteps to exit the outside door and clumsily navigate the loud wooden steps to street level, I darted into the hallway. Mark came back in about ten seconds later, keeping his gaze low, and wore a downward smirk. Unable to properly describe Mark's facial expression except, his puzzled eyes looked up the stairs toward me as he walked, and all I could say was *oh my God I'm sorry, I'm so very sorry*. Mark said Rodney took off running once they got outside.

We moved 'round lethargically for several minutes then left, after giving Rodney and his damn gun a buffer to take off to wherever the hell they were going. Once walking down the road shoulder to shoulder with my friends, my Roger Ray rageful temper flared boiled and bubbled. Thankful no one got shot in my house tonight, but my brain quickly switched gears and I made the sound commitment to fuck Rodney up the next time I saw him, fuck him up big time, unless he gets to me first…handgun, fucking handgun.

Broken

Hey-Hey There Mister Rodney

Improperly could I attempt a rightful explanation of the matter, how much of a crazy motherfucker Rodney was. Although not a large or otherwise viscerally billowing guy at the time, I recollect the razored ice chards in his eyes, well as his general sound position, practically monofuckinglithic, meaning there was no moving that dude from where he stood. Such attributes could have perhaps caused New York One to walk off, if ever fictionally coming toe-to-toe with Rodney on neutral turf. Fuck to the no, I was neither bad ass nor could I fake such toughness, rather an ignorant punk, me absolutely turned inside out and far fucking apart from reality. I was a wimpy fucking loser-loser lowlife loser while Rodney had casually shot people before, and hah, probably since, unless, as I recall him telling me prior, unless Rodney is already drug-deal-dead-murdered, like one of his brothers was, or unless imprisoned for life, like another one of his brothers was.

Although I perhaps back-when factually knew any move made against Rodney would not fall in my favor, even if utilizing my biggest protectiveness muscles, I trudged forward regardless and without restraint. My run at Rodney was nothing but a blind 120 MPH pitch-black slalom course between impenetrable steel buildings, aka nothing but a soon upcoming fall upon my sword. Kamikaze driving the machine was my sheer viscous rage, which fueled 100% of my fucking feelings, thoughts, intentions, actions, and behavior in such regard. Here I step out of the room to cook the books for a couple minutes…if viewing your log of the situation and it lists my claim of skill, wherewithal, or even opportunity to inflict damage upon Rodney, there ain't no fucking way. Such parading is in fact my dumb ass bird brain march to slaughter, just needed to pause one fucked-up moment and set the record straight on that shit before proceeding, just sayin'.

Deeper Than Deep

The teased European ski trip with Ryan was far away and beyond a want or a notation on a wish list. The high mountain adventure futures was actually a pinnacle need, aka a principal life dream that without margin had to materialize, or else.

I believed the Swiss Alps possessed a metaphysical filler, a special sticky something to fill the void, a transcending emotional plug matching the shape and size of hole in my heart, least hoping for such ends if enacting my faith of intention, possibilities, and willingness.

Yet within reality were my cold hard truths…accomplishing nothing I started, I achieved nothing aimed at the good. I fulfilled nothing imperative to my well being, I abandoned all aspirations for sport and legal pleasure. I dismantled possible chances for a livable work career, me enroute to nowhere but darkness, me unworthy of even sunshine. I found solace and sanctuary nowhere but amid my foundational shallow pool of tears.

My head heavy, my heart weak…spinelessly I should lie down, or forced to. I deserve not to walk, I deserve not these legs, I deserve no verticalness, I deserve not to stay. Maybe I should shatter both these my lower limbs, maybe I should just lie down, just lie down, just lie down and drown.

Five

~

Liar

Staring Down that Lowlife Piece Of Shit Loser in the Mirror

Chapter Five, Liar ~

On the train from Grindelwald to Zermatt, it just happened, and, well…it was, it was fucking religious.

After days skiing Grindelwald's expansive Swiss peaks and snow filled meadows, with the mighty Eiger mountain smack dab in the middle of town, Ryan and I boarded the singular railroad line and headed out the opposite way we came in, en route to Zermatt.

Aside the hard Euro adjustment and sans cocaine needle stressors, once again back on the train and rolling, afforded no other opportunity but to sit and enjoy the show, then only…then only sheer bewilderment sprawled into my heart from our previous week in Grindelwald.

The breathtaking train ride ducked in and out of avalanche-proofed tunnels and literally I felt entranced inside a come to life Christmas wish.

Playfully I poked my right index finger into the muscle of my right thigh…push, push, push, totally enamored with the scenery and wanting everything to stop…pause, pause, pause, wishing to become wondrously encased inside my own real life European snowglobe right now…now…now.

Religious, the realization collected as we rolled past foots of mountain after mountain, and I felt its heft plop down in my lap. I laughingly admitted to myself…*that wasn't so hard, I could do that*. I could do that. I could do that…from then on I realized wherever I went in the world, although forever having the challenges of housing, language, train schedules, plane schedules and currency, I now knew how it all worked. There was no secrecy to this travel thing and I could do it, I could really do it…I could do it on my own. Quite literally I could come back here next season and do this by myself, going where I wanted and staying long as I pleased.

In the flash of a moment right there on the train, a whole new world opened up to me, whole…new…world. There was certainly much more I did not know and more I needed to learn, but I recognized to know enough…in the future I could do it, or least figure it out, I could ramble-travel and explore alone. For so long before this trip, I sunk deeper into myself, losing strength, losing steam, and losing hope.

Now I realize something paradoxically different, opposite of all known to me before…assemble the courage to get up and go, I can do it, rise up, rise up, rise up and follow my heart.

Now I realize something astronomically powerful, something able to carry me for the rest of my life…I am not so frail, I am not unworthy, I can do it, I can actually do any darn thing I can dream.

The humble sensations of empowerment were absolutely overwhelming. I turned far away from Ryan as I could, almost smashing my nose against the train's large window. I pulled my right sweater sleeve up and over my clenched-up fist to use as a tissue implement. I put my left hand low across my brow like a visor, hiding my face from other human peeking creeper eyes, staying frozen against the glass, peering at the mountains for almost an hour, just crying my damn eyes out.

Something remarkable just happened.

In an instant, the comfort, the love, and the beauty of these mountains engulfed me as I hoped they would. Despite the chaos of the last week in Grindelwald, despite my bullet riddled heart, none of that mattered anymore, least for a while, I hurt no more, my heart was warm, my heart was full. Immediately I felt ok, I felt more whole than I ever had in my life, ever, fucking ever…I felt safe, even outside a roof, and even being oh so far away from home. I also bloomed, growing two feet taller in opportunistic stature…yes I still had issues to return to, but now, least for now, I was eight feet tall.

The train ride itself from Grindelwald was more magical than any single experience I ever lived thus-then so far in my twenty years. We began to slow, approaching Zermatt and barely did I want to unload. Joking soft-quiet out loud with an accent of extreme desire, I spoke to the imaginary personality of the train, like I would hear you my lovely Lauren say to me twenty years later, after I finish reading aloud one of your favorite books and you push it back to me…*please, again, again*. Ahhh…I was frozen, part-time emotionally crippled by the self-empowered religious-like realization, but mostly, *incredible*…the visual splendor of Zermatt structurally weakened me.

Ryan walked forward up the train car aisle, but glanced back at yours bird-truly with puzzlement. The Swiss railroad crew would not sit here for long, not for me, hah, not for anyone…this bird almost unable and unwilling to exit. Somehow I rose to weight my feet…stepping slowly, cautiously, gingerly, then out onto the train platform. The town majorly surreal, like make believe…absolutely breathtaking. Zermatt destroyed my standard of alpine mountaintown awe, shattering such notion into bits. The sheer spectacle of the place was something far beyond anything I had ever seen anywhere, in pictures video or otherwise. Zermatt was more polished than my imagination allowed me to believe, this place the paramount picture postcard of Switzerland come to life, with the glowing aura of the mighty Matterhorn mountain hovering over town. Prior apprehensions of climbing were now stripped away, gone. I was thrilled with the notion of gearing up in a few days and setting off pre-dawn for the Matterhorn summit.

All lingering mistrusts of old were completely erased, vanished. The exaulted stupe-oh-wow-faction quieted my upset mind and settled my aching heart. With anticipated forwardness when Ryan's back was turned, I whispered moderately out loud to myself, demanding, no, in fact instructing of this bag of bones and skin self, "I could live here."

Bountiful as the yesterday of what Grindelwald was, its Eiger's imminence constrained the glee I missed, and perhaps the previous town fell victim to my drug adjustments and sensory overload. Big gnarly mountains thrill me but in retrospect, maybe some decompression time in Germany or Amsterdam before rolling into Switzerland proper would have been wise. Ashamed to have struggled with such slumbering disorientation, such my Grindelwald menace, I also recounted my previous 16 years of fear fright and flee. But then, but then deeply entranced in the here of now, I felt awakened, replanted, and beginning anew, I embraced Zermatt with a grace I had never known.

The train pulled away and I stood there pinned to the wooden decking, dropped my bags and performed a low speed pirouette, absorbing the local marvel with still watered and still puffy humbled new eyes.

Ryan walked off to investigate a large public map of town, but I kept rounding in place, speechless and mind blown. The town's classic European roads similarly narrow, but not so steep as Grindelwald, and the topography looks easier to navigate by foot, especially while carrying around almost 100 pounds of gear. Beyond the exhilaration of this paradise found, Zermatt presented as more spread out geographically and therefore, more casual and inviting…my tautness loosened dramatically. I noticed a softer speak of German, maybe with a more prominent something, a supplementation of French or maybe perhaps Italian mixed in, or the like, not at all sure. The culture more cush, the town more inviting, and not even off the train platform yet, I was not in no way hurry to leave.

Ridiculousness

Ridiculous, it was ridiculous. Ridiculous I thought previously…ridiculous the fact I was finally sitting on a plane heading for the Swiss Alps, a destination I dreamed of for over a decade, to finally live out my first big-ass life dream after all previous aspirations fizzled. *Ah, the Alps*…I couldn't believe it. My eyelids slowly draped closed, my bird bottom sunk deeper into the seated airline leather, thoroughly losing thyself amid the pleasureful thoughts of alpine joy soon coming my way.

Just to visit, me unpretentiously standing amongst the peaks contained by the marvel, what a triumphant life accomplishment…my eyes welled amidst the brain bespeak.

Without elaboration, to be in their vicinity, to be in their presence I thought surely, artlessly, by physical association the mountains will change me, yes…change me for the better, change me for the good. The embrace of the mountains back in the states comforted and loved me. The peace and calm consuming me when taken in the arms of the highlands is something magnetic, truly an uncontrollable force of nurture and grace.

Yeah sure, I am only visiting the European peaks but perhaps during our short time together I thought…perhaps I can heal a little, perhaps I can grow a smidge, perhaps I can strengthen somewhat. Now on my way to Europe, maybe I gain the knowledge to live in the mountains. Hopefully in a year or three I can travel to the peaks again, somewhere else. Then staying longer, like a year, or three, or ten…or forever. I knew to need what the mountains held, a loving peaceful calm capable of altering my darkness, truly dismantling the shadow.

Feeling incredibly blissful, seeped within such thoughts, I attempted a cognitive linger longer before minding much about the ancillary life complexities of my past, present, or future. Shaking all recent stressors from my awareness…the anxiety-riddled drive to BWI, the bathroom shooting session, Laura's phone-spewed chew-out, the re-route to LaGuardia, none of that shit mattered anymore. I attempted a dismiss of short-term irrelevant memories too, it didn't matter…losing Wolfman, least I knew him, least I treasured the transformative time we shared. The mountainbike race failure…oh well, I can perhaps try again if I want to, if willing, least I learned something, hah, learned what NOT to do. Rodney and fucking him up for ripping off me and my friends…oh man fuck it just fuck it, I'm gonna let that shit go, it just doesn't matter anymore. All that matters is this…this is all I have and all I should spend my energy on…this, just this.

I sought a mere few more minutes galivanting 'round my high Swiss daydream, before giving thought to the rest of it. Dang, the silly bothersome worries crept in quickly though…how would I survive without marijuana and cocaine for two months, what would I do when I get back, but, no, but no, I tried to brush off the at-time pointless dilemmas. Settling back into the wonderment of the Alps, I hoped the in life version of mountainous Europe to be even better than imagined. Heavenly seeped in this blissful mind space, oops…I was not able to relax for long. Ryan rocked me out of my alpine daydream and brought me back to reality. Soon as he started talking, Ryan's words shocked me and my eyelids sprung open…I…I…I was flabbergasted.

Ryan began matter-of-factly, with his signature emotionless delivery…"After skiing and climbing we're going to Amsterdam."

My eyes wide ablaze and trying to adjust to the light, I shook my head side to side. *Say what*…I thought…*what are you talking about?* Amsterdam, I pondered…*that's news to me*. Ryan continued, "We'll sell our gear in Amsterdam, except our packs. We're going to switch our homebound plane tickets and fly to Spain instead. Changing plane tickets shouldn't cost anything and we might even get money back, we'll buy a bunch of food and bottled water. We'll find a seaside town on the west coast of Spain, steal a sailboat, and sail home."

Mistakenly, I then chuckled aloud and said, *What?*, then chuckled some more, but, oops, wrong…I knew better than to chuckle. I knew better than to doubt anything Ryan said. Ryan halfheartedly jested in response using his traditional undertone, "Ha-ha what do you mean?". I never knew Ryan to joke about anything.

He certainly wasn't pulling my leg about the 3,500-mile sailing escapade across the Atlantic, but I would have much more preferred he told me the plan before we boarded the damn plane. Now I felt ready to hurl-up my dinner, and moderate panic set in. I was not the traveler Ryan was, not even close. I did not know where I was going or what I was doing, but Ryan did. The thought of splitting apart mid-trip and flying home alone if I said no to the stolen sailboat caper terrified me.

Ryan was a certified adventurer, an accomplished sailor and I believed an experienced open ocean explorer. With a forbidding frame at 6'6" he's hiddenly-whimsical while outwardly stoic, a great skier, of course a motorcycle guy, and a big-mountain mountaineer. Ryan previously summited the massive and remote Mount McKinley in Alaska, a three-week ordeal with its 20,000-feet peak elevation, well as summiting the iconic Devil's Tower monolith in Wyoming and other genuine mountains, aka he is one badass motherfucker. Additionally, Ryan sometimes operates as he pleases, outside and boldly in defiance of the law, aka he is one *crazy* badass motherfucker. Suddenly my whole world changed…contemplating one of my biggest life gambles upcoming. In a matter of mere seconds I processed the messy menu…*sail-it-because-you-stole-it*, or if nabbed, *international felon*.

Pack List

Packing my bags pre-Europe, while the lowlights of the *Midnight Express* movie played loop repeat in my head, I chose to leave the pot at home. Marijuana besides smelly, occupies the largest physical space of any street drug. Not only is there a higher chance of weed being found if airport security searched or x-rayed my pack, but I also did not have room alongside all my ski and climbing gear. As you might envision, there was no available real estate for a big bag of stinky skunk bud in my pack.

Also I feared a large stash of pills would be found out, but I had to take something. I believed I could not, and did not want to attempt a cold turkey of all drugs on this trip. So I stashed a sheet of acid within my travel belongings, aka 100 doses of paper tab LSD, hidden nicely in my wallet amid my driver's license and a business card or three. I considered carrying nothing, alternatively hauling ass to Amsterdam once deplaning in Luxembourg, but I already arranged for Laura to pick us up. The varied waste and risk while backtracking from Germany to Amsterdam, The City of Legal Drugs, then leapfrogging back to Switzerland didn't make good sense to me, although such an itinerary was a choice. In the end, I decided to carry the acid because of low volume physical space and hopeful concealment.

Pass Through

Some of my Grindelwald out of orderliness before heading to Zermatt certainly resulted from my radical drug dosage changes lately. Multiple days had passed since I smoked pot last or consumed any cocaine, barbiturates, or amphetamines. Before airborne and for the prior seven years, I smoked least three grams of pot a day no doubt, every single day without fail and many times double that. I was shooting least two grams of coke or coke/dope a day, every single day for like a couple years now.

For the last six and a half years or so, I consumed a multitude of speed, barbie downers, coke, crack, dope, or meth every day. For the last six and a half years or so, I dropped hits of acid multiple times per week, sometimes every day for a month or more. For over a week I've been dropping acid every day, usually multiple hits during wake-wake hours. So although when earlier back home I might tie dye trip every day for a month or so at a time, I had layered other drugs on top of my hallucinogens. Never before doing acid by itself, maybe this chemical adjustment was playing out oddly harder than anticipated.

Additional movie regrets included then another flick before leaving home…Clint Eastwood's darn *The Eiger Sanction* movie. Yeah sure, the cinematic threat of the Eiger in Grindelwald was far removed from the eased reality we should face on the upcoming Matterhorn but still…um, *but still*. Based on everything I knew or heard, our planned climb on the Matterhorn in Zermatt was not so death-defying as the Eiger could have been, but still…but still the comprehension of mountaineering techniques and emergency maneuvers during high-altitude icy conditions were entirely foreign to me, and wreaked slight havoc deep in my head. Previously, I never swung an ice axe, never mind affixed ice climbing boots or crampons to my feet, but still…although Ryan and I would be tethered together and theoretically anchored into the snow and glacier surface as we leap-frogged our ice screws up and down the Swiss massive, my complexities of such a climb were completely unknown.

Back in Grindelwald, I had desired to stay longer and settle into the routine, the culture, and the language least slightly before moving on. Desperately I wanted to come to terms with both the locals and my own emotions, unwinding within the should-be surrounding comfort and magic of nature. Feeling deflated and slightly weakened, not yet defeated, I desired to stand taller over the multiple streams of stress flowing upon me. Or rather, I thought…ah screw it and let's hurry up and leave for Zermatt sooner than later, to get the looming job of climbing the Matterhorn started. Mostly due to my rickety and undefinable emotions, I did not mention anything to Ryan but rather just rode along…off to Zermatt and the awaiting Matterhorn. Profoundly, the archetypal Mount Everest in Nepal, the world's highest peak at 29,032' summit elevation, is considered one of the most life-extinguishing mountains in the world with 200 deaths, so far and counting.

The high death toll on the Matterhorn in Zermatt is due to the mistaken presumptive ease of the up and down walk, famously not requiring any climbing gear in warm weather, and the underestimation taking a heavy toll of 500 deaths, so far and counting. The terminal Matterhorn misjudgment is similar to the Grand Canyon death dynamic, a rather simple seven mile hike from either the north or south rim of the canyon, down to the Colorado River. Partially 'cause of poor planning and a 50-degree or more temperature variance between the rim and the river, almost 1,000 people have died in the canyon. The dozen deaths per year or so in the Grand Canyon resulting mostly because of dehydration and heat stroke. Such a tragedy slightly out of my comprehension because of my diligent preparation for most similar things. Pre-drugs I pursued time with the Scout leader BigBird, me an active Cub Scout and an aspiring Boy Scout for goodness sake, and if you my darling daughter don't know, the Boy Scout's motto is…*Be Prepared.*

The general claim then portrays the Matterhorn challenge as not so tough. Parents with their children and dogs, so they say, are capable of completing the day trek up and down its Swiss peak during the summer time's canopy of sun and breeze. Of course conditions become more serious in winter but still, but still the air not so dangerously thin at its 14,692' summit elevation, so they say. And no, as you truly *do* know my beautiful Birdy, no I am not Grand-Canyon-speaking from my butthole, I've backpacked from the rim to the river, or from the river to the rim eight times total and that Arizona canyon temperature variance is legitimately freakish.

Homebound Bounce

Oh boy…finally after securing concluding travel, I had plenty of time to gaze out across the glimmering ocean and reflect. Heading home to the states I was still seven feet tall, losing only one emotional foot of height during the tussle over return transport. Allowing myself to recall the favorable parts of the trip, I scribbled some Swiss summaries in my small carry-along notebook, although now paraphrasing.

Primarily, the splendor of Zermatt and a huge sense of accomplishment…I dreamt it, when the opportunity arose I said yes, I stood up and did it, this time I actually did *something*. Additionally, the gush of prideful completeness, bringing the previous one-dimensional wonderment of printed European ski photos into focus, and into 3-D hands-on life, hah, although Mother Nature threw us a death-defying curveball enroute to the Matterhorn summit. A definite healing within, least the beginnings of curing movements. An absolute strengthening of self, least a temporary emotional height enhancement. A yearning for travel now birthed and, *and now I know*…now I know to not sit around so much from now on…*now I know.* I should not stew, I should dream more, I should rise more, I should journey more, I should believe. I should believe in possibilities, I should believe in myself, I should. I must dream, I must rise, I must journey, I must adventure, I must travel. I must believe more in possibilities, I must believe more in myself, I must.

Back At It

Re-entering reality, getting back to work at the shop, and getting back on the bike, I tried to maintain my positive self-belief mojo from Europe, but began to slip.

Closing my eyes, trying to slow and revisit the boundless thoughts afront me a short time before, you know, trying to regenerate some of the recent uplifting notions, well…I tried, I really fucking tried.

Trying to hold onto those positive remnants though, in short order I somewhat and with ambivalence realized my notions as amusement…hah, what a joke, nothing but a ride, nothing but a silly undulating rollercoaster ride.

Crumbling yet again, I self-convinced that the grand adventure of Europe was outside my scope or span of sustainable reality, well…no, I actually thought worse than that. Such exotic travel is for people who have money, is for people who have their lives together, for people who know what they're doing, people who know where they're going. Such ambitions, such directions are afforded people who are smart, who are educated, who earned it, who deserve it. I wasn't educated, I wasn't smart, I didn't deserve it, maybe I should have never been allowed to go there at all. Maybe I somehow snuck in when they weren't paying attention for punks, and quite possibly maybe a loser-loser junkie lowlife loser like me will never be afforded a chance like that again.

The months before leaving for Europe were extremely hard on me, well…I made those months hard on myself. Before Ryan pulled me up, resuscitated me, and pitched Switzerland my way, I was laying down face-first in the cesspool of my own life's shittyness. Before flopping into said shallow swamp…*echo*…I attempted but failed my brand new big-ass cool thing endeavor, mountainbike racing. Going into my first off-road bike race I sat atop a self-inflated healthy-ego optimism balloon, wanting to float off to somewhere better, somewhere I could do something real. My hopes and desires for a life dream realized were high but my mountainbike activity attempt was certifiably fucking pathetic, not realizing what I did not know about endurance athletics before I began.

My balloon popped and I toppled…down, down, down to my dark-dark place, motherfucker I fell fast. I tried to align against the mirror, looking objectively to see what the fuck just happened, but the mirror she showed me nothing, nothing but a weird hazy and shadowed fog. *Meh*…I then however cared little to none of her dense unshown, aka mine the blacked-out future…*yeah whatever fine, go ahead, go ahead and do what you want to me, I don't care, I don't at all care, I just don't fucking care.*

I dismantled, thinking nothing remained for me, nothing realistic anyway, accompanied by my second overdose, aka the scary weird Park Heights heroin maybe it-was-just-a multi-day shoot-sesh blackout.

Ryan's European adventure quite literally pulled me up and out of my dark place, allowing me to breathe and giving me the opportunity to see, but what I saw is what I chose and of course, these here hands alone tinted my seeing-colored lenses. So thereupon after a slight reprieve from the needle in Europe, my enhanced emotional stature was, *oh fuck me*…short lived.

Europe was the high point of the tracks and now back home, the rollercoaster let loose and dropped, hurling towards the bottom and nobody sat ahold of the brakes.

Back to it then in Baltimore, I also went back on the damn needle. Obviously, *duh*…I was not ready to be done shooting after home from Europe and to some degree, now back within shadow, I doubted the belief I could ever really be done with the damn needle at all ever. Rolling back my sleeves after months away, the initial danger was my low tolerance and the high risk for overdose but hah…I placed my bets indifferently on the goddamn gamble, placed my bets indifferently on the goddamn roulette.

Dark Skies at Night
It was nighttime, I was sleeping, and I was dreaming.

I was dreaming a typical type dream while sleeping a typical type sleep and in accordance with such conditions, I did not realize I was sleeping, or dreaming.

My dream was vividly real per typical, until quickly…*it was not.*

My dream then…*atypical.*

My dream was unlike any I ever had, or heard of ever, still to this day.

Within my atypical dream there was no sound, no movement, no plot.

No implications, least nothing presented as immediately apparent.

Simply framed it was a lowly and stalled scene, stagnant, frozen…full-stopped.

My perception attempted a slight zoom-in on the focal point.

It was a simple stage but strange…strange, and…and, um…*unwholesome.*

A single solo character existed there…the person was stationary, no movement.

In a room the character existed passively, not a piece of movement elsewhere.

Instantly I grew nauseated.

I presumed the character to be *me.*

But no, I was not the character, I was the viewer, I was the camera, *I was the lens.*

He looked like me, or perhaps I was led to believe he looked like me.

I could not see his face…his head slumped forward, and to the left…his paltry chin down as far as it could go upon that unhallowed chest.

His hair, same shade as mine, close enough. His hair, greasy long, unkept and flopped in his face. I believe…*hum*, I believe he was my older self. He my older self, maybe beginning to middle 50 within his years. He was seated upon the floor, upon the old dirty plank wood floor with scattered trash about…snack-sized potato chip bags, unsheathed hypodermic needles, ripped-open plastic grocery bags, unsmoked cigarettes with their filters torn off, empty RC soda cans, orange plastic shooting needle caps…hundreds of 'em, and the such. Affixed to his faint person…tattered jeans open-kneed, threadbare bottoms and crusted with some sort of dragged-along pickup like dried dog poop or mud, t-shirt dark green almost greyish, dark flat sneakers with holes under each forefoot like low lace-up Vans, his kicks covering some maybe once-white socks. He was half-sitting up, looking like the stench of pee, propped-up lifeless in the corner of the room. The room, the corner of the room actually, presented itself to me as existing inside a downtown Baltimore abandoned rowhouse, like mid-Saint Paul Street or something. Within the dream, the room was old, the house was old with old house windows on each of the two walls in the still frame. Both windows were boarded-up but one of the boards was broken so some slight light crept in, enough light anyway for my private seeing.

I viewed the sleep dream, again, and again, and again nightly for at least four weeks and maybe up to a few months, aka a while, hard to know how long precisely while enthralled in my junkie-world disheveled non-patterned sleep. I viewed for weeks the presumptive propped-up me in that supposed Baltimore abandoned raunch rowhouse dream, with the drug needle hanging out of my right forearm…the room almost lightless and my body entirely lifeless. My attempted zoom-in was only allowed to get so close. Not permitted to focus much but I got hyper-intently nearby best I could, rushing past the unsuccessful face identification and not wasting time on body shape recognition assumptions. Past the rest of it, I tried to see if he was breathing…was he alive, was there any movement amongst his torso, was there a slight hissing noise, was there a faint fog *poofing* out of his mouth or nose, was there anything signifying outbreaths? I saw nothing of the sort. He was pestilence permanent, he was dead, he overdosed. There was no one there to save him, seemed he died alone, all alone and maybe won't even be discovered for weeks or months or years…poor guy.

Besides the implied stench of death, a muddled overspread of loneliness hazed the room, least within the picture-framed corner of the room. His arms were entirely ravaged. I could see them but paid little attention to those upper limbs…his upper limbs…or was it factually *these* upper limbs…I think they were actually *my* upper limbs. But it didn't fucking for-real matter to guesstimate or gauge how long I might cipher that shit had been going on based on his arm scars, that being the shooting affliction of his…the desperation, the aloneness of the dead man, the dead-endness of that lifeless man. Like maybe a tree expert counting rings on a now-fallen old-school redwood…*how old is it?* I'm no junkie expert to decipher such things…how long had he been booting, how long had he been able to survive that shit? What the fuck do I know? I barely know a single thing, maybe three, but the guy lived long enough it seemed, hard and lonely enough it seemed, however he could and while he could…it seemed. Clearly, something churned within my subconscious to fabricate such a dream, such a dream playing loop repeat in my sleeping head every night for weeks, maybe months.

Liar

Surrender the Mirror

I couldn't see things as they really were

I only saw what I desired to see

I surrendered the tears that were waiting in line

I stand witness to the mirror now broken

I did it…I did all of it

I smashed that mirror and am leaving it there

Don't need it anymore

Don't want to bleed from it ever again

Don't want to see what I have seen

I'm basing hope on the visible chance to change.

Soar High, My Phoenix…Soar High

The dream, the dead junkie dream, the atypical dead junkie dream was the phoenix, my beginning process to quit drugs in earnest. When on the train from Grindelwald to Zermatt when I was 20, I began building emotional stature, although for over a year afterward the needle still ruled me. The phoenix however was now in flight, tracking me, floating above, adjusting and gaining the inspection of my true meanings, and of my true potential. The mighty winged one of transformational change lofted high, higher than a human eye can see, drifting, soaring, and waiting to dive upon me.

Dissecting this reoccurring older dead junkie me dream during waking hours of performing the exact practices leading to my assumed future death, I paid great service to my nightmare. If the man is me, if he is the future me and the certainty of me, and if this nightmare actually came true, then what? *Then what?* I had to do the math…then what?

My eight-foot emotional frame ballooned in Europe, then shrunk, but the opportunity of expanse for my self-confidence and self-worth lay waiting.

After my dead junkie dream, the eclipsing phoenix of change finally descended towards me. My out of orderliness sank low enough and the final straw was dropped into my hands with only one step left. Only one step left, break the straw…break the damn last straw.

Extending the next set of quotients and formulating a resulting day vision, I did the math…if I died like that man did, like I will if I honor the nightmare, die with a needle in my arm, the math showed that next then is my funeral, so I imagined it clearly, my funeral, I daytime imagined it crystal fucking clearly. Consciously framing the funeral scene, I let the movie play.

Firstly, foremost and principally, I identified the distraught slumped-forward walking physical trainwreck fabric of my father, moving slowly without cause and upright but barely…sharp black suit, white pressed shirt with a tight buttoned-down collar, a perfectly-bound solid black tie with slight sheen, his black shoes shining, but seemingly an inch away from lifeless, both in form and face. There too I see, secondarily and not far from my father but engaged separately, standing still and huddled around a few other attendees was, *oh my God* and this is when I lost it…perfectly appointed in a long black dress, a black patent leather closed-toe flat, with a thin black stretch fashion neckband, a black scrunchie hairband on her right wrist and her waist-length blonde hair fuller than I've ever seen it, was my best friend little sister Beth. I saw her, I saw her face, I saw her absolutely fucking destroyed self-face. Filling in the rest of the crowded scene were not extras, but the specific sobbing face of every single person I might have ever meant anything to. It was a large overwhelming scene, every single person there for me, there to say goodbye to me, their eyes towards the ground, not the heavens…this my fabricated daytime movie set of dread.

I viewed this scene once, only once, *that's all it fucking took.*

Clearly envisioning my funeral scene and it sunk in, the final twig snapped and weird…my dead junkie dream ended, I saw it no more. After weeks or months of haunting me, my nightmare played out, that movie now over…that frightful film reel now broken. The funeral day vision now ruled over my highlighted thoughts. My factually fabricated funeral sights now threatened me more than a lifeless form in a rowhome corner sleep dream, multitudes more. Now with subconscious dream visions gone and conscious math-driven realities slapping me in my fucking face, shit got real.

The hope I found in Europe, my failed mountainbike race, my Redline rock bottom, and now with the final-final funeral scene tattooed in my memory, *I decided.* Fucking once and for fucking all, *I fucking decided.*

I decided I needed to quit the needle…I wanted to quit the needle…I wanted to quit the fucking needle…I decided.
I fucking decided.

No way, no way, no way will I allow this funeral scene to be my reality, least not without a fucking fight. That is what the nightmare implied, my certain death after a long struggle. Next, the resulting day vision of my funeral showed only pain. Only pain but no, not my pain. For a long-long time, I believed death to be an adventurous relief. But no, but no…I will not, I will not, I will not hurt my father like that, *fuck to the no.* I will not hurt Beth like that. No way will I hurt Beth, not like that, no fucking way, fuck to the no way forget it, *least not without a motherfucking goddamn fight.*

Facing the Mirror
Recognizing the aftereffects of my reoccurring dead junkie nightmare, I aligned myself against the mirror, then seeing clearly the conscious truth of the matter.

Entirely embracing the committed to task, I spoke sternly into the reflective pane…do not, do not, do not break my father's heart, or demolish Beth's sisterly quintessence, nor smash the crux of each my friends, aka stop shooting up drugs you big fucking dummy.

Unmixed within daytime consciousness I knew for truth-be-crystal-certain-100 that my days ahead were decided for me, unless me myself changed my days. No time was wasted pondering specifics, it didn't fucking matter. I had no earthly idea how to quit the needle, no not none…it didn't…fucking…matter. Before the sprawl of stupid fucking irrelevant-at-the-moment details, I put first things fucking first…I needed my heart and head fixated on course. Even if my actuals ran opposite of intention, I withheld the truth I needed to believe this now my path no matter how many times I strayed…this my path, this my path, this now my path, this my path period, this my path period fucking period.

Token Mention Of A 'Nother One

Funny my depth of thought ran phantoms deep but admittedly, not always without implements. Let me explain. It feels weird to admit, but the planned exit from my thus-then lifelong comatose state of fearful running most often occurred when gazing into the physical mirror.

Oh yes and for certain sure, most often LSD swirled throughout the entirety of my cellular structure but still…but still, gazing deeper than deep into the mystical lair of these eyes blues, I finally began to face my own God's-Honest Personal Truth.

Straight-up truth…for the previous ten years I had wanted to die. Yet I could not adequately act on my end-it-all desires, because of not pausing long enough to learn the truth of my death-wish-wants entirely.

Truthfully I decided…for the first time in my life, I intentionally wanted to live on purpose, and for the sole benefit of not hurting those around me.

Oh crap no…no, no, fuck to the no-way bitch bird and just wait up a fucking second would ya', jeeze that's not really true and fact-one actually that ain't accurate at all…factually-actually the real decision made was that I intentionally wanted *not* to die. Strange to even attempt explanation, but the two comments are dramatically different.

Wanting to live could also mean that I did not mind if I died. My position was the opposite however, factually I was entirely indifferent on future breaths, aka *honestly I did not at all care about or focus on living.*

Alternatively awhile definitively, I wanted to *not* die. Any sunny dreams escaped me but rather, I was trying to *not* cast darkened shadows upon those I love.

Only once and no matter fucking what…only once facing the total truth and comprehensive reality of my current life throughout my entire periphery and beyond, only then, only then was I able to reorient myself towards the good, aka me self-protecting thy future heart a beating, aka me oriented towards *not* hurting others no matter fucking what, period fucking period.

Subsurface Living

Please let me not laze on the surface of a fanciful fake life.

Please let me journey below, with the strength to linger longer than mere seconds...yes, risking the drown but perchance slight, finding the known.

Please let me persevere in the place of the few...finding truth, purpose, and tools to fend off predators excited to drag my shelled frame up top...endeavoring to beach me, belly up.

~

Tantamount a sage sea turtle...breezing effortlessly underneath, sailing unencumbered for hours...this way then that, that way then this. Strolling, strolling, now and again drawn to the uptown light, a single quick exhale-inhalation, gracefully then dropping...such exquisite silent perfection, perfect, just perfect...down, down, down, back to their breathtaking boundless utopia below.

The Motivating Why

Although still extremely defiant towards my father, I performed a paradigm shift of sorts, ignoring my parental aversions and dealing solely with the factual truth of the malicious matter. Realizing the life-ending path I was on would hurt him beyond measure, hence damaging him permanently, awhile meantime my self-inflicted termination would negatively impact so many others, I decided. I decided, no more needle. I decided, but still I could not entirely subsume the motivating why, until I did.

If I do this, letting the needle continue its consumption of me, allowing my however thus-unknown glimmering star inside to blacken, well, well...they would be pissed.

If my father did the same thing, haphazardly letting his breath extinguish, I would be pissed. If Beth did some similar thing, letting her light go out unbothered, I would be pissed. Pissed, more than pissed, I would be hurt, I would be very, very, very-very hurt. Such hurt would be hurt beyond hurt. I hurt enough already, my hurt box runneth over. Oh shit, *oh fucking shit wait*...my father hurt much as me, *probably more*, Beth hurt much as me, *probably more*. If they did this to me, such dark endings might destroy me, so...so if I do it to them, I might destroy them as a result. I did not want to cause such pain, I could not handle such pain myself, so if I can't handle it, I presume they can't either.

Still up to this very day I see the one-time-viewed funeral scene I created in my hyper-mindful bird brain's eye. Clearly I see my father's face, clearly I see Beth's face. No way was I going to intentionally cause such harm, no way no how, not without a fight, not without a fucking fight. Right then, in that precise moment, it was *game on*...on the spot it was game on and I was serious about my quest to get off the needle, I was serious AF. It was game on and I decided with conviction, *I am fucking doing this.*

Dejected Thoughts- Restricted Movements

He's in his 40's, no younger, no older.

He was but is no longer, an active drug addict.

I would describe him as 'little rough 'round the edges, but extremely wise.

Additionally caring whilst patient simultaneous to, potentially available.

A good listener it seems, someone who was once where I am now, a junkie.

He is BigBird's friend, and said 40's friendman resides in Baltimore.

Not sure if he works as a drug counselor or simply holds a large street-wise heart.

I do not find him, my father introduces us.

He can help me, if willing to accept this one me under his wing.

He is hesitant at first, not at all sure this here struggling one me is worth his effort.

He's seen my type too many times before, he's not sure this one me is ready to change.

But I want him to take an interest in me.

I want him to get involved, I need his wisdom, I want his help.

I need his help, otherwise I'll die soon, both him 'n I know this truth as pure-fact-100.

Oh wow, amazing…we hit it off right away, he's super cool.

He offers his time for free or maybe my father is paying him, not sure which.

He always takes my call. He welcomes me to pop in when I'm out running 'bout town.

He only loses his cool when pushing this one me to stop being so stupid.

He helps this here one me, he helps this one to see a better me, and I follow him.

He takes this one my troubled me under his wing.

He grabs me, shakes me, and roughs me up a little bit but it's ok.

It's ok, it's ok, it's really ok, I deserve it.

More than deserve it, I need it, more than need it, I want it, I really, really, really want it.

He steps forward and does the good work…he reaches me.

We connect, he protects me, he loves me, he saves me.

He saves me once and for all, I am free of the needle and away from drugs forever.

This my daydream but unfortunately, such occurrences strictly fantasy.

I never met such a man, the imagined hopeful scenario never played out.

These factual envisions were conceived earlier, when I saw no way through to the light.

This divine guardian, BigBird's friend, only a painted angel, only a strong desire of mine.

My closest proximity brush to this angelman was bumping up against a similar cool dude during early times on the mountainbike, my beautiful friend Mason Day. Mister Mason lived in Columbia Maryland and worked as a gifted drug intervention counselor, now retired in Florida. My anticipated helpful intrusion, my developed portrait of savior, was composed before I met Mister Mason. I thought myself beyond hope until returning from Europe but likely, I was still not ready for rescue, and I waffled. Maybe my sacrificial walk amid the final hour towards emancipation would never come, or maybe I would never let anyone else do the saving. Maybe if righting of self was even possible, such salvation could only arrive by my own hand, maybe.

Subsequent to my first overdose, I was turned away from a local drug treatment center. Attempting to enter the program all on my own, the center told me no. With tears full rolling, requesting to just talk to a counselor…*Please, please, I overdosed yesterday, *sniff-sniff*, don't think I'm gonna make it much longer…the center told me, ah, no.*

Following my fucked-up multi-day Park Heights disrobed spanking, aka my malfunctionally-probable *second overdose*, I consulted with Mister Mason, me deferentially proposing general questions. My heavenly friend seemed to comprehend my mounting demise…he'll be in his car within seconds coming to get me, he said, doing everything he thought needed to be done, he promised he said, scooping me up and taking me where he thought I needed to go that would really work, won't cost me a penny, he said, the second I gave him the word…*I heard jingling keys*…actually he's on his way right now, stay right there Roger and don't move, don't move, I'll be right there for you, stay and wait for me, just wait, wait right there Roger, stay Roger STAY, he said.

                    Chapter FIVE

Embarrassed and emotionally bottom-floored, I thought Mister Mason would think less of me. Stupid I know and I subsurface knew it stupid then…I lied, I took the baddest parts back, *no actually my situation wasn't so horrible, I was earlier exaggerating…it's not so bad, I'll be ok.* But ok I was not, not even fucking close, I was hanging on by a mere spindly thread. Mister Mason responded with headstrong hesitancy but then amongst his likely learned dignity of the damn matter, he slowed his roll, maybe wrongly believing I was more put together than I factually was, or maybe I was *that* good of a liar, at the time.

Now not then, now thinking what I think, believing what I believe and knowing what I know, I spy Mister Mason's wicked smartness of back when…I was not ready. Although no one pushed me but myself, seemed I was not committed to the truth of my reality, although Mister Mason was making it ridiculously accessible for me to say yes, like *yes come get me, I'm ready, yes ok I will, I'll wait right here.* Seems Mister Mason knew intrinsically that if me myself was not fully committed, if me not entirely good to go, if me not willing-100 to embark on the path of a whatever it takes drug free life, least my honest intent and best effort, then it won't fucking work.

Mister Mason listened and casted a few tempting carrots, but then reeled it back in and let me be, even though…even though I wanted him to do the absolute opposite. I wanted his help, I wanted him to grab me, grab me harder, *harder still if you pretty please,* shake me and rough me up, even imprison me within his care…I wanted all this from Mister Mason, and more than needing I wanted, but couldn't open my heart, mind, or mouth enough to admit it. Although I wanted nothing else, my devil within won that battle…I panicked and snuck out the window of opportunity. The treatment center turned me away indifferently…no insurance meant zero chance for entry, or even brief counsel. And the scraped together nerve to pick up that damn phone proclaiming my surrender, asking the center for help, well, it is a dynamic I cannot even begin to attempt describe.

I felt omitted, disallowed, insulted, nothing then but my brand new shiny out of package semblance resided within…doormat.

Last Known Truth

I attempt to live intentionally. I can neither promise nor claim I will absolutely live intentionally. My ability to live intentionally is not one of my three absolutes. The totality of my world minute by minute is a turbulent weather forecast, downright boisterous and variable, aka ever-changing.

My navigation…my navigation is up to me.

My life asks me to attempt…do my best or let go of the bother, do my best or let go of the worry. Truth is, even when visible indicators push my sails opposite directions, no one nor any condition has big of an impact on me as my ability to orient my own mind this way or the next, you know, to steer my own damn ship and just fucking go get after it, stormy high seas be damned…that is all, bird truth out.

Do We?

During good times, can we shed every worry, every fear, and every negative thought in our heads?

Do we naturally seek understanding, do we...do we accept unconditionally, do we...do we let go? It appears not.

We sit waiting, unwilling to get up or move...we aim for no new reality at all.

We judge and dirty-assume willfully, we blame and complain, resting in our same old bullshit kiddie pool.

Change? Hell no, change is scary and change is hard, change might hurt and change might make it worse.

Yet change we must.

How will we face to embrace change if we do not try, our assured success be damned?

Effectively organizing our own shit we should, preparing for life's dark hardships, awhile trying for betterment of days, thus thereupon they are fucking coming, one after the next after the next after the next, like it or not.

Six

~

Bravery

Standing Tall Over the Pain

Serendipitously, I found myself in tears. On display to Mark and Mike was perhaps the totality of my dysfunction, telling them I wanted to quit shooting drugs and was trying but, but no, on my own I only failed. I wanted to quit but couldn't, I tried, I really tried but couldn't, I just couldn't fucking do it.

My botched attempts to shake the needle had dragged on for months and finally, I broke down. Following the great winged one collecting me, once seeing the damage I'd cause, even after *deciding,* I fucking *decided*…still, still, I…just…couldn't…fucking…do it.

During a weakened moment of total despair and emotional shambles, I was sitting with my best guy pal Mark Weinreich in his at-home bedroom alongside a very good friend of ours Mike Welsh. Because of my needle corruption and general patheticism, I fell away from these guys in the last year because they didn't participate in either such shit.

> I was bearing my soul unfiltered, truthfully admitting my doubt of prolonged existence much past that time.

Neither these guys were around for my overdoses but I think they heard about the first one. I was neither forthcoming nor honest, the same sort of bullshit I had pulled with Mister Mason, I held back, me not revealing to Mike and Mark the severity of my situation, but as it turned out I didn't have to, it didn't fucking matter. Fuck-pathetic months before, I loitered no more than 20 feet from the phone after hanging up with Mister Mason, camouflage-praying he shows up to collect me anyway. I would have gone if he ignored my dismissal, but show he did not…half an hour later I just slithered away to score some shit and find some works, like whatever who cares. But if Mister Mason had showed, could I have then shook that naughty little monkey? Was I ready, or not? Hum, don't know, impossible to say.

    I sat there in front of Mark and Mike crying, absolutely losing my fucking shit, shaking my balling baby bird head in disbelief, totally hopeless and saying my life's become what it is, and will only forever be what it is now. My eyes came to rest on the floor, and my mitts nervously played hands with my fingernails, that is when not wiping back tears and sniffles. The guys knew what I meant…I wanted to kick the damn needle.

    Mike Welsh opened his mouth first. I looked up slightly through my punk-ass-bitch long hair…Mike was sitting directly on Mark's left, both of them across from me. "Well then…", Mike said, him looking at me but now turning to Mark. It seemed Mike was seeking approval and support from Mark as he spoke. Their eyes met briefly, Mike turned away from Mark and glared at me stone-hard, powerful and very serious, straight-up 100 more aggressive than I have ever seen Mike Welsh behave before, *ever.*

Mike continued, "Well then, we will help you". Mike looked at Mark, almost implying for *a little help here please*, and Mark chimed in immediately, "You're damn right". So there you go, and that was it, end of conversation. I had no idea what just happened, or if anything truly happened at all. There was no discussion, no plan, no sharing of scheming plots to wrangle the needle's death-grip away from me, nothing, we didn't say anything else about it. Later that night I drifted away from Mike and Mark and found myself squandered inside my room at home, dark and down, silently shooting dope for a couple hours, long after my fav sis Beth was asleep.

unholy and in a simply injurious manner, despite desires and attempts otherwise, I put drugs first in front of all else, therefore giving barely one singular shit about continued breathing, at the time.

Still, and despite the bang-bang at home, the next day I arrived to work as scheduled, right before 10 AM. Mark called me mid-day at the shop and asked what time I was done. *On the clock 'til six* I said, but asked *why*? Mark did not answer my question. He said he'll see me later and hung up quickly. Oh well…I gave Mark's mystery phone call no added consideration, hah…I had been shooting up coke during the workday awhile remaining on task, so my thoughts shifted quickly to other concerns.

Around 5:30 PM I began futzing at my workbench in the basement of Mount Washington Bike shop putting my tools away, finishing paperwork for the last completed repair, and I walked upstairs with work sheets in hand. I filed away the service ticket and made my way to the bathroom for final clean-up. Walking across the sales floor, some commotion caught my eye through the big front window. A clear view outside the store was blocked because of a raised display of high-end featured bikes. Two guys were fooling around, pushing and shoving each other playfully on the sidewalk in front of the store. I could not see who it was, I walked on and gave the on-display fake wrestle session no more never mind.

In the tiny old previously-a-house sink, I scrubbed my hands with special dirty mitts hand cleaner for several minutes then dried off. Walking out the bathroom, *yikes*…Mark was standing right in front of me inside the store, in a creepy and surprising way. I said oh hi, what are you doing here, do you need something, but he did not answer my questions. He informed me with semi-sternness…he was there to *pick* me *up*. He and Mike will be waiting for me *out front,* he pronounced with force. Trying to puzzle me more it seemed, he added another short burst of speak…they called Beth and she is *waiting to meet us.* I thought to myself…what the heck, I wanted to know where all this was coming from, what is he talking about, we did not make plans, I was thinking of doing something else tonight, what are we doing and where are we going, why is Beth meeting us and where are we supposed to meet her? I had so many questions but was not given a chance to say anything. Mark turned around and walked away, marching for the front door and shouted slightly over his shoulder, "We'll be out front".

Mildly pissed, yet…hum, they were up to something, it seemed like their scheme was for my benefit, so instead of arguing or wrecking a potential surprise, I played along. I clocked out and hesitantly walked through the front door. *Oh fuck*, Mike Welsh jumped me immediately, basically assaulting me with a standing tackle. Mike more than startled me at first, he scared almost the piss out of me. Mike was a football player in school and shackled me easily with the wrap-around hug of his stout grizzly bear arms. Encaging skinny junkie me, Mike started shaking me and said with his signature enthused extension of my name, "We got you Roggg, we got you Roggg". He squeezed and squeezed, shaking me with enthusiasm like reinforcing through physical constriction what he previously said seconds ago…he's got me, do I see that he's got me, do I feel it, he's really got me, he's got me good. Mike Welsh did not loosen his goshdarn grip, and some sort of weird but humbling guy friend love billowed over me entirely.

At first I had no idea what the heck was going on, but considering my personal state of affairs recently, my eyes teared up in nothing flat.

Without ratcheting loose one single strain of his constrictive grip, Mike started walking me towards the car and I suddenly remembered the chat we had last night. *Oh*, I thought, *hum*…they said they were going to help me, although I had no idea what that meant, but it looked like it was going down, looked like it was going down right now.

And so it was, and so it did…for months.

For months. For months they babysat me, even when I tried to sneak out the basement side door of the bike shop, even when I lied and ran away, they chased me down, trapped me, and held me lovingly tight, for months…for motherfucking months.

I still can't believe they did what they did…trying to save my pathetic fucking loser down low life when I was entirely incapable of doing that stupid shit myself because I tried, I really fucking tried. Mark Weinreich and Mike Welsh, along with my best friend little sister Beth, the three of them battled ridiculously hard…tolerating my stupid lying and manipulative bullshit, them battling the Prince of Darkness himself, all to try and free me from the malevolent death clench of that motherfucker the needle.

My three circulatory system prison guards, my three supremely-loved human heartbeat champions absolutely cared more for my life than I did myself, absofuckinglutely no doubt.

The Inadmissible Admission
Oh such my desire to ditch the needle, but an uninformed slant still opposed me. Rejoining day to day living, I could not see my factual physical future past the needle, and I possessed not a single darn notion of how to get started.

                                         Chapter SIX

Much as I creatively envisioned my funeral by way of math, I could not begin to calculate my in-person reality…*I could not see it*. I only knew I needed to try, I wanted to try, and try I must. So thereupon fucking hell…I tried, I really tried. My desire and attempt to ditch the needle was, to say the least, hah…many times nothing more than a contempted trial of self judgments and blame. Much as I told myself I wanted to stop shooting, I could not do it. Boldly I would announce to Beth Mark or Mike…*I'm not doing it anymore, I'm done.*

Hah, the second their back was even a twist, I was out the door running to get more needles and coke or needles and dope. My main and secondary coke dealers were also in my friend circle so avoiding getting found out, I spent more and more time with people I barely knew in Park Heights. The collective Park Heights mostly dealt in dope, but I was able to hide when with them, and they had coke here and there. I appreciated their unmasked straightforwardness during our dealings, not hidden contrived or two-faced like some of my caucasian drug contacts, not judgin' just sayin'.

Maybe not yet did I…maybe not yet did I want it bad enough.

Maybe not yet was I…maybe not yet was I fully committed.

Maybe still I was not…maybe still I was not willing.

Hard to say what held me back but regardless, well…by my own accord I could not for gosh darn sake get started. Everything coming out of my mouth was a lie. Most thoughts swirling around inside my head were lies, even lying that I am quitting the needle because thus far, I myself had not done shit about it, rather just rode along with my three circulatory escorts. While creating such disaster within and without, I did however uniquely recognize that such struggle is necessary.

Frankly, I long ago grew accustomed to pain and suffering, hence irrationally comfortable amidst the turmoil and periodic self abuse.

Although I was not yet convinced that heightened difficulties will get me off the needle, I believed it will be the only thing that could.

Naughty Little Monkey
The trial of trying to shake the needle was a real fucking bitch.

I was kinda-sorta somewhat interested in doing something great with my life but of course, the constraint was my pre-existing condition of…still a junkie.

I juggled a few different breath balls, experimenting with some time off the needle, some time on the bike, and attempts to live life for real, yet truthfully…deep down doubting myself and half-heartedly waiting bemused to see how it all works out, or not. My first ever mountainbike race attempt the year before was a literal fucking disaster. Mike and Mark white-glove chauffeured me to that challenge and still to this day, it was the most defeating event of my life…I did not finish, not even fricking close.

Pre-event I tried to imagine the possibilities of latching onto this new sport, while facing my most pressing bleak hard truths…I was still on the needle and I really fucking sucked at all things. During the three hours in the car heading to the inaugural big boy bike event that morning, I was royalized in the front seat, both guys praising and pumping me up for what we all thought was going to be something really fricking cool. *Haha*…then to say that my once-cheerleading guy pals were mad when I quit less than two minutes after starting my race is an understatement. Our retreating three hour drive made for a proper time-out punishment session, me shun-relegated-pouting in the back seat all the way home. The aftermath then was ugly, extremely ugly. I gave up on myself, as did my two pals and we went our separate ways a while.

Later home from Europe then feeling some brief 'flation of self, trying to pull some bird shit together, yet hah…factually I desired to beat myself up more, seeing if this bike race endeavor crap might kill me because it held such threat, I would self-abusively try again. Mike Welsh and Mark Weinreich then pulled a paradigm shift and gave up on me not, rejoining and leading the Roger Ray crusade beginning with Mike's *Well Then* statement and his stout arm constriction. Laughingly, my second race attempt flushed out polar-opposite of the first, I won. Racing became more regular as I went along, and much to the delight of Mike and Mark, I collected a foundation of fitness well as an understanding of endurance competition in general. I then competed in the highest level existing on the regional level, expert class. I on many occasions put every ounce of effort into my racing and training, plus some. I was running fast from all I desired to leave in my rear mirror, and thought there was somewhere for me to go, not yet sure where, but away from here. The hospital trips came regular, along too the broken bones and blows to the head. A new notebook opened, my amassed injury rollup rivaling Evel Knievel himself, but I cared less than none…I was doing *something*, I was going *somewhere*.

While the mountainbike events were highly competitive, most racers were minimally, pot smokers. Before any of us held mentionable money, we slept in tents and converged at the morning campfire to smoke weed before starting the day's race. I believe the fact we were high lessened much of the aggressive must-win mentality. Although everyone raced hard, at the end of the competition, most of us grew to be good friends. I do not recall any mountainbike specific expert racers at the time who did not smoke pot, so it was a level wake and bake field in such regard. With plenty of mountainbike races happening in the mid-Atlantic, I tried to think bigger once in a while. It was hard AF to imagine myself more than I was at the time but the early beginnings of my healthy-ego and inner expanse began germinating, thinking bigger hence staying aligned to my European religious experience of *get up and go* and *yes I can do it*.

Transpiring solely from the urging and financial sponsorship of my life adventuring godfather Wolfman, I previously rose to test a few downhill ski races too, but never finished within the recognition zone. This bird all but despondent after tripping the on-snow finish line timing light, yet Wolfman congratulated me always, shaking me from my depressive loser fog using his cheer, *but what did you learn? Let's talk about what you learned, and next time you'll remember today,* he'd say with bright eyed enthusiasm.

                    Chapter SIX

I believe much because of my mounting purposeful intention on the mountainbike and wanting to make Wolfman more proud of me from the beyond, I also grew to not suck at racing skis. I did not win my first ski race medal until after Wolfman was earth-gone, but I argue to have never tried or learned his wicked smart *improvement by day* process if not for my beloved Wolfman Roy Turner. My string of medals earned skiing mean perhaps more to me than the average recreational pay-to-race skier, I don't know, but even today I retain every on-snow race medal I ever earned, well…imaginably in part as also some sorta trophy case tribute to Wolfman. Somehow, those stupid little pin-on medals and my bike race trophies mean something, hum…maybe, maybe it's knowing I traded my literal death for said small throw-away event placement trinkets, and in part I like to believe that Wolfman sacrificed his life for motherfucking something.

So anyway…keeping my eyes open for a bigger and grander bike race adventure challenging me than before, I found it, and thought it an event my girlfriend Kim could attend with me. She deserved a better boyfriend than me…I was trying to improve. I thought maybe during some travel we could grow closer or least, it wouldn't push us further apart. Arriving to the inaugural *Ross Race* in Massachusetts with Kim and her kitty on a leash, I was beyond giddy with excitement to be in the presence of the sport's greatest stars, the California pro women and men I had only previously met in magazine pictures. My talents on the bike at the time were more so my technical riding abilities than pure aerobic fitness and with that, I was enthused to be racing in the shared expert/pro class for both the varied cross country challenges but most of all, the downhill event.

I was later told my intermediary split during the Ross Race solo declined time trial was amongst the top pros, but sadly I would not collect a finish time that day. I crashed badly and awoke hours later in a Vermont hospital, strapped down to a rock-hard flat backboard, bound in a constrictive AF neck brace, and entirely forbid to look in the mirror. Kim stood by me for the days I couldn't leave my emergency room then intensive care beds, as the team of plastic surgeons orthopedics and neurologists tried to put my cracked shell back together again. Although the journey north from Baltimore with my girlfriend and her socialized travel kitty didn't end as planned, I learned gobs about my physical limits, about competitive logistics, and about how to prepare proper purified nutrition.

Chaw…Fucking Possible
After resting easy a while, then beginning to recover from my splattermatic brain injury and broken jaw, I got back on the bike soon as it made good sense for me to do so. My equilibrium stabilized somewhat, or rather, hah…least I wasn't puking from the swirling dizziness. My migraines lessened, my jaw wires removed, and my shrinking upper story stain damage allowed for some slight jostling while jiggling down the trail on my mountainbike.

I didn't give the mountainbike enough legitimate training time, focus or respect in my life. Well, *plausibly*, I considered…but then no, *no*, I offered no advanced charter of allegiance to the bike, nor did I think the oath worth it, until I did. Following my Redline rock bottom, after my post-Europe hard analysis, past my junkie nightmare and funeral daydream, then baby bird balling afront my two bike race doormen, I considered the mountainbike my only chance to escape my shitty-ass pathetic druggie-loser fucking life.

Once Beth, Mike and Mark started fighting for me in ways I could not fight for myself, them trying to wrestle this here animated bag of bones and skin away from the clench of the drug needle's chaw, I spied a slight glimmer of chance. Perchance I could start something, conceivably I could start to gather some hope, if collecting enough hope, would the initiation of a dream to dream produce something, is there something, is there something else for me, is there something else I could do with my life, is there something more than this, is there something more to me than this here shitty me…is there something for all that is goodness sake really?

My mind wandered.

I knew not how to think of something else, least think of much, *meh*…most of what I knew was this here pain, what I knew best was this here hurt, this damn place, this crappy life, and these fricking drugs. I tried to dream, I really tried. Dreaming was hard, very-very hard. I barely knew how to dream and mostly, I believed myself not worth the effort so why bother, why even start, why even try to try? Earlier in life I dreamed so much and none of it worked, well, no…wait up that's not true, none of it worked until I carried a ski bag a backpack and a sheet of acid into Europe. Europe created a part-time glimmer of possible hope…*possible* I thought, something different was possible for me.

Meanwhile, *reality check*…I lived to know that despite attempts, shit unravels unexpectedly and often, so I charted course to lead with intention, regardless of how the fuck anything turns out. My self-taught lesson plan pronounced that because so much sat outside my controls, I knew to not always reach anticipated harbors, yet hah, I thought myself maybe able to steer my own damn ship, regardless playing dodgeball within an open sea of icebergs.

The results of course, *duh*, were still hit or miss. We could only keep the needle hidden for a short while, but even with slight reprieve, a gap began to appear. What should I do with my newfound time? Yes sure I could sit around and slurp down more and more drugs while trying to resist the needle itself, but the temptation too-too great and the risk too high. Once creating a slight gap with the needle oh for fuck's sake, my tolerance dropped and several times I ran ridiculously close to overdosing again. Insanely, I justified some of my shooting so to not lose tolerance, thinking longer term it would help to keep me alive…dumb ass bird.

     Chapter SIX

What is my best chance for change...change towards the better, change towards the good?

Infected with a new enhanced feeling or three, I thought to believe I could possibly get up and do something more, do something that works, something unfaltering. Maybe not something ginormously cool and super fantastical but do something real, least a little more real...truthfully real. If I can really do something this time, which way do I go to try, what do I do to try, so not to die here? But, but no...won't the what?

What about-holdup hum...won't I grow bored and go back to the needle anyway?
Won't the numbing escape of the needle pull me back every time I'm blue?
I will be up and down blue all my life.
I will be in and out of shadow all my life, I already knew so for fact...I had no choice.
How do I build sound footings, rock solid pillars that survive even my tsunami of self?
Something I can stand upon that won't wobble, will not leave, won't let go, or yell?
Could I trick myself that anything else was even possible?
The doubt seeped in between the cracks of my thinking.
My doubt drip-dripped like a spring glacier melt, then billowed into a raging river run.
I paused. I sunk. I felt smaller. I felt weakened...white flag, where's the damn white flag?

Ok no, fuck to the no I'm not going there...I'm not going to crucify myself again, dragged into the gutter and dropped by my own hand. I have to stay put, stay here, stay here, right here, right here, stay right here, stay right here stay right now, I must stay grounded in these here my shoes. I must deal with this shit truthfully and not weakly fabricate more lies to then whisper in my own ear. So right here now, what is true, but more so...*what is possible?*

Possible. What is possible? *Hum*...what if, what if I ended up back on the needle fulltime, what would happen, what would that look like? Haha...I remembered my funeral day vision, I knew what would happen and likely happen fast, aka feet-up dead bird.

Possible. What is possible? *Hum*...what if, what if I held steady a while, could I really stay off the needle for an extra afternoon? What if I pushed the needle off for an extra day? A week? A month? Oh God I think my brain is about to start bleeding, *and*...and oh hell-upon-the-earth what the fuck ever, *if then*...if then, why not a year? Why not three years? Five years? Yet what would that look like and how would that even work? I could barely imagine, it was...it was so distant...it was so hard to consider, an almost unimaginable force to even think about, a vision too blurry to see remotely close to real life. But yet *could I*...could I even...is that even possible, *to stay away*, and oh good lord for fuck's sake wait...could I even stay away...stay away...like...*like forever?* Oh motherfucking hell...nervously flushed, my head pounded and I began to sweat. I tried to look away for a second and think of something else because my brain was spinning...I needed a break from such ridiculous far-away notions before my dizziness knocks me on my keister.

No-no…no and oh fuck wait.

Wait a fucking minute.

My mind ran back to the train in Europe, before pulling into Zermatt.

What the fuck am I doing?

Can I not see that no one else is doing this to me?

No one else no one.

There is no force holding me down, *none*…there is no force holding me back, *none*.

I am the motherfucking force, *I am doing this*…I am doing this to myself.

I am causing this pain, *all of it…me*, no one else and nothing else but me.

Oh fuck it that's it, that's really it.

I'm sick and tired of this back and forth fucking bullshit.

Why the fuck isn't this shit working?

What's holding me back?

Duh, nothing is holding me back but me, no one is holding me back but me.

It is all because of me…*fucking all.*

I will not hold myself back anymore, *I am fucking done.*

I decided definitively, the possibility to get off the needle exists…*it is actually possible.*

I thought back to Europe with resolve…I assembled my strength puzzle pieces.

I thought yes, yes it is possible.

Yes I can do it, I can do it and I can do it alone, I do not need anyone else.

I *can* do this…I will *not* doubt, I *will* believe.

I will believe yes I can, I can do it…I can do anything I dream to dream.

I will not sit.

I will not wait.

I will get up, I will get up and go, I will not be lost.

I will not go back, I will not go back, I will not go back to that fucking house.

I will not go back to that fucking house, fuck to the no ever.

Never ever fucking never.

I saw it, *I finally saw it*…and it was religious.

The misstep I suffered before was my environment. I believed I was done with my habituated behavior and maybe I honestly believed so, but not enough in my real world changed for anything to truly happen as intended. I left too many things to chance and I allowed my routines and bad habits to auto-play. I thought my discipline and forced-will withheld the strength to do the work for me but no, I was wrong, my approach was riddled with faults.

But no longer, fuck to the no…I now knew what to do, and I fucking did it.

    I grabbed my bike.

    I grabbed my bike and I rode.

 Chapter SIX

I rode and rode, hour after hour, day after day, riding past my friend's house, aka my main coke dealer's house. Sometimes five passes per day I'd ride by…sprinting past, not stopping, racing past the temptation and onto change towards the better, change towards the good. Not necessarily still running from my fears or doubts, but proving to self I had more power over it than it had over me…proving to myself I was bigger and stronger, I was bigger and stronger than the damn needle, well, least for now. My defiance mounted, of both the house and substances inside…I will not…I will not…I will not stop…I will not fucking stop there. I rode my brains out and it began to appear, the realization I was finally distancing myself from the needle, by myself. Now I was doing it…not Mike, not Mark, not Beth, but me…I was doing this and doing it now. Although still consuming plenty of drugs, I was not so close to death…I gained time, I created distance, and I built multi channels of strength throughout my entire structure.

Then, and then *oh man motherfucker*…after a couple weeks, remorsefully I refocused…the people inside that house, the regulars, my friends…*they are my friends*. If I continue detouring that house, if I never stop there again, I might not see those people again…my friends, I might not see my friends again, *ever*.

Hum, I thought, is that what I want? Is that what I need?

Do I not want to see them again, *ever*?

Well, I was not at all sure, until I fucking was.

It became the topper choice of zenith fucking choices…I decided more than wanting to hang with my friends, more than wanting to shoot up, more than wanting to keep those friends, more than wanting what pleasures that house held for me, more than all of that, I decided I wanted the other thing.

Originating from my deepest and most-central core orientation, *I decided*.

I decided, I fucking decided.

Principally and without a motherfucking doubt, I wanted to *not* shoot up, I wanted to *not* stop at that house, I wanted to *not* go inside of that house. More than any of the relatively positive desires, I chose *not* to do the bad. I put my need and want and desire to *not* shoot up first and foremost in front of everything else, everything…fucking everything, because I knew nothing else would work for me…fucking nothing. I put first things fucking first and I never stepped inside that goddamn house again, ever, motherfucking never ever never. I put first things fucking first and I never talked to most of those people again, ever, period.

A Long-Long Way From Home
After Johnny Powell drowned, I associated the hurt inside me as, hum, well…injured, bleeding in anguish, barren and broken. Pulling back, I spent many more moments of day woefully withdrawn, apart and departed from where I would normally be.

Those were confusing times for me, me behaving like an emotional runaway, and I, I just…I just went, not knowing what I was fleeing from or running towards. I barely understood what I was doing and once I got there, somewhere, anywhere…my internal unsettledness at times reached boil-over proportions. The sadness and guilt sat heavily atop my head and laid viscously mid-chest, like troubling and bubbling acid slopped across my heart. Much as I tried to theorize the rescue what-if's or empathize with Johnny's family…tasting or adopting some of the loss they might be processing, the pain compliantly piled atop my tall legacy heap of hurt.

Predominantly I absorbed my disconnected hours slowly, riding my bike alone or walking in the woods, alone. While off with me myself, I aimed for majorly the time not to think but simply be, them being the let-go days…hoping for diffusion of the shock and awe, or least attempt to control my emotional hyperventilation. I previously observed the example of people breathing into paper bags attempting inhalation regulation, but I never felt or thought the need for such exercise. Well then…several times as I walked silently the trails around Lake Roland, sheepishly peering out across the water where I recently lived to learn death by drowning more intimately, I cupped both hands and breathed heavily into my own makeshift paper bag, but, well…that shit didn't fucking work.

Other times being the reasoning days, when the occupied off-by-self moments played out in minor not major, my cognitive gaze reflected intentionally, struggling to see…struggling through an improvised private performance of *What the Hell is Going on in My Life?* My recounting began slowly. Backing up but not spending too much time there I recognized the unsettledness at home began and grew rapidly due to my mother's functional mental capacity that went downhill like a speeding rollercoaster, no brakes. The unrest in that monster house would have been a magnitude greater than ever recorded in human history if there were a scale for Familia Familiar Spirit, but Mr. Richter seemed to be more focused on the with-out than the within when he developed his shake-shake-shake the world earthquake scale however long ago.

A simultaneous circumstance of expendable misfortune rained down as I practiced my introspection, both the acceptance of my outdoor here and now, in juxtaposition to my amassed wobbly lifehood. Much as I attempted a horror show sort-out and rushed from my past, the more the realization all frights transferred with me, no matter where I ran or how fast.

More the thinking produced more the hurt, but thankful to learn that until I faced that fucked-up shit, I could not shake that fucked-up shit.

Maybe I did ok with some of the figuring-it-out part, but still I really sucked at the doing-it part. Aspirations of easier and breezier often remained bottom of mind, buried by *Modern Day The Precarious.* All of it, fucking all of it…the unshakable motherly fear, the fatherly resentment, the self-disgust, the fuckcontempt, thereupon screw it all anyway, my consumed time theorizing was mostly negative and self-blaming, despite a far-far-and-away hidden hope for even a neutral day every fuck in a while, or three.

     Chapter SIX

Unforsaken Needs

If not honest, wherein do we harmonize?

If never vulnerable, can we claim we have grown?

If not remaining connected, credibly can we live?

If recluse, does it mean we've lost, does it mean we've given up?

We want for togetherness, nurture, and ever-lasting love. Yet we tear each other apart, thinking more riches are gained from the freedom.

Certainly, strength arrives through our self knowings. Quality alone time is non-negotiable but off alone and apart forever we cannot.

The pants about our bottoms, the shirts across our backs, the tooled implements we wield, our supplies, most all of which others produce…these things not wants but unforsaken needs.

We need time with others, the togetherness. We need least part-time comfort, support, and safety found within other's arms, that which is sustainably unobtanium to our solo single oneself.

We need the share, we need the receive.

Ride On By

Although the drug needle still fucked with me, I raced around on the bike detouring most of the inner shitty parts trying to end me. Teasingly I'd ride past my main coke dealer's house, proudly defiant and building resolve every time I sprinted by. Certainly with an unlimited offering of remaining sources to score coke dope and meth, like everywhere, well as available opportunities to find a needle if even a used one, I was not out of the woods yet. Yes the shots continued, but the sit-down on-site deep supply availability was avoided, the all-day lounging safe haven in my friend's homebase shooting den was over, and the wakeup-and-shoot-til-pass-out-sleep benders were greatly lessened.

My number one primary main focused goal was to stay out of that damn house, and I fricking did.

By February after my head-dart episode at the Massachusetts Ross Race months before, I was racing again, learning more about athletic training, the dynamics of competition, and understanding slightly better the inner workings of this here bird brain. Gaining new friends throughout the racing community boosted my self-confidence greatly, especially because I didn't suck so much on the bike. I was fast enough to be competitive and I believe most of the event promoters and peer expert/pro racers accepted me, or least they did not openly admit the opposite.

Reviewing the published east coast mountainbike calendar for the year, I was thrilled by the listed opportunities…*yes-yes*, race every weekend 'til Christmas, all within a four-hour drive from home. Mapping out my race-travel schedule, I over-optimistically planned to compete every weekend. Although still smoking a shit ton of pot, doing plenty of cocaine, throwing back pills and dropping acid throughout the week, my drug use had lessened. I was not calling in *sick* anymore…code name for still shooting up from the night before. I desired weekends off for racing so if not better satisfying my job accountabilities and making it to work on time, I might be unemployed. If I got fired, how the hell could I afford drugs gas money and race entry fees, in that order?

My betterment of technical skills and aerobic training on the bike became more serious, and I carved out more time away from drugs to spend in the saddle. With the option and variability of idleness versus non-free-time, I tried to use the situation to my advantage, attempting to stay entirely away from the meth, the dope and that damn needle. In an endeavor to avoid that shit, sometimes it worked and sometimes it didn't, but then my secondary goal after stay out of that house was do-not, do-not, do-not sit still. I was either actively doing drugs, working, riding my bike, eating sleeping or skiing.

Re-Do

My somewhat naughty neighborhood friend Ryan called my father's house again. Ryan asked if I would like to join him on another trip. Immediately I said yes, but then oh shit, *oops*…I took it back. I said oh actually wait…are we going to Europe again? He said *no*. Ok, are we going to Canada? *No.* Hum, Mexico? *No.* Darn it, secretly I wanted to do a big multi-day dirtbike expedition in the desert of Mex-Mex-Mexicali Baja.

Are we flying, I asked? *No*. Hum, wow, ok, I was intrigued. Are we going climbing? *No but that sounds good, maybe we should*, he said. Are we going sailing? He chuckled slightly but said *no*, and I chuckled right back, because both the specific question and his answer was legitimately fucking funny. I thought sure to be nearing the riddle conclusion. Are we going skiing, I asked? *Yes*. Oh ok cool, skiing, count me in for sure, I said.

Driving across eastern Colorado sucked and *yuck*, it was exactly like Kansas…flat and boring. I began to worry, *oh shit*, I might have developed this film reel opposite of correct, I thought all of Colorado would look awesome. Growing fearful, maybe my expected exposure was dead-duck wrong. We drove over a large sort-of ridge in the landscape barely east of Denver and with extreme caution I sucked in a big breath of *oh fucking hell*, afraid of what I would see next. Once rolling into Denver proper, wow, my worries unreservedly vanished, I saw it there in front of me…True Heaven on Earth. We were still some miles away but I could see them, the Rockies, and for a moment they entirely took my breath away…*wow, oh man wow, that's amazing*. Uncontrollably then, my eyes welled, legit I was…I was *awe-struck humbled*. No more than a three second in-person flash viewing of these mountains needed to occur…wholeheartedly yes, yes, deal done-done deal, this is where I needed to be, without a singular fricking doubt I knew it, I needed what the Rockies held for me, I knew it straight-up, needed…I had no choice.

Still a couple hours from the slopes but it was like doing the first shot of a brand new to me high-alpine pleasure juice and…and it was just a car ride away and…and in no way did I need to see anything more, I was solidly sold, sold, sold…done, deal, done.

Once viewing the 13,000-foot peaks, even from afar, gladly I could have turned around right that second, went home, packed my bags, and moved to Colorado, like forever.

The awestruck bewilderment for a certain spot on the globe captivates me virtually through print or film, then my thrill is uprooted by the multiplicity of in-person stupefaction…the face-to-face dismay of the here-now touch it wonderment, many times a near religious experience for me, and far beyond what is seen or felt through the audio-media experience. When seeing an amazing place in print or video, once occupying the frame in person, the comparison is not even close, *uh yeah no way*…the real thing hundreds or thousands times better, without compare…every damn time.

On my 21st birthday, legitimately straight-up 100…for the first time in my life, I finally found a true reason to celebrate the anniversary of my coming into this world, unlike all mediocre or non-existent birthdays before. Celebrate…we skied at several Colorado resorts then continued west. I was sitting inside the *Mangy Moose Saloon* at the foot of Jackson Hole resort, and nestled graciously tight by the mighty Teton mountains. Although despising beer, I sipped a celebratory birthday brew with Ryan after a long hard day of skiing in paradise, and only a stone's throw from Yellowstone National Park.

Successfully fulfilling my desire to explore the western United States, and furthering my need to be in the mountains, I contemplated more seriously moving out west someday.

I dared not dream too long about living in the Alps, although I coveted greatly such dream come true. Realizing a European relocation was beyond my resources, maybe someday I will go back and might even stay, but no time soon. Besides and moreover, I need to play out this mountainbike thing and far as I knew or could tell, they were not racing mountainbikes in Europe yet, it was only an American thing, so far.

Hum, maybe…maybe it is possible I could somehow make it work, to move here, to live in this paradise found, sky-high amid the massive western peaks of America.

I began formulating ideas, not yet plans, to move out west. I needed to, I needed to do it, I needed to go, maybe next year or the year after or after that but I needed to go absolutely no doubt. Driving east I was eight-feet tall again, intending not to lose much blissful height of emotional dominance once I got home, this shit felt way too good. Save for a big fat speeding ticket and jailbird napping in a cell overnight so to assure our appearance before the morning judge, the western states ski trip adventure was fantastic. Doubly fantastic that the Wyoming State Troopers did not search the car better and find my huge stash of cocaine weed and pills, them distracted by the tall heap of downhill boards they believed were stolen. Well, maybe they were not and maybe they were, oh well hard to tell…Ryan not speaking freely the where or how he procured 20 pairs of brand new skis.

Twisty Return Route
Once home from out west, bringing glorious future happenings into determined focus became easier and easier. I tried kicking myself in the pants regularly…*hey dummy*, quit sitting stagnant for so long, get your ass up, go travel and do it often. Recognizing whole heartedly the damaging self-minimization befalling me when aimlessly lingering round my home hood, I began to accept the undeniable need to travel, not want but *need*.

The wonderment and fullness of life experienced when out and about warms and fills my soul in ways sitting at home never could, or will.

Why…why do I need to derail my hopes and dreams of living in the mountains just because I don't have the fricking money?

Fuck to the no…I certainly do not have to do any fricking thing of the sort, fuck to the no. Why should I believe my residential alpine life goal is unachievable? I certainly do not have to get stuck on that stupid fucking bird brain shit, no I do not.

Believe…I tried to believe, I tried to imagine believing in myself was possible. Thinking I was beginning to go somewhere least in mind, hum, I wondered…was there something more possible for me than I have seen felt or known before, out there, somewhere? If something more is really possible, more of what, and where the hell is it?

Retribution…for the second year's Ross Race in Massachusetts, my bad ass sister Beth and I threw a bike rack on the back of BigBird's Fiat Spider convertible and drove north, because my shitty blue Subaru wagon daily driver was broken down again.

My hotshot straight-laced lovable pal George Hebner met us at the event, him competing with me in the expert-pro class, uh yeah…it being my retribution of sorts. I knew handfuls of fellow competitors from previous events in the year and the scene was jovial. Several new friendships were solidified, and the connections continued to expand my hopeful horizons. My follow-up trip to the Ross Race sealed the deal that this stuff was for me, not only the invigorating national level mountainbike race scene, but also my critical connection to travel.

Humboldt…one of the coolest people we met at the Ross Race was a guy touring around the world on his mountainbike, after cashing out and retiring from his job. Barely 30 years young, he recently sold his farming business back in California. Wise Successful One visited me weeks later in Baltimore and stayed a while. A smallish but heavy 10-pound FedEx box showed up at my house addressed to visiting retired dude. It was stuffed with exotic sweet sticky bud, and weird purple strands ran throughout the dense formations of pot, *my recipe*, he said. Vaguely he teased that his recently sold business was very lucrative, picking up one of the buds and twirling it around, proudly showing off the non-monetary side dividends.

Competitive…I was competitive at the second Ross Race and I avoided ambulances, hospitals, and additional brain injuries, thank goodness. I performed ok, least good enough by my measure to mark my first national-level pro race as successfully completed. I needed more large venue bike races in my life…needed.

Closer…I used my motivational results from the Ross Race to help keep me on the straight and narrow at times, moving further from the needle, distancing myself from some more of the drugs, and moving my heart and mind closer to the mountains.

Needed…I needed to keep racing, I needed to travel, I needed to continue filling and healing my heart…needed to.

I was not only running, I was also going somewhere, I was going somewhere better, I was going somewhere good. I needed to, well…I have to, yet…I must, I must leave. I knew I had to leave Baltimore, had to…I needed a larger and more comprehensive environment change, needed it…I fricking needed it.

Yet, intrinsically, damn it, I was still stuck.
Ok, fuck this stupid fucking shit…what's the fucking problem bitch boy?
Well, the temptation still too strong, and the risk too great.
This stupid fucking shit is not working, not good enough anyway.
The needle was still messing with me.
I needed to get the fuck away…far-far fucking away.
I needed to move west and live in the mountains…needed.
Needed, fucking needed fucking period, period fucking period needed.

Magazine Pictures

For months the hard truths of my life's disorder accumulated a pile high in my mind.
Driving home from the Ross Race in BigBird's Fiat, Beth helped me sort through some of
my many thoughts, now mildly paraphrasing but not much.

What did I want out of life?
I want a reasonable level of self-controllable guidance.
I want inner peace and the ability to live peacefully in my future.

What did I need in order to calm, grow, and strengthen?
I need to breathe, sit, think, and sort shit out.
I need the right environment to do it.

What did I need to stay away from the needle?
I need to place myself in the correct location geographically long enough, or die.
I need to gain, leapfrog and sustain an upward emotional trend, or die.
I need distance away from my shooting scene and I need inner growth.
Simply trying to forgo the needle is not sustainable.

What are the things messing me up or in my way?
One main thing, *me*. I am my biggest challenge awhile my greatest opportunity.
I must discover my true self inside, then put my true self to work in the outside world.

What actions or inactions will pull me back to where I was as a miserable junkie?
Staying in Baltimore will drag me back to the needle and put me to death.
Not making and taking the time to find and enact my true self will drag me back.
Continuing to reside on the east coast meant only pain and prolonged misery for me.

*Baltimore is the dark alternative world to the bright peaceful mountain
meadows I knew I needed. My life's discontentment would never
change until I change. I needed to change dramatically more than ever
before, and change right fricking now.*

Motorcycle racing was not going to save me now.
Skiing was not going to save me now.
Bicycles were not going to save me now.
Big mountains can save me, and only they could, I knew it inherently, if I can get there.

The bike might be pulling me away from the drugs a bit for now…too soon to tell.
But only the mountains can save me from myself forever, I know it.
The deepest and truest comfort I have ever known is while in the mountains.
So I will move to the mountains.
Yes I am financially disadvantaged, but money will not bind me.

I need to go, I need to go and I want to go, I will go and I will try my best try.
The shadow over me cleared. If I can rise and go, I saw my life's possibilities as limitless.

I was already feeling relief, a betterment of self once Beth helped me see so clearly.
I held zero plan how to assemble a workable life out west logistically or financially…zero.
Zero plan, and zero care…I did not fucking care.
Zero fucks given, no not none. Absolutely, fuck…care…zero.
No, money was not the fricking problem, money was a small bothersome issue, like taxes.
I trusted the adventure will lead me…full faith 100.

Best Buddy…not only did I decide but we both decided, we are moving west, together, soon as I could replace one of the Subaru's front drive axles. Well, factually I'm not sure how much Beth wanted to go versus her attempt to help me regain operational control of my own life. Anyway, after some additional back and forth wrenching on the Subaru, I finally got the car sorted out and we were ready to travel. Anxious to leave, I started pulling levers…giving notice at work, packing and saying goodbye to friends. Beth then stuttered, sounding hesitant about the move. As it turned out, my best friend little sister had too many things going right in her life to exit Baltimore now. She changed her mind, Beth declined on the mountainous expedition. She loved her job at Pimlico race track while making good money, well as getting along great with her hyper-cool boyfriend Mark Rhoderick. I believe Beth was scared to tell me of her second guessing, so we did not have our heart to heart about her staying behind until a week or so before planning to leave. Seemingly she felt guilty about the late realization but I was not upset. Yes I wanted her to join me for such a grand adventure, yes I would have preferred to know of her change of heart earlier so I could mentally adjust, but in the end I would not be stopped, I was for certain going, and I would not leave whilst sour.

I was going, no matter fucking what.

The thrilling juxtaposition of fleeing death in Baltimore while venturing west to create a brand new me certainly left no room for hesitation. I was attempting to shed my supereminent junkie disposition, leave the Baltimore drug trade in my rearview, and amend my general shitty outlook on life. The western mountains offered me all of that, *I knew it*…I just had to get there. Although still consuming the same bulk of substances, I intently planned my future, highlighted by the headline of liberation from that motherfucker the needle, period. Expanding on my intentional westward two-fold life path I preconceived my highest intentions as the following.

1. ONE. Put great distance between me and my well-known east coast drug contacts.
   a. Move away from my known accessible needle connections for a substantial amount of time. I believed the further I travelled away from the needle and the longer I stayed away, the better chance I had to quit shooting forever.
   I believed two years was the minimum time required to create life-sustaining distance from the devilish little poker sticks.

b. Distance myself from the Baltimore drug community and continue my wind-down of meth, heroin, and cocaine. I did not imagine to struggle discontinuing meth and dope entirely long as I did not find a new source out west and hang around it. Remaining realistic, I did not intend to abandon cocaine, no way. I was not ready to give up the coke but once on the edge of leaving, I felt intently committed and somewhat maybe mostly confident to never put a needle in my veins again, ever, fucking never ever, well, such was my intent anyway. I did not imagine quitting all drugs was a possibility or even option available, so I did not set myself up for failure in that regard, besides, I loved the drugs…loved.

2. TWO. Find peace calm and beauty, first within the mountains, second within myself.
    a. Open my heart to meet touch and grab Mother Nature's hand when she reaches out to me. Open my heart to find my core self, my truthful center, a person and place I have never known.
    b. Drop my deep inner anger, even if I miss comprehension of the core fury origination or reason…set free the distemper from my person. Soak deep in the beauty, power and resolve of the mountains, letting go of my emotional discontentment.
    c. Try to live and work as high in the mountains as possible, embraced by Mother Nature's magical alpine healing and strengthening powers.

Synopsizing:
I need to find and retain my true self and inner strength once away from the needle.
I need to establish some moderate level of controllable guidance with my actions.
I need to find and retain my inner peace afforded me by the engross of the mountains.

Yes of course I was leaving my father, my sisters, and a hundred friends and friendly contacts behind, but due to the horrific precariousness of my escalating nine-year addiction, chiefly I desired to leave the east coast drug scene behind me, forever. Yet having it rather good in Maryland, it was hard to leave, very hard. About to turn my back on many friends became a heavier decision, as was leaving a real job, walking away from a possible restarted career in the bicycle retail business, and sans-course driving off to only God knows where. But no, no, fuck to the no…no time to calculate what was about to be nothing but behind me, I knew I had to force change upon myself in order to survive.

Death was legitimately nipping at my ankles for more than seven years now, and if not flexing my self-discipline muscle and leave Baltimore soon, I knew the Prince of Darkness would catch me…game over.

Not *feel* it. Not *think* it. Not *fear* it, I *knew* it instinctively.

            Chapter SIX

With $400 cash in my pocket, no credit card, no debit card or overdraft protection cushion, no checking account, I readied. BigBird was a struggling single father with a demanding full-time job paying him barely enough to stay afloat. Certainly no cash donations will come from my father before I blew town, nor did I fricking want any. Besides, for everything I put BigBird through, I certainly did not deserve a single damn thing from him, no way, not a slight morsel of nothing. I worked a multitude of jobs since eight years old, and at thirteen I was buying many of my own clothes, not interested to wear the polyester tops and bottoms my father was making for me and my sisters. These era-correct works of art were hand-cut pieces of material stenciled from paper patterns and assembled on BigBird's old Singer sewing machine. Though I spent most everything I had on drugs, I did find a few bucks now and then for a new pair of jeans and some t-shirts.

I held inadequate funds to move fricking anywhere, yet loungy comforting cash was not going to stop me, hells to the no...I HAD to go.

I did not share the fact I was near broke with anyone. I was going to get in my car and leave, deferring the stupid money thing for later. Viewing my life comprehensively I had one intentional destination: locating the meadow of continued breaths. The greatest challenge revealing itself to me on my journey will be the wavering of my willingness, I knew so. Factually, money was one of the least things I worried about, I had bigger problems than the fill of my fucking pockets.

Money would not fix my void.
Money will not mend my heart.
Money won't lift me...money cannot carry me or pump me up emotionally.
Money loves me not, not in ways I feel loved.
Money affords me no subsidiary dreams.
Money does not provide me the courage to face my monsters, no way forget it.

From the northwest side of the city it's an easy route...take Northern Parkway east, jump on the I-83 expressway north, go west around the Baltimore beltway, turn right on I-70 west and aim for, hum...I have no clue where I am going, only big westward mountains. Within the next few days, I would choose one of the many beckoning ski towns to call the new place home. No idea where I might land, zero inclination what I would do when I got there, and I did not at all fricking care. Feeling slightly nauseous and with an instantaneous lump in my throat, I knew not when or if ever I would be back again. After making pretty much the same drive less than a year ago with Ryan, I was not only familiar with the road but knew it rather well. For the last two years I drove Interstate 70 west for mountainbike races in West Virginia, Pennsylvania and Ohio. Past the Ohio turnpike, the road is not as familiar but I grasped and embraced the basic operational logistics...stay on I-70W and it will take me straight through Denver, up into the Rockies then towards Utah.

Heading for a glorious ski resort somewhere in Colorado I was, maybe not stopping until I reached Northern California. Telluride Colorado was stuck in my mind as a probable target destination and some certain magnetism for Jackson Hole lingered in my bird brain after skiing there the previous year with Ryan. Utah eluded my travels before this time and although I could not imagine anywhere better than Colorado, most other hand-first humans I consulted proclaimed Utah snow puts Colorado to shame. When I previously worked for Sonny, his eldest son Alan managed the ski department at Princeton Sports and Alan was the most globally-traveled skier I knew. Nothing more was known to me about these towns except what I experienced myself, saw in ski magazines, or the tales Alan told me.

My mind ran wild as the journey began…back and forth my thoughts darted, trying to decide and commit to a new geographical home, worrying about finding a job and a place to live, well as tasting the probable creep of the needle. I let the devil and the angel run around playing hide and seek on my shoulders as I wriggled snugly lower into my driver's seat, cranked up the music, and tried to clear my head as I drove moderately-blissful into the setting sun.

No real matter where I ended, I was going, feeling excitedly scared while surplus sad, leaving so much familiarity and supreme love behind me.

I cared nor planned not for any set destination. Five years earlier when self-expelling from high school, I pompously imagined to know what I was doing. But I did not know, I did not know much of anything. Once the educational continuation options were laid on the table, all I consulted was my half-baked juvenile indifference. My approach was, quit everything in my way of getting and selling more drugs, and going to school was an absolute barrier to my drugs. Then despite brief interludes of the sun's ray's shining through, still not enough had changed in order for me to survive.

I had to leave, had to, seeing in my mind's eye vividly only hopelessness and this total truth…poignantly stagnant, adrift in a cesspool of mediocrity, just waiting to die in Baltimore.

Bizarrely then and hah…with zero premeditation, just an instinctual and defiantly solemn forceful reaction, almost immediately once off the Baltimore Beltway and planted firmly on Interstate 70 west, I turned down the rear-view mirror inside my Subaru, thus deeming it dysfunctional. "Turn it down…", I chanted to myself soft and rhythmically, "Turn it down, turn it down, turn it down and go…just fricking go". The weakened dam of both my eye sockets leaked salty droplets over their walls, the falling tears quickly collected by my lower puffy and quivering lip. The foundational source of such emotions, although yet undefined, was blindly understood as I keenly glared out the windshield looking towards a new world, a new day, a new life, and intentionally, a brand new me.

     Chapter SIX

Only once in St. Louis during rush hour would I reinstall the operational rear view functionality, then turning it down again outside the chaotic Arched City bustle. Then through Denver proper and slowly chugging up the Rockies, I reinstituted my rear sight mirror for good, giggling out loud to see the big city skyline grow smaller and finally fade out of sight, *and good riddance to you* I chirped out loud, as I drove up into the clouds of my let's-go-do-this big mountain dreams.

There was nothing left for me in life except forward of where I faced, not from where I came.

I constructed my precarious and programmed dead end chaotic path by my own hand, and my career options seemed extremely limited to achieve anything of decent value in my life. Saying not ever a single prayer for grand corporate success, I also wished none and held no desire or notion for wealth. Wanting to steer clear and hide from everything remotely similar to outward public fame, I also possessed otherwise, mostly zero clues about anything.

I blame fucking nothing, fucking no one, for landing me here…I did this, I did all of it.

Withholding minimal formal education, I thought therefore no chance ever offered my way for a real career of any kind. Choosing instead to get up, so as to not otherwise die…just get up and go. My hope…try and quite possibly maybe live more within myself, aligned with what brought me joy and provided some purpose. Hoping also, to live simultaneously no longer outside myself running, hiding, hustling, slinging, stealing, lying, and drugging. Chancing too, a satisfied longing of comforting love in the mountains, after accumulated years of hurt by the hand of conditions outside my influence. My final dream…reside within the frame of a stunning landscape, allowing and affording me the opening to live out loud as my best self, mostly free and far from the pain fear and anger consuming me back in Baltimore. I aimed for peace, calm, letting go, a continued heartbeat, blooming nature, and big bold mountains. Envisioning a chilled-vibe ski town out west where I could settle into for a while, maybe stay forever, and see if I could turn my otherwise shitty little life into something slightly bigger, slightly better. True-true, a tall order, but I had to try, had to, I had no choice.

My eyes glistened with hope as the leave behind life tears slowly dissipated.

I accounted my path as en route to the proverbial pot of gold at the end of the rainbow, a livable dream, a new beginning, this being my self-reinvention. I was on my way, using the western sun to help guide me as I motored down the highway away from Baltimore.

I wanted the simplest job paying me barely enough to eat and cover rent, then spend the rest of my time skiing the big mountains of the western United States. More than *needing*…finally once and for all I *wanted* to find and reside deep within my true self, a self I never knew before. Consensually, after nine years dancing hand in hand with The Prince of Darkness, I was tired, and many days thought myself better off giving up. I was close, but not entirely done with this here life, just not yet. I had to try something dramatically different than ever done before, to see if I could change, least change enough. The doubt in myself was strong, and after unsuccessfully wanting and hoping and trying elsewhere best I could, this here my last attempt with something brand new. So, I began my grand adventure, to open…clearly seeing for the first time what I have never seen, blossom and feel what I have never felt, breakthrough and think what I have never thought, finding what I have never found and learning the truth of my findings, then learning my life my way and in a manner I have never understood, working intently towards a new way and hoping my new way to be sustainable for me.

I am who I am because I choose to be this here me
I change only when I decide to be a new me.

Picnic Table Religion

My second week working at Spruce Saddle restaurant flipping burgers midway atop Beaver Creek ski resort in Vail Valley Colorado, it happened, and it was fucking religious. On the front deck of the place, a couple dozen picnic tables lay inviting for guests to dine outside under the warm 10,208 feet high altitude sun. I ate amid the picnic tables whenever reasonable weather, so I could be close, closer, closest to the mountains…I needed to, I had no choice. Deck mealtime was mostly alone time because of split shift lunches, we could not afford to have more than one person gone from the grill. I tried to carry my backpack to the deck, filled with writing tools. Otherwise I aimed to include a notebook or minimally, a pen or pencil so I could scribble notes atop a paper towel.

Surrounded by the bosom of Mother Nature's wrap, I pecked away at my plans. And yet, a resonance pulsated gently against the walls of my heart. Although on scene to settle, most times I was preoccupied with the task at hand too much to notice, until I did. While writing thoughts to self on deck one midday, I lifted my head to contemplate a better word than just noted. I gazed innocently to my left, eastbound as it was, and got snagged staring at the peaked Gore Range of the Rockies. Instantly the symphonic notes entranced me…oh shit, here I was, a world away from all I desired to leave behind. Here I was, close to heaven as I had ever been. Here I was in the correct locale, if willing to do the fucking work and not flood my back-of-face brain matter with more and more lies.

The reinforcement came fast and hard…my life's path is mine to
create, is mine to navigate and stay the course, is mine and no one else
is capable to hold me on or push me off my intended route, fucking no
one none.

Picnic Table Extensions

Outside one sunny new day on the Spruce Saddle deck during a deep contemplative session, I undertook the thought path of…the needle. Since leaving Baltimore months before I had remained off the needle, but how will I STAY off the needle? While already committed to the notion but duh, the DOING is the true fricking problem, aka the doing is the rock-hard challenge far above and beyond the rather simplistic shuffle of deciding. So, how specifically will I try to remain apart from the needle, like fucking forever? Because like are you kidding me…I lived to learn and know that just wanting and wishing and praying no way won't get the job done, least not for me, by my measure.

Hum, well, oh shit hold up wait, I need to stop. I need to stop, back up, and stay a while…try. Try. What is *try*? That word try feels bothersome. Try feels caught between here and there, stuck amid truth and not. Try. Is try a true word or an untrue word? Is try an accurate word for me or should I strike it from my diction and not use that word ever again? Well, while the while, I know for fact I cannot say anything else, because truthfully I cannot guarantee myself I will stay away from the needle forever, like not really able to say that at all. To say I definitely *will* stay away is an untruth, aka a lie. The only truth I can speak is that I will *try*. Also, to stand around *trying* to avoid the needle physically, or fight the needle mentally sounds really fricking dumb, because when I tried that shit before I couldn't do it, I just couldn't.

Ok, so that won't work, my notion of TRYING to detour the needle while still in proximity to it or not, but, well…but what DID factually work?

1. Sharing my truth and letting close friends join the crusade worked, partially.
2. Staying away from my main coke dealer's house worked, partially.
3. Leaving those friends in that coke house behind worked, partially.
4. Riding my bike past that house and not stopping worked, partially.
5. Staying busy, committing effort to working training and racing worked, partially.
6. Leaving Baltimore and the east coast as a whole worked, for now.
7. Remaining away from heavy use or users of cocaine with needles worked, for now.

Summarizing what has worked so far…I became me myself mostly truthful, shared my struggle with friends, and allowed them to help me. Also I stayed apart from the needle, and that is much of the functional recipe, so far. *Ok, good, nice job, now, what should work best going forward?*

1. ONE. Extend it. Keep doing the same things I am doing already.
2. TWO. Extend it. Distance myself more from my Baltimore contacts, if even possible.
3. THREE. Double down. Share my truth and let my close Vail friends join my crusade.

Breakdown on ONE. Extend it. Keep doing what I am already doing. I should try and not let my thoughts get the best of me, try not to mess myself up with excessive doubting notions. Try and avoid any catastrophes so I don't overreact and sabotage the good momentum I have.

Yes, keep trucking forward but hum, it's more so…well, oh wow, it's not what I need to do, I need to try and NOT do any of the bad stupid shit foreign to my current path. The importance now is what I will try NOT to do, period. *Ok cool, good job, let's keep going.*

Number TWO is a duh-no-brainer so I'm skipping it.

Breakdown on THREE. Double down. Recruit members to the bird brain sans-needle crusade. Find a few Vail people and let them join my battle against the needle, like with Beth Mike and Mark. Well, but hum…I built my strength in Baltimore right before I left by kinda staying away from the needle on my own. Unless finding myself inching too close or seeing the increased temptation to pick up another evil poker stick coming into vision, maybe I will try to carry this one by myself. *Uh no you idiot, that's a dumb idea.* Yeah, maybe you're right, am I fooling the fool that such self-regulation is possible? Regrettably, I might not yet possess the strength, and this strategy might backfire. Hum, well…I will not always have others around to help me. If I am doing this and doing it for real, by my measure it appears I must do it alone. Staying steady with my solo needle effort seems correct, for now. If I start slipping, then I will try to bring in reinforcements although I do not know who that would be. Maybe I do not hold enough chips for this gamble, aka the bet of catching myself and asking for help before it's too late, IDK, but I will try my best try.

Loop-around and down on TWO. Extend it. Distance myself further from my Baltimore contacts if possible. *Hum you dummy no, that makes no sense, aka duh…already distanced.* Yes and for sure, I skipped this one but I'm coming back to it now, I have to, I have no choice. *What the frick are you talking about bitch boy?* Well, reality check, I am not calling my shooting friends or in touch with them. They are not coming to visit and they are not mailing me drugs or needles, so I'm fine. Yet veritably, maybe there is SOMETHING I could be doing to distance myself more, something, because, gut checker…they are the true threat. *Uh no you idiot, no not really, fuck to the no not really at all.*

Ok yes, I am the true threat but my old contacts still hold the weight.

For sure, the weight, fair enough…what else you got? I do not plan to ever move back to Baltimore, I think I will stay here, or leapfrog mountain peaks to elsewhere nearby. Too soon to tell but this feels right, least big western mountains feel right. But, plainly thinking about not going back isn't enough. I don't think I'll go back but to say I won't ever is a lie…truth is I cannot guarantee I won't go back. *Yeah but for holy-shit Pete's sake probably won't go back for a long time, so what the frick or frack does it matter?* Well, it kind of matters a fuck-ton, it matters to try my best fucking try to never go back to my old ways, back to that coke house or back to hanging with those old shooting friends. So although here now, what if I go back? *Dude, it's willpower asshole, that's all, just don't contact them if going back.* No, there's more, there has to be least one thing I could do from here now. *No, fucking stop dude, there's not, quit overthinking shit.*

                                    Chapter SIX

On the Saddle deck that day…well, oops, actually, hold up a little, let me back up one sentence. Hah, more tech history…pre-cellphones, all I had was a little pocket phone book with my contacts recorded alphabetically, and no other way to reach people besides calling directory assistance or recounting numbers from memory. Ok and catchup onward…on the Saddle deck that day I reached into my backpack, pulled out my phonebook and scratch-out-scribbled the phone numbers for my drug dealers and dealing contacts back in Baltimore, you know, the people I was attempting to stay away from, so to safeguard myself from the needle. I scribbled them out. Although still knowing where they lived and had some numbers memorized, scratching out the numbers was something I could fricking do, something to build increased distance. It seemed like a silly little no-nothing thing, but within the workings of me, I felt extremely proud I did SOMETHING.

So there ya go, I'm good, now I'm good to go. That's all I can do in that regard. I could not think of anything else. And yet, hah, no, fuck to the no actually wait, I am a asshole fucking lowlife loser drug addict, so I had to check this here shady-ass character at the door, yeah…frisk this fucker but good. Yes-yes I played along, pathetically, so true…laughingly I might look at the backside of the scrib-scrib-scribbled pages and decipher the scratched out numbers later. *No, that's dumb, bro…just fricking stop already.* Shut up no it's not, it's not dumb at all, it's fucking true…what the fuck? I am fighting for my fucking life here, and nothing is dumb in this fucking regard, fucking nothing, fuck you…asshole. So, I did something else, I did something more, I did, one…more…thing.

That night after work I was almost out of food so duh, of course I went to the grocery store for more cheap white bread and smooth generic peanut butter. It's all I could afford outside of my foodservice job at Spruce Saddle, but on this day I splurged, I afforded an extra ninety-nine cents. I could swing that, not always but this week I could swing it. I splurged my over budget ninety-nine cents for a new paper pocket phonebook and I went home. While chomping on a PB sammie, I copied the keeper numbers, and I threw the old wretched phone book away…gone, now it was really gone, and haha no, the devil on this my one shoulder never dug it out of the trash and stashed it from the angel on that my other shoulder. Ok, now I was doubly-proud of myself, I did something truly effective. I totally destroyed the extensions of connecting to the shit I knew would hurt me. I avoided doing the shit that was bad for me…I deleted the damn extensions.

Close to Touch

Outside thy food service job on that, thine the magical deck, I got hit with the embracing love of the peaks and an initial calm came over me, soothing and quieting my discontented heart. The mountains whispered their message and because I was close enough to literally touch them, I heard what they had to teach me. No of course not and fuck to the no-100 did I change in an instant, I was not immediately and forever transformed and righted. Rather I merely felt the medicinal power I desired kick in, least for now, and this time I wasn't leaving for a while, hopefully maybe never.

Day after day and month after month I began to find my center and my heart's truth, meeting my true self for the first time in my life. I began to meet my core self and began to emulate a better me, inside and out, and it was fucking religious.

I had befriended two guys, as it was the only other two humanoids in the Vail Valley who raced mountainbikes, and we regularly carpooled to races together all over Colorado. Mike and Dave's drive and energy as athletes, racers, and humans was unquestionably infectious. Drugs were never involved or discussed, these guys didn't do that shit. Instead of thinking maybe one day my life could be better, they afforded me the lens to see the necessary pieces existed within me already.

Instead of hoping and fantasizing, Dave and Mike displayed to me that I already possessed what I needed, I only had to grab hold of it and go.

Spending time with Dave and Mike also helped me realize I did not have to be high all the time, and I began to link together some more days here and there free of drugs, although sporadic. And to crystal clarify, I had not yet admitted to Dave or Mike I was a druggie, rather I hid this at-time irrelevant truth from my two closest Colorado friends.

Jellyfished
The first person I met only seconds after pulling over in Colorado for a brief unplanned hangry bird lunchbreak, unplanned because I thought to be travelling further west to Telluride, was a burly mountainbike riding dude named Paul Jankauskas, alongside his behemoth golden retriever mountain dog, Marmot. Although I found Paul to be gruff, I quickly learned he was a legitimate bespoke craftsman beyond scale, and one of Paul's ventures was operating his miniscule but hyper-high-end bike shop in the heart of Vail's retail village, Custom Wheel Building. Paul teased a summer session fulltime bike mechanic job in front of me within minutes of our first meet up that December, and the following Spring I was working for Paul inside his tiny ultra-cool shop.

Often my primary orientation was just stay out of Paul's grumpy way, while spending joy filled minutes between tasks playing with Marmot, who arrived to work with his hooman every single day. Paul's wife Joanne was a gem of a sweetheart, and stopped by the bike shop now and then to bring Paul lunch. Marmot was such a darling boy, albeit an absolute monster…he had the biggest head I have ever seen on any retriever-type dog. I affectionately nicknamed Marmot thy darling Woolley The Mammoth.

During winters I relied on my day job working for big boss Otto at his Spruce Saddle mid-mountain restaurant for a paycheck, a complementary season ski pass, and free food when on the clock. Winter evenings I was employed at an exotic ski boot fitting shop next to Paul's bike store, working for the masterful Don Lamson at his Boot Lab.

Come summertime I realized the need for a second job to pay bills and frankly, it had to be a foodservice job. Lacking adequate funds to feed my face at home, I was then a cook at the local Pizza Hut franchise after concluding work at Paul's bike shop.

My sophomore year working for Paul, I had raced my mountainbike tons the year before, spending many hours behind the windshield with Dave Turner and Mike Kloser carpooling to mountainbike events all over the state. But two months earlier at my most recent race, I broke my collarbone. Still waffling on turning pro although I was beating multiple card carrying professionals every weekend, I struggled somedays to keep pointing forward with my racing aspirations beyond expert class, and lately struggled slightly to even maintain my mood. Coming off my broken collarbone I was trying to rally my front facing mojo and get back on the road with Dave and Mike. I found the endeavor of racing and the potential it held for me was perhaps the only at-time thing capable of saving me from my most vicious inescapable enemy.

I was trying, I was really trying to stand taller than my pain, stand taller than my fears, stand taller than all inside that held me back from my best capable life, but that shit was hard AF to face and reside over. I was trying to commit to a new life, a sustainable life, and I began to see the truth clearly that only such chance danced around in front of me by way of the bike. I was trying, but it was hard as fuck to even begin to believe that me myself was worth the goddamn effort.

Already I knew I could be pro but I wanted to be the correct type of pro, by my measure. Wanting it somewhat but not yet wanting it more than anything else in the world, I considered a new path. I contemplated coming clean with Dave Turner about my drug addiction, and see if he could maybe help me, I believed he was the only person anywhere in my life at the time who could. Dave is a smart, loving, driven, and charming human, unique and far above average. The second I met him, I felt as I did with Miss Freed and Mister Thomas…Dave would not look away, Dave cared, Dave cared deeply, it was obvious.

As it could be with Dave...this my providence?

Could it be, this my once-and-for-all push me over the clean edge nudge to a pro racing license? Yes, I think so, I thought I was correct and I tried to believe in the notion, attempting to broach the issue with Dave. Then however...no, I can't, I can't do it, I jellyfished, afraid Dave would think less of me and immediately an emotional divide would part us. Yes dumb I know, and I'm sure he would never but I was scared of losing the great connection him and I truthfully shared. Clearly, I was not ready to step up.

Figurine
At the end of the days' time, when night comes for me and I lay down to bed, a small lifelike figurine climbs upon my chest and speaks softly into my closed eyes…this being my *neutrally-alert subconscious.*

Walking about this island with no bridge, no ferry, no flights, and no way off, other people mill about but yet I am alone, sans-seeing and unseen…this being my *self-defeating subconscious*. I am trapped here a while under my half-alert half-unknown snowglobe that is my pilgrimage out west, this betterment-of-self crusade of mine. My arm outstretches to those around me, reaching for them to help or comfort me but no, our hands cannot touch, an invisible wall ensconced between us. The prison bars, perchance my silence. My misstep and the chains binding me are the feared avoidances to build my squad, not allowing others to join me, skipping out on inviting my team to help lift me, guide me, push me, pull me…this being my *backward-sliding subconscious*.

Thus then and therefore, some eye opening conscious analysis…this suffrage of mine, this supposed hardship, this cage of bars I have built around me, is it in fact my noiseless speak? Is it my inadmissible liabilities, my lack of quest shared, my sans-purpose stated, my path unpictured, my intention non-crystal clarified? Have others here been held back from helping, am I muffled with this solo sheltering, this shielding in place? Was I missing the opportunity lay waiting by not opening, by not asking for help from those who could assist to save me…save me from myself? Was I inefficiently doing the work of five women and men, struggling senselessly on my own instead of opening my damn mouth? Was my self-inflicted life holdback the fact I was not telling of myself to others, that I could not do it alone? Could I not allow them to see me as I truly was? Would I not let them join, if they even cared at all? Oh for Christ's sake, I must, I must recount, I must remember. Before leaving Baltimore, I lived to learn know and grow to go it alone, to do it on my own, to hold myself up. I was doing it, least for a while, partially. Yes I knew I couldn't stay and do it forever but I was doing it, me, me, only me. Now do I need such support, cannot I continue to build myself tall and strong alone? Should I shirk and retreat, asking Dave *DT* Turner for help? He's only one man, but I knew no others so valiant enough in appearance to even include. Good as DT was, I did not think if I surrendered could one man carry me entirely.

No and no, I must not slide backward, I must stand and perpetuate thyself. Yes, I suppose yes if I reach for the needle, yes if I crave an uncontrollable craving, yes then I will speak, but til then, I believe it is up to me and least til I falter, I will try to keep going it alone and try my best try…this my *paused bewildered thinking*, partially alert and mostly awake.

My consciousness stepped forward into the light and all other bits of me knew better…they stepped the fuck off. Heretofore and onward then comprehensively, I viewed my overall life outlook as ok, it's fine, pretty damn good actually, with only a few small things to tweak. The updated Vail forecast…sunny, while my wrist-tied anchor string to the little black raincloud overhead tugs at me now and again yet hence and oh well I'm ok, I'm ok, I'm really ok for now, no true bother no less better.

Something Revered

My leading life lessons eventuate out of my missed steps, my slipped footings, what might otherwise be called. . . mistakes.

My lessons learned proper however they leave a mark, a memento, a scar, something revered, the easy stuff does not.

The non-challenging is invisible. . . not recognized, recalled, nor memorized.

Rolling Up to the Wrong Beach on D-Day

I tried to have Paul order it for me, it was just a little thing, but he tuned me out. It was just a little thing, then after a few ignored pleas too many regarding my personal needs, I felt stonewalled. The simple single sealed bearing part needed to arrive that week and although I was maybe breaking an unspoken protocol, I ordered the item myself, adding it to our main weekly requisition with *QBP*, aka Quality Bicycle Products, and I'll settle up with Paul when the coin-sized bearing arrives. Attempting to pay for it upfront when ordered, there was no resolution, I echo-possessed no credit or debit card. The critical part, the bearing, was scheduled to arrive in our weekly Quality shipment on Thursday. Thursday was barely enough time for me to install it, frankly a complicated process, perform a thorough break-in and test ride over the weekend, then hopefully be properly prepared for my comeback race the following week.

I needed to race, *needed to*…I needed to get back to the start line, even if I didn't reach the finish line. My injured downtime was challenging my healthy thoughts and actions. While collarbone-broken in Colorado and not outside on my bike, I worried more about my social ineptness. Pondering my social ineptness, I misdoubted if I was really good enough for someone like Shannon The Stunning, my too-good-for-the-likes-of-me somewhat flirty treasured cutie coworker at Spruce Saddle. Fretting while broken, feeling dodgy on my unsociability and questioning my caliber with Stunning Shannon, I found myself slipping back under the warm emotional blanket of the drugs.

But no, no, no…I did not want to be snuggled by the drugs, not at all, I wanted to stand tall and strong over my weaknesses, one day breaking free of these emotional leg irons forever, and I needed the racing to help get me where I wanted to go.

Thursday morning I arrived for work slightly before 10am and per always, Paul and Marmot were already on the job site. Unknowingly, the parts order was inside, unboxed and received. Stepping in the door after riding my bike to work, Paul ripped my damn head off. Immediately I felt like he was going to punch me. Paul screamed violently…how dare I order anything without his permission, that is not my job, this is his business not mine, I am not allowed to ever order anything.

I tried to apologize and explain the situation but he was having zip-zero none of it. I tried, I really tried…attempting to walk to the back of the shop and put my things away, hoping he might calm down. But Paul with wall-like force blocked me in a confrontational manner. Ok gee whiz I get it, we were legitimately doing battle over this three-dollar broken protocol thing, right now. Pleading, I apologized in excess and asked, "How can I fix this?" Paul snapped back angrily, "You can't, it's not fixable."

FUCK…FUCK…FUCK.

Not exactly knowing what he meant, I inferred I was fired for ordering the part without approval. Looking away, I tried to break the tension. Marmot was cowering near the front door, seemingly desperate to go outside and escape his hooman's rage.

　　　　　　　　　Chapter SIX

Both arms straight down at his sides with fists clenched, Paul was borderline hyperventilating, his bright red face literally puffing big breaths. It was a long five seconds…*well*, I thought, *well*…one more speedily dismissed *I'm sorry*, and…and I…and I swallowed a big breath of *oh fuck it* courage. Struggling to maintain only these deluged droopy eyes, and not let things go any further I said, "Well…I'm sorry, I am very sorry Paul and I'm sorry this didn't work out, I loved working here and I am going to miss it, please tell Joanne I said goodbye."

I hesitated momentarily for any slight response…none… none…none, and with nothing else going for me, I backed up, then turned my bike around. Paul was fuming in place as indisputably…*Puff The Mad-Mad Dragon* collecting a regenerated charge before another blast of flamed fury. *I hope he doesn't*…I hope he doesn't throw anything at the back of my head, but I was still wearing my helmet, so there was that. Walking towards the front, Marmot anxiously nuzzled his nose into the corner of the heavy wood door and its frame. Wriggling his huge hind quarters and wagging his tail that it was me, frantic to get the heck outside and desperately escape this yelling and the thick fog of tension in here, thy darling Woolley almost pushed open the emergency exit hatch himself.

I, I had to…I stopped.

I had to, I…I had no choice.

Flooded with emotional effects aimed at myself, I shifted around and leaned my bike against my right hip. Reaching down with both hands, I cradled Marmot's darling face and brought his big wet nose right up against mine, touching…now my nose wet too. Because Paul was behind and couldn't see, I released the darn tears, letting them raindrop off the edges of both my cheeks. Surprisingly, Marmot didn't flinch as they landed on his snout. Thy beloved Woolley seemed keenly connected to what was happening here…such a smart dog. My enduring kiss landed atop Marmot's head with a dull thud, and with my lips buried in his lovely locks I mumbled daintily…"Goodbye sweetboy".

Lingering for almost a long-ass minute and fixing a gaze out the front door window, I kept both hands under Marmot's massive chin, giving him long slow and heavy love rubs in a favored place. Some sort of connection was happening here, an astronomically-heightened heartspeak, and how the heck does my link with a dog, not even *my* dog, supersede the connection with another heavily-associated work family human?

Paul loves his Marmot dearly but I wondered…*could I possibly flee a Woolley The Mammoth dognapping charge here?* I needed something to hug, something strong, soft, and that wouldn't shake me off them. Minutely I moved my head, a shaking of side to side disbelief, a mild physical misreckoning of self, knowing Paul was watching from behind…*what the hell did I just do here, man I really screwed that shit up, and what the heck do I do now?* My tears rolling steady and although Paul couldn't see my face, I resisted the wiping away, not wanting him to infer it. I let go of Marmot slowly, and reluctantly, highly reluctantly. Opening the door at half speed, still my hope, Paul's mention of something…one…single…thing, anything. No, no, no…Paul said not a peep. Marmot tried to race me outside and I struggled to push thy darling Mammoth back with my leg, not at all wanting to tangle with Paul over anything else. I then let myself out, I…I left…I fricking left…pushing the door closed with finality. My fingers lay lingered on the wood and glass barrier, to what was perhaps a grand opportunity now lost. Slow-motioning my entire bodyweight off the door, like lethargically starting to swim off a wall, I…I just, oh damn it…within seconds I just…I just lost, I just lost my mojo, all of it…*fucking all of it.*

Escapism…Release-ism…Let-go-ism…Just-done-ism

I ducked around to the right, towards The Boot Lab. Inappropriately, *fucking hell's damnation and why did I do this*…I looked back at the door. Marmot's nose was up against the glass, the window steamed and oh my God my sagged knees almost fucking dropped me. I remained propped up by my bike, but barely. The far-away wretchedness of Marmot's chagrined eyes hurt me more than anything I was carrying and…and probably everything upcoming I would have to handle as well. I cannot imagine anything in my future to feel worse than my heart hurts this second, walking away from thy beloved darling Marmot's stare. How is it that the goodbye look from a dog dismantles me so? *Oh good Lord*…the mental melting intensified, this now a volcanic explosion of sorts.

Holding the handlebars with my right, I remained on my feet but trembling, tragically unsteady…the back of my left hand wiped away the first pipeline of tears. I am not entirely sure why I didn't want Paul to see or guess me crying. Maybe deep down I believed he would grow even more mad if I showed such weakness, mostly because he was such a rough and tumble sort of man's man, you know, the football player type of guy he factually was…never cries and gets mad when other wimpy guys cry. Anyway, I was not pissed at Paul, not at all, I screwed up and I should have known better.

Once reaching for Marmot's face, I realized I'll probably never see my dear furry friend again, and the crazily-unsettled notion hurt me more profoundly than I could understand. In a multitude of ways, I interpreted I was kissing the entire Vail Valley goodbye as I planted my lips on Woolly The Mammoth's crown. Before consciously processing any of it, I was already thinking of being done, just done…go…just leave…run away…quit, just quit…quit it all. Well, no…no wait, but I did not want to go, I wanted to stay, I wanted to stay long time.

I took about ten steps away from the shop, walking past the Boot Lab under the arch of the open courtyard building structure, and pushed my bike towards the street, not sure where to go, not sure what to do, not sure how I felt about anything.

 Chapter SIX

Mostly out of sight from the shop, I leaned the top tube of my bike against my right thigh, then wiping tsunami tears wave number two back with both hands, I thought with annoyed recoil…*now what?* Now what…what the fuck do I do now?

I did not slow, I did not pause, don't think I even took a single breath for almost two minutes, I weakened, and just…kept…moving. With perverse self-disgust I boarded my bike, asking the mighty mountains their advice as I moviescreen-spun by.

Their provisional lifesoul adjusted, speaking to me as I rode…the snow peaks filmrolling along on my sides, the grandiose scale zooming in and adjusting bigger ahead of me, the fantabulous picture fading out and shrinking smaller behind me.

Fuck it, fuck it all, just fuck it all then. Once after 'a couple hours fleeing eastbound in the Subaru, blatantly ignoring my alpine lucidity, I no longer felt strong or tall…well, hah, until I did. With the Rockies almost entirely in my rearview I re-bloomed when figuring…hum, wait a damn second, *this* is my reality now, *this right here*, at my *hands*, under my *feet*, and in my *lap*…*not* behind me, *not* in front of me and *not* to my sides…*here*, right here, right fricking here…*this*, this, *only this mattered,* and I rolled with it.

Where I've been and what I've done shapes me, but where I'm heading fuels me.

Interset Kismet
Hum, as I sampled to cipher while driving, the inexplicable everything-just-fell-into-place Vail episode…meeting Paul, receiving his job offer within minutes, and finding an apartment in less than an hour, what did this teach me, what did this experience offer me? Such destinations alignment enhanced my get-up-and-go gumption. Two years earlier when leaving Baltimore for who-knows-where, mostly the kismet of my life reinvention pilgrimage out west lined up pretty good ok and fine, by my measure.

My pockets practically pauperized, I had left Baltimore for the mountains anyway, yes I was taking a chance leaving, but I believed my chances none if I stayed.

Ski-bum fiscally challenged, I survived ok fine on white bread 'n peanut butter. Lacking a doorknob to call home for a few weeks, I resourced a roof within the Subaru and tried to pay for stink-shedding showers at the nearby health club regularly.

Getting barked at often by the master while the dog Mammoth hid, I stuck, and my emotional skin thickened, calloused actually. And hah, no there will be not none take-backs this time…my wrangle with Paul was the antithesis of prior boss yelling.

I was just trying to navigate Paul's frustration with me, not fit self-blame concrete anklets on and shove myself into a lake. Thereupon then under review, I comprehended myself capable of the same thing again and again if I choose, and able to survive elsewhere, same-same or better as in Vail…*I can, I can, and I will*. Learning more out west than guessed was there to see or overcome, doing what I came to do and then some, I studied the still-wet and striking wall art…*I am not so weak, I am not so dumb, I can do it, I am good enough, I am strong enough, I can do it, I can do anything*. The forevermore portrait of myself sat there, a blank canvas complete with paint and brushes, anxiously awaiting me to pick them up and use them, pick them up and begin.

Alignments

Once deciding a run to the mountains was in order, knowing the safe loving arms of the peaks was my only path, that shit right there was the first major defining moment of betterment in my life. Every nano-detail, every do or do-not amounted to make me who I was at the time. I spent all prior years worrying and second-guessing myself, well…until I mostly didn't.

> A decision made, I lived to learn and know, is a *choice*.
> A decision made, I lived to learn and know, is a *reorientation*.
> A decision made, I lived to learn and know, is a *direction*.
> A decision made, I lived to learn and know, is a *piece of me*.

I learned, I learned it fast and learned it honestly, that a decision is a *decision*. For the most part, once decided, I have thought it through enough to go, just go, and not look back. Encircling my decision to move west and pre-Vail, oh bloody hell the darkness had rolled in…the drug deals grew sketchier and I pushed heavier bets into the center of the table, unconcerned for how it might play out. I'd blow an eight ball in a few hours and leave negative-cashflow broke. I told outlandish lies to have people front me more and more shit, knowing I would never make good on the drug debt.

The second overdose or whatever the heck it was, the damage deeper and the residue dirtier than willing to live through again. I was absolutely flat out exhausted and ready to let it all go, *yeah whatever*, freewill journeying then to The Other Side. So yes for sure, whole-heartedly I believe if not for my Vail experience, I would have absolutely died within months, without hesitation I proclaim this. Why would I have died? Because I wasn't strong enough to commandeer and grow into the knowledge of guiding my own life, until I was.

Expanse, In and Out

Within a matter of minutes I quit my job at Paul's shop, well, technically I think to have been fired, oh well regardless and anyway…then packed up and left Colorado, in a huff. Being so huffed up on many levels, I wanted to puff up, aka smoke a shit ton of weed and soft-pad my sorrows. No, but no, I hadn't been high in a while, a few days, and when able to string together a few clean days, I felt, well, I felt…I felt proud. I felt strong. I felt better than the me prior to the last sunset past. I felt strong-stronger, I felt tall-taller.

I felt like if Dave Turner knew everything I was up against or put myself through, I felt like he would be very proud of me the days I didn't touch drugs noon to night.

After grumble driving all huffed up for a couple hours on Interstate 70 east, a self-inventory found my heart at organic peace, not elsewise in conflict or struggle. My head…smarter than previous. My comprehensive self…expanded more than before. In no way whatsoever did I leave Vail smaller or weaker than I arrived, no fricking way forget it, and in no way did I need or want to be high, just to try and feel another way, or to try and not feel something real. Hum…ok, more mental math…drugs created coverup fake feelings. Well, I'd rather live with feels of real, than unreal. Well, but what's real…meaning, what really happened in Vail?

1.   ONE. Reviewing my beginning motivational initiatives for moving west
     a.   Yes, *check*, I possessed absolute accomplishment with what I set out to do
2.   TWO. Regarding my intentions once landing out west
     a.   Yes, *check*, I realized them all, and then some
3.   THREE. Regarding my planned not-to-do's once I got there
     a.   Yes, *check*, my plan was most definitely carried out successfully

In Colorado I calmed, I centered and I found much of my own truth within. I grew and expanded in ways I could have never dreamed. I would have loved to stay in Vail but the conditions suddenly presented as wrong, blanketed by shouting and unfairness. Maybe I am *that* fragile, for good reason or not. As the life dominoes began to topple, I decided to pull out and change my world. Then in short order, my realized thankfulness sat down beside me as I drove, thrilled to be heading where I'm heading and no, not once touching my rear view mirror or making any mental gestures towards it either. I had one direction now…forward, and I faced it…forward. Forward…back to Maryland.

Finally, I have met this bird heads up and mostly understood my true self.

Finally, I am well on my way to living as my complete true self.

Finally, once back home I believe to stay-stay standing tall-taller over my fears, my darkest doubts and the needle itself, least this my strong-strongest intentional try.

Waffle-Waffle

Just before storming off from Colorful Colorado I wondered bizarrely if some shit was about to blow up in my face, because I thought it just might, right before I twisted the ignition key forward. Meaning to say, I doubted my inner strength to leave the warm bosom of the mountains, awhile bail on my friends, probably to beat myself up about it, then possibly return home to the needle. On many levels, leaving Vail was a huge roll of the chamber for me, and one I was not sure to turn out favorably, no not sure at all.

Also I struggled greatly with self-imposed dilemmas associated with turning pro. When training on my bike, I trained intently. When racing I exerted every possible output. However unconsciously but at the end of the day, I avoided the comprehensive commitment of proper nutrition, adequate rest, specified speed training, and a stress reductive home life. Comparatively, I didn't have the horsepower the top guys had, but did I lack the speed potency, or was my velocity still underdeveloped?

Easily I could have already turned pro, based purely on results, but I did not want to plainly *exist* in the pro field, ah, no, I wanted to live up to my own expectations. Yet I struggled to visualize the correct image of what being pro looked like…my satisfied result placings, level of sponsorship, and overall fiscal viability. I could not commit to a pro career while still using drugs, and those facts of the matter blocked me from believing such a bona fide athlete dynamic was even possible. I reckon focused on my probable core potential, but was not nearly situated for an unsupported stand without the prop up of my long time daily street substances. I waffled, I was not ready. If not yet committed by my measure, what would I call myself in this regard, being the space between current efforts and maximum abilities? Hum, well, I claim…part-time passionate.

 Part-time passionate…what is part-time passionate? Some planned training days, I never touched my bike. I was still smoking too much pot, plus other occasional binges of pills, cocaine, acid, and more. Even when enthused to train, the rain or snow or wind would get the better of me at times. I couldn't pull together enough hyper focused training, I wasn't ready, although I desired it greatly. Yes I was probably getting close to a full commitment, long as I did not stay too busy or overly-distracted doing mostly senseless shit, or work too much and delay the jump turning pro another year, another year, another year. I was part-time passionate but not yet engulfed in the critical state of *whatever it fucking takes*, aka committed-100-willing-100, by my measure.

Monkey-Monkey Naughty-Naughty Monkey-Monkey

Yes the recipe included the ingredients of mountains and time away, then it was maybe the added special spice of the reprieve finally making the bird-bake mix delectable. Yet, hum, dang…could growings and learnings come my way honestly if doing the same amount of time elsewhere, like two years of committed rehab, *committed* meaning I walked in myself, fueled and driven by my own motivations, within my own accordance, to take this thing on, my progressive monkey shedding? Could I have lasted long enough within a facility of sorts while doing intense self uplifting work? Would I not have jetted way earlier from such the hard scene? What if I moved to live in a place where there were those to talk to, with regular check in's but they did not own me, where they would not *lord over me* as my Friendwords pal Tyler TJ Schmidt so eloquently rattles off? What if it were an extreme outdoor compound where I could come and go as I please, yet receive semi regular counseling and somehow it kept me from the worst of the worst, aka kept me from the needle? A place with loving, comforting, and non-judgmental therapists who never gave up on me despite my dysfunction and maybe self-giving-up?

 Yes, the primary driver was my committed readiness, but I think for the most part, it was plainly something I had to go through on my own, solely under my own power, using my self-fabricated tools and resources, aka not receiving or taking a damn penny from my father. Although I would like to believe such a fix-it recovery center to be a possibility, I don't think I was ready for such a factually fabricated utopian meadow, while the while and anyway, how could any administration for goodness sake accurately screen or sheepman marshal over me and my peer incoming damaged flock?

Holding Up the Sky

Nonstop change
Constant challenge

Only me my one solo self can step up
I cannot grant burden its victory

I've always endured
Strength is willing

The switch gets flipped
This sky will not fall

Only within
Only within

Only within
Do I win.

Running Out of Gas and Broken Down at the Crossroads

Back on the clock in Baltimore, I went to work for Alan Davis at the brand new second location of Princeton Sports in Columbia Maryland, about 40 minutes south from his dad Sonny's original location in Baltimore, and it was glorious. Alan took great care of me, and it was glorious. For a couple years under Alan's bike and ski shop work roof, I was operating at extremes, doing most all work things righter than right, and it was glorious.

It was a Tuesday…it was an average springtime Tuesday. It was another Tuesday working at the bike shop. My mountainbike racing buddy Paul Smith Junior was employed in the workshop with me at Princeton Columbia. For more than a week I had not consumed any drug substances. Not in months had I sold drugs, but I was still using.

My seriousness concerning work and racing was increasing dramatically, and my drug use had lessened substantially.

Hah, besides, for the last two weeks Baltimore was suffering through a marijuana drought. The only pot around was dirt weed. This dirt weed was shit so weak and pathetic I couldn't even bring myself to buy or smoke it…I'd rather do without than pay for some illegal pseudo-substance lacking enough active ingredients to even get me high. This shit even looked like shit…dry brown loose flakes in bags or wrapped up in foil, no sweet smell, no green color, and certainly no sticky bud formations. Once in a while a strain of dirt weed might get me slightly high, but most times I resented spending money on that crap and what I gained was only a paid-for headache. This shitty shit weed lately was worthless of even an attempt, which really aggravated me.

My younger mountainbike racer protégé friend and co-worker Paul Smith Junior and I stopped at a dude buddy's place after work for a social smoke call, hoping he had some decent pot. Quick side note here if you pretty please, Paul was a regular pot smoker before we met, that was not on me…just sayin'. Ok, back to the dirt weed train…I practically reeled backward in frustration once inside and seated in my buddy's condo, seeing the shit brown color of the pot bag he just pulled out. Our hosting dude claimed it was *ok*…and I begrudgingly accepted a bong hit as the junior Paul choked on one of his own. Soon as I began to cook the bowl and taste the smoke, my stomach started to turn. Smoking the entire hit and taking in the imitation illegal, I quickly blew it out of my mouth, sick and tired of trying to catch a buzz off the damn brown dirt weed.

Proclaiming to both Paul Junior and our host pal that I'm fed up to the moon with shitty shit weed, I stood up to leave for home. Paul had his own car and chose to stay behind, to *hang out a while* with our buddy. I walked out the door shaking my head side to side slightly, saying to myself *that's not ok dude…that shit was not ok*. No I was not mad at my hosting friend, I was slightly pissed at the weed itself but cast resentment out unto the world that there wasn't any good pot in town. I was off balance emotionally, and now legitimately mad. I began my drive back to Baltimore mad, but hum…wait a minute, *mad,* what is mad? Was I truly mad? Hum, no…*angry,* I was angry.

'Litrilly once to highway 29 north I started slamming my fist on the steering wheel, angrily. *Ouch motherfucker…*on the third punch of the wheel I felt something twinge, think I just broke my fucking hand, dumb ass fucking angry bird. Why the hell am I so angry, why am I so ridiculously upset, what the hell do I have to be angry about? Many things were moving in my direction of betterment, I came so far in the last five years since leaving the drug needle behind…why the hell can't I relax in the good I have created for myself? Why am I carrying this up and down angst, what the hell is my problem? I tried settling into the 30-minute drive home and figure some shit out. I wriggled lower into a comfy spot and started my dissection of this here dumb ass angry bird shit.

    Ok asshole, what's the damn problem? The dirt weed is the problem, the stupid dirt weed. *No you big dummy, no.* Pot in general is the problem. *Yes, better.* The marijuana is the problem, and the blockage it creates within me, that's the problem. The pills are also the problem, when I do them. The acid is the problem, although I imagine to face no trouble giving that crap up. The coke is certainly still a problem. This drug shit, all of it…this stupid blockage shit. Blockage, this shit creates blockage. Much as I want to do better in life, this shit is blocking me. Much as I want to do better on the bike, this shit is still blocking me. The drugs are the fucking problem, that's what's wrong. The drugs are the problem, their blockage, the drugs are blocking me.

    Ha-ha, hey dummy, knock-knock. Huh, say what? Who's there, oh wait…dang it, the drugs are not the problem. *Correct.* The blockage is not the problem, the blockage is not the problem and I know it. *Correct.* I am the problem, it's me, I am the damn problem, I am the blockage. *Correct.* Here we fucking go again but, but now at an entirely new level never considered before. Is this what I want, is it, is this, is this what I need? It's been over thirteen years, are the drugs what I really want? It's been thirteen motherfucking goddamn years, are the drugs what I really need? Oh what the fucking fuck? How long am I going to keep doing this shit to myself? I am sick and tired of the damn dirt weed, I am sick and tired of the blockage, so now what? *Yeah right, now what…now…what?*

    As my wheels rolled I puzzled, all-thought lost and seeking direction…I slowed. Emotionally I sat there out of gas and spiritually broken down at the crossroads. It was time. It was really, really, really time. It was time to choose, I had to choose. Now what, do what? And do not what? Where do I go from here? I am sick and fucking tired of getting in my own way. I had to pick a path, one path. One path one, there were only two routes from which to choose. Only two avenues available, and I knew it. One, stand up and journey my glorious unknown and adventurous but intentional drug free path. Two, stay sat on my habitually blocked stupid ass substance stoop.

Here both of which I will allow and either of which I will afford, by these here my own damn hands. Either of which I will choose to live with, as desired and wanted by me myself alone.

Pick a path, pick a path, pick a fucking path, pick a fucking path and go…go, go, go right fucking now.

Dynamo

We're not so damn tough, until we choose to be.

Sometimes we step up to the plate, and sometimes we step off.

Now and again camped in bed, tear filled...all day.

Reflecting across everything survived thus far, realizing we're a lot tougher than we think we are, this recall our asylum...a shelter to weather the storms, storms absolutely and positively coming for us.

Now knowing, hopefully we can face forward and gain strength as we go, a human dynamo...being the one who mostly holds it together when shit really hits the fan.

Seven

~

Willing

Dragging Thou's Indifferent Ass to the Curb

Chapter Seven, Willing ~

Angrily…angrily I stormed out of my pal's condo, me now all alone after leaving Paul Smith Junior behind at our mutual friend's place. I planned my pitstop, a nearby gas station convenience store to buy a bottle of Coca-Cola and rinse the taste of rank dirt weed bong hit from my mouth. Also I hoped the caffeine would help starve away the approaching ache inside my noggin, while the liquid utilized to wash down three Ibuprofen's.

That single skank bong hit stripped me of my previous one week clean time, although I incessantly broke my damn short stints of intentional drug free days, broke them time after time in the last five years, so it really didn't much fricking matter anymore whatever why bother who cares.

Feeling sky high levels of frustration, then accepting the tiredness of utter exhaustion from over a dozen straight years of daily hustling, stealing, lying, scamming and searching for drugs, I pulled into the convenience store parking lot and switched off my car.

It was a post-Monday working day at the bike shop, evening time, an hour after clocking out at Princeton Sports Columbia. I sat soundless, completely still behind the wheel for about four minutes, a factual long-ass time to remain in reserved silence. Self-shame flooded me…I aimlessly pinned my *Lowlife Loser* nametag back on, glaring down at its badly marred but familiar finish of repulsiveness. My bird butt bottom grew heavier as I sat, *ugh*…physically unconfident, I sank shamefully lower into my seat. My short-while-ago spoken words, "sick and tired of this shitty dirt weed" still rang in my ears irately.

I shook my head back and forth in disgust then posed the self-proposition out loud…"What the hell am I doing?".

For the last couple years since moving back to Baltimore from Colorado, my unsettledness compiled. My mental wrangling orchestrated a faint repeating jingle in my head…*I really don't know what the fuck I am doing*, hah, with but discrete mere scantness did I possess any guidance of cognizant orientation at all. Most days I awoke and…whatever happened, happened. Indisputably, I maintained vocation of life passenger, not driver. The distinction of what I was working towards, or however fighting for, well…such positioning was a crapshoot gamble, at best. Although my ascending trajectory was somewhat encouraging, still, barely did I have a flipping clue. My approach was not much more than a tattered feeble paltry indifference of how to act out any life movement at all.

Loitering quietly in the convenience store parking lot, slightly rocking my bird frame forward and back in my seat, my aching hands rubbing my knees, glaring ahead while focusing on nothing but this bird's bleak blankness through the windshield...something changed.

Something changed, something really changed…I was disgusted with myself, disgusted I still travelled the path pursuing drugs, pursued that shit most every…single…day. I accepted the coming-into-focus image of myself as only half a person, me still lying to myself, me still lying to the world. Lying…*lying* the drugs were assisting me. *Lying* I needed drugs to function and survive. *Lying* I could operate my best life while also maintaining my drug use. I wanted to get serious about competing on the mountainbike but on several opposing levels, I was unsure of my capabilities and waffled on my commitment to the seriousness required to race at the pro level, because I was still semi-childlike. I did not accept the responsibilities of my operational life, and solidly, I could not stand soundly within my true place of opportunity in the world.

However then providentially, I found myself afront a paned reflective glass glaring back into this mind's eye. Unequivocally, and conclusively, the raw marrow of my truth then exposed itself like never before, fucking ever. Quick to follow like a one-two punch was my comprehensive constitution of committed readiness…I was ready. I was ready, I was really, really, really *ready*. Instinctually upon abridged review, I was repulsed by my expansive catalog of legacy lies. I wanted a new me…more than *needing* a new me, I *wanted*. My self-tiredness had been radiating brightly from the mirror whenever I walked by, years now…hah, I could even see the beaming rays of Roger Ray repugnance splashing the walls around the corner from another room.

Time for a supreme change, time to do life different, time to accept the truthful responsibility that no one, nor not a single motherfucking thing was coming to rescue me or would show up to do the work for me.

I wanted a different life, I decided to try for a different life, different than this old shitty one anyway.

Since then steering in the direction of a new me, I comprehended clearly...deciding I myself would have to construct the life I desired.

Purchasing a plastic encased twist-top-cap Coca-Cola 20-ouncer, I decided also, today, *fucking today*…today I would begin living anew, flushing down the drain much of my self-shame and blame, intentionally doing more right things, and doing least a fewer wrong things, most every…single…day. I decided. Then and there I decided, I fucking decided.

PFP, P…F…P, I decided. I decided…those dirt weed bong hits would be the last bong hits I will take, I absolutely fucking decided.

Factually, I was sick and tired of the life I patch work fabricated for myself…truthfully run down, worn out, deflated and depleted, exceedingly exhausted. Not all such surface shit was individually unmanageable but rather, sick of the deep undertones of my life I was, my abysmally-true unsettled self…my quitting, lying, stealing, drug addict self…absolutely fucking sick and tired of it. I wanted a new life, I wanted a different feeling, I wanted alternative comfort, I wanted controllable guidance. I wanted a different umbrella to shield me, I wanted a new-to-me patch of ground to stand upon. I thought deeper, not actually seeing the totality of the life I wanted, but I knew much of the parts I un-desired…I wanted a life void of running, I wanted a life free from fear. Wanting the ability to look forward, not having to watch over my shoulder always. I wanted a sense of completion, a feeling I could do something successfully. Wanting a life of forward positive momentum I did, able to go fast as I could and not have to slow down or pause. I wanted a head free from drug fog, a life of semi-responsible humanhood, wanting to achieve all I desired without reservation, and without the barrier of lies that I was not good enough…not good enough, not good enough for anything.

I decided, I decided to unravel dirty assumptions, strive for goodness, and turn my life in a new direction, I fucking decided. I constructed course…a path towards *not sure where*, but a direction *away from here*. More than life challenge, more than fear more than threat, and more than the void of resources I did not possess, I lived to learn and know that willingness to endure is my primary superpower.

I had to oblige death in order to leave the drugs behind because, well…henceforth I knew myself unable to organically stay away and if I could not stay away from the drugs, they would happily carry me off, aka belly-up dead bird, aka I would die anyway. So then *why not*…why not die trying for something better than wallow in complacent nothingness? *Nothingness*…nothing but sitting still and residing in the bad, nothing more than hiding, nothing 'cept waiting for the bad-badness to come take me away. The easiest thing to do was nothing…sit and wait but no, but no, I would not auto pilot into the brick wall, I would not close my eyes and let the vehicle of my life high speed drive itself, no fucking no. I determined, I decided, I decided to finally do something different.

I was willing to do whatever it takes to move in my desired direction. I would not, would not, would not give up wimpily this time, even if the attempted try terminates me. I fucking decided.

Outboard Safe Harbors

Barely could I recognize the criticalness of the proceeding…I missed the viewing. At the time, the significance of my irrevocable decision at the crossroads escaped me. Perhaps, perhaps my non-thinking on the matter was partially due to the fact, well, no, wait up a sec…the scenario was not an occurrence of *perhaps* at all.

I am sure-sure-100 my brain did not absorb the future impact of my commitment to rid myself of drugs and ultimately steer my own ship, due to the fact I was not yet within calm waters.

Residing far apart from any comparative language did this the finality of my decision to quit all drugs come close to any hopes, dreams, claims, promises or attempts I held previously, aka this was something brand new. Finding myself in a place never been before, I knew I was ready, I was ready, I was fucking ready. Truth-truth of the matter, I was never more serious about anything in my life until when I decided.

Alas I tried to remain realistic yes, yes, yes, the lure of drugs will be with me for rest of days, total…for-certain…truth 100. Although my orientation was that I'd rather jump bare butt naked into a hungry-hungry great white shark-filled bottomless pool with slippery stainless steel mile-high sidewalls sans escape ladder before using drugs again, I knew I could not control my future and anything was possible. Awhile this my biggest life reinvention ever was conclusive and profound alongside uncertain, I was steadfast AF with my path. Hah, knowing despite all pain and fear determined to depart, I also accepted the truth of more darkness awaiting me over the horizon no doubt. But I cared less than none, this bird now fixated on course, I prepared to take flight.

For an amassed five years, the only taste and smell of the drug needle originated from the legacy recalls in my head, not from physical shots in my arms hands or feet. My quest to break away from the needle had little almost none to do with me at all, *echo-echo*…but was done to spare others the pain of my funeral, my death an absolute certainty I knew it, and soon. Then with the needle a handful years gone, this was something else now, this was for me.

I had an opportunity, what my precise probable advantage was I did not at all know, but I developed the notion of a *chanced maybe* to do something…for me myself to do something justifiable with my life, instead of *duh*, just throw it all away. Yes, I believed to have found an opening, but it was more than just getting onto my bike and speeding off into the sunset. The fears frights shouts and sights of my mother still clung to me negatively, but I believed myself ready to shed most all that stupid sticky shit, like a snake slithering free and leaving its old stinky skin behind. My vision looked outward into the blue, far-far-farther ahead than I had ever envisioned before.

Laying Abottom My Own Nothingness

Even once first *deciding* to try and shake the needle, breaking free of the absolute stranglehold that dark malevolence of death soon upcoming had on me, the doing was the hard part, those five inexorable years of inner turbulence, well…they were neither fucking fast nor easy. The while, following a few feeble years half heartedly *trying*, I nonetheless accumulated moments of memorialized clean time, all of which added up to my final decision to act with certainty, aka quit all drugs with dominating determination you big dummy stupidhead. Yet, I must also say…previous and admittedly, barely did I cling to the truthful train of *trying* to quit, aka I was just riding along, I was just mouthing the words. I believe such stringer of half-hearted try's withhold clean time memory, however slight. These stretches of clean time akin a stand alone internal generator that runs strong a while, then the fuse blows, the train engine's outboard light dies, but the internal flame is still there long as the breath breathes, and the fire returns to burn brighter and run stronger once rekindled. I believe alongside every stretch of clean time, however short or slight, however successful or dysfunctional, my inner expanse grows. My inner expanse is the totality of me, well, least all of what I *could* be.

Only by way of my earlier attempts trying to get clean did the resonance of possibilities ring.

Only by way of earlier attempts trying and trying and trying to get clean did the narrative of possibilities speak to me…whispering the story into my inner ear of how much better I did last time, and how it is *possible* for me to do even better next time still. Only by way of earlier wanting, then trying and trying and trying by way of truth did I reach the place I finally found myself in, understanding my inner expanse had not yet filled, aka I still had more room within me…I had more room left inside than I could even begin to understand. Sitting behind the wheel in the convenience store parking lot, that was it, I was done, I was totally fucking done. I decided, I decided I was done, I was *fucking done* once and for all…no more drugs, no more drugs, even if it kills me I was fuck to the fucking done, starting right fucking then. Oh shit but no, straight-up fuck to the no, oh for fucking shit's sake no and slow the fuck down fuck no…jesusfuckingchrist, just wait a fucking second, just stop. Stop, just…fucking…stop, fuck that shit and factually-actually no fucking way, that's bullshit, that's fucking bullshit bird boy.

That fucked-up shit, that fucked-up shit ain't so goddamn easy.

    Not so goddamn easy at all.

    While fucking factually, it's fucking harder than fucking hard.

    That fucked-up shit's beyond reason hard.

    Beyond human limits hard.

    Beyond fathomability hard.

    It's harder than…it's harder than trying to imitate the sun.

    The sun, the fucking sun…it's harder than trying to mock the moon, the stars.

    The stars, the motherfucking stars, aka that shit's harder…than…fucking…hard.

So what was it really? More than my spillage page prior, what brought me to just *deciding,* and how did a decisive mental thought pattern overpower my deep down 13 year addiction? Hum…well, lemme see…perhaps some echoing resonance here, but the return dissection I believe valuable and the lookback worthy of producing additional clarity. It was the finality then, me broken down and destitute at the end of end lines…upon a deep, a dark, and a painful exploration into my heart of hearts, trying to figure out an escape from this certain death sentence, I fell soundly on the realization and the commitment more than I *wanted to* get high, I must be steadfast with my resolve to *NOT* get high, least for the next five minutes, which was all I could hope to possibly relegate anyway.

Just For Today is a phrase I assume was crafted to help us manage pain, trauma, and addiction while building strength and momentum, but the notion always foreign to me. I could never do it…hell's bells, like are you kidding me or what, a whole entire *today* felt so incredibly long, as if a decade away. So let me get this straight…an entire day at a time just praying wishing or trying to stay away from drugs? Are you fucking kidding me, I'd be drop down dead to the ground by noon. I had to live minute by minute, then in fifteen minute blocks, then hour by hour and finally with a slight breeze at my back, I tried to survive a few hours at a time. Maybe I'd stay clean from wake til breakfast, if eating that day. Maybe til lunch or dinner or midnight, or bedtime, if sleeping that night.

The Devil strolled cockily about in my consciousness, awhile camouflage-lurked below the seeable watch of the surface, anxiously waiting for me to slip an inch.

I was intimately mindful of the dark underlord hiding in the tall grass nearby. I felt the master of death scratching at my heels whenever I slowed forward momentum. I had to keep pushing, keep going, and could not stop no matter fucking what. If pausing even a nano second, I could and most likely would find myself back within the darkest of places…at the bottom of the pit inside my own nothingness. This cavity the last holding cell, the gap between the world that once gave oxygen freely but alternatively I struggle, my breath under arrest, slightly distracted I begin to barely adjust my grip then without a hint of notice, he strikes. With lightning speed and unbearable nuclear force I'm then gone, done, game over, fatally consumed…end, ender, end…of…story.

Assuming an angered position against the drugs, I determined to stand above them and tower over the smaller weaker drug addict me, challenging to see if the contest was capable of killing me, because it just might. My assembled oak tree boldness was a taller, stronger, and wiser sense of self than ever perceived before, ever, motherfucking ever. Such orientation also precision aligned with truth…I was going to see this one through to the end, surpassing the checkered flag, I was going to win this one, exceeding the weighted power drugs once held over me.

This being the factual first-move jumpstart of my healthy ego…I laid everything within me on the line, everything, and if I presumed wrong, oh well, least I would have no regrets, no regrets.

No regrets…least I did every single possible fucking thing within my humanoid power to reorient myself towards the good, no matter fucking what, period fucking period. My strength optimism and resolve improved as I continued experimenting with how much drug free brutal shit I could endure. Besides needing to stay in the lead of the race against the Prince of Darkness, I discovered through total unwavering commitment I could actually find success with linked minor victories, giving my heart of hearts a small taste of hope…hope to try and keep trying, try to keep growing, try to keep elevating above all that which once held me down. Comically, even when thinking myself comprehensively clean and surviving the toughest thing ever, alas tougher things just kept coming for me.

Major turns in life direction take time tenacity and my total try.

My process became one of digging deep to find self-truth, then assuming the rather painful position of willingness to accept any and all physical and mental blows of trauma and heartache. The evolution was intentional commitment, even when sitting to think. My routine became the absolute clarification of focus, force rank, and prioritizing my options or to-do's. Then viably, filling in the most critical gaps, I identified my *not* to-do's. From scratch I fabricated most things, or least heavily re-engineered stuff already in play. Thinking ahead with a filtered sustainability lens, I systemized shit best I could, then pulled it off effectively as possible, even if just an experiment.

    Like what dad? Well my Birdy…like putting fricking first things flipping first.

1. *First things first*…like my commitment to *not* use drugs foremost in line of everything else, even in front of my factual desire to still use drugs.
2. *First things first*…like how I placed an associated-materials reading ban on myself while writing this book, so not to be influenced. Or how I pushed work aside for years and burned all paychecks in favor of producing these here your pages.
3. *First things first*…like how many times I remove the Facebook and Instagram apps on my phone while trying to better focus on other things, thus removing the temptation.
4. *First things first*…like when tired or intimidated or lacking the money, I go to special social show-up events anyway, knowing the effort of being there for others always worth it in the end, always, always, fucking always.

I will not be a bystander, no, no flipping way, I will not be a passenger, no way forget it, I will be the driver of my own life direction, fuck to the yes…me plotting my own course, me packing my own gear, me, me, it's all on me, period fucking period.

Set Adrift Upon the Sea of Mediocrity

I dove into situations capable of hurting me, both physically and neurologically. Awhile recognizing...a knock down blow doing something I love tastes like the most amazing and scrumptious birthday cake, set against the gluttony of those vicious self-inflicted poisonous death pills. My fuel is my intention, my destination is forward.

It is hard for most people to comprehend but I skirted death during my dance with the devil, certain death, and there was no way I was going to sit around and just coast...you know, taking it easy, floating adrift upon a sea of mediocrity.

I hesitated none to jump, even if unable to first spy a landing place. Mid-flight I knew...mid-flight and flying I knew myself safer than sitting still. I cultivated skills and developed talents thus-then unspoken to even me, discovering elements of self to celebrate wildly this here life with fervor, celebrate wildly, and joyfully.

It was not recklessness, no way, but a pursuit of living boldly out in the light, far away from that damn dark death pit as I could position, a pursuit of life with 101% effort, entirely fuck-void concerned of a slip, a fall, or a break.

My own safety came last because I thought nothing to fear, long as I kept moving, long as I kept going. However then un-gloriously the faster I went, the bigger lead I would have on those things chasing me, those things trying to devour me.

If I ciphered something doable, often I threw precaution to the wind. If deeming the challenge possible I went for it, hah...or as my fantastical fat-tired flying friend Andrew Shandro once told me, "Huck and Hold". This here battered bird swallowing 40+ broken bones, 13 surgeries, and 60+ concussions to date, I am thankful to be vertical and operating under my own power today.

Given the chance to go back and do things over, I would not have slowed so to otherwise avoid the blows, no, no way not at all but rather, methodically and wisely developed methods to go faster, thus able to make it cleanly up and over the obstacles previously stopping me cold.

Face Down in the Mud

Day one clean from drugs felt not much different than any prior. Highly charged enthused and focused though, my intent was sound AF…no, no way, there would be no resting, no coasting, and no fucking freewheeling. My initiative soundly secure…get up, get going, keep moving, and do…not…fucking stop. Yeah right, take a break? Hah, fat fucking chance, when unmindful my hands knew not what to do or how to do, and solely the stretch of purified darkness reached out to collect me.

I slipped on gloves of virtuousness and sparred that lowlife loser reflection of mine in the mirror. No and no, I had come too fucking far to tap out now.

I knew not where, I knew not how, yet I found…*possibility*. I found possibility of hope, and I found willingness to pursue all what I had not yet seen, felt, held, or known.

No, no, fuck to the not on your life, I will not yield to the dark feebleness of death's chaw now, no nor never, me thinks. Yet do I even know what I know, and that which I do not? Hum, well…ah fuck it, *huck and hold*.

Finally, I have duly strengthened. I fittingly heightened in emotional stature, and I have unquestionably expanded…greatly expanded.

Rudder

Who remains in these here shoes once the cloud cover of fear worry and want have cleared…for it is I, my singular solo oneself, free to dream, sing, and dance as I choose.

They the clouds however, they the clouds will return for me soon enough, the veil of shadow then to be lifted afront these eyes in alternative short order, only then to repeat again and again…and again, I know such intimately.

But to maintain my rudder regardless the storm amid this here sea of life…such is, who I hope to be…such is, precisely that which I will try.

Supporting Truth

Scars…figuratively. Scars…literally. I am a junkie…this, a forever piece of me. This piece of shit junkie lowlife me formed scars fast. Scars formed first atop the bag of skin covering my gangly little man arms. Coloring in with *fantastical narrative crayons*…this here easy to rip pale sheathing righteously ravaged by her the poker stick needle, when coming 'round to nurse me her medicinal magic, mollifying my mortified mind…least a while. Our first date was sweet…she was so nice and older than me but still wore pink, kicking a pair of cute white lace-up Oxford flats, purple sparkly laces, ladies size 8. I was blanketed, my entire person draped with her glorious warm love wrap, a comfort thereupon me never known before. Without adequate shielding over these here eyes, my love blindness and her administered emotional remedy lasted clear through our second date. I did not think my highest powered truth lenses were required for any courtships, but perhaps I knew better. Yes, truthfully I grasped the risk and willfully chose to ignore the onset of untruths, choosing to ignore the onset of her the drug needle. The wickedness of her outfit for date night two was strikingly different…a tight black blouse, red skirt, and bejeweled five inch heels. Her highness the hellion arrived for date three dressed to the nines…half her face painted ablaze with the hideosity of her heavy handed harm, absolutely intending to hurt, mainly meaning to maim. She strutted up laughingly and pinned both hands to my sides, suffocating my available breath with her one naked-sided two-face half-lips, just as the needle went in.

My intravenous drug addiction began as an almost romantic kiss and ended by its nature, a practiced taunting…the open-and-close slamming session of my coffin lid.

Meagerly, the horrendous personality shift and disorderliness of the needle's intent did major damage but duh…of course, the 20-plus daily injections of coke dope and meth these here hands performed certainly banged up this human pin cushion quite proper. The literal junkie scars I wear are announcements to the world, that is when brazen enough to live my life uncovered, these statements unto the world of precisely who I am.

My darling Birdy, this supporting scars entry is an emotionally immersed pool of bled tears residing deep within my heart, but…but is a portrait I feel obliged to paint, and a hurt I am compelled to share. My lived to learn then known concept of scars is wildly multidimensional, and stretches into an even much bigger issue, well…I believe you will understand what I mean in about six minutes. Your cousin Ananda, aka my niece, aka my littlest sister Christy's oldest daughter, carries these scars still on her arms, while mine have mostly faded to the uneducated eye. On the inside, Ananda carries scars still like me, aka these our residual sad pains. Little ways back Ananda wrote a Facebook post regarding life as a drug addict but mostly, it was her verbal wrangling with the associated judgement of the term *lowlife*. Ananda's social media share least on the surface and to the inexpert eye, was perhaps understood as a simple and basic rant, possessing a moderate level of idealism, and perceived as slightly whiny. Me then, I did not view her social platform post as containing any negativity whatsoever, no not at all.

I wore my lowlife screwed up drug addict nametag around for two decades, although long ago put away. I wore the same sleeves as Ananda does now, and to me her note was a cry for understanding and support.

Slightly late to the perhaps public pity party, I was maybe the tenth person to comment on Ananda's wall. The other notes amounted to roughly eight or nine words each, them lending high level sympathy support or encouragement. Others shared words like…*hang in there we love you*, or *you got this*, etcetera. No way I was staying surface level on this one, no fucking way. I love this girl too much, and the history between us ran too-too deep for me to just splash her a quick one liner. For your upcoming reference, *Jimmy* is the name of Ananda's beautiful, loving, and super cool ginger paramedic firefighter husband…I love that guy. Here now my exact post on Ananda's wall concerning her slight shameful admission of being a lowlife drug addict, no edits.

Ananda,

My love, we ARE drug addicts, and we will always be drug addicts. At first, we hid this fact to stay out of jail. We hid this fact from ourselves by lying. We hid this fact from the world by lying. Then we hid this fact because we were convinced, and the world convinced us, that we WERE fucking lowlifes and that we should cower, cover, and hide. But the wording that we are fucking lowlifes is a lie. Today, and for now, some of us try to hide our addiction, even if we are clean, because of the present or residual lowlife feelings still inside of us.

You are not a lowlife and neither am I, no fucking way. I would argue that we are the opposite of that, we are the ones that should face the day and face the world with our backs tall, our chests out, and our heads high. We bear our scars of addiction, some with our outside scars and some with our inside scars, and usually both.

Wear your outside scars like a badge of courage. Wear your outside scars like a badge of courage from a battle that you fought and won, and of a war that will follow you for all your days. Wear your outside scars proudly to remind yourself and show the world that at least for now, you are winning this war and the world has not defeated you on this day.

Wear your inside scars and face them, talk to them, look at them, look at them so long that they walk off, because today, if only for today, you are the tougher motherfucker and you have won the war so far. Wear your inside scars to build strength and resolve, a reminder that either with your five weeks clean or my 31 years clean, it is a relentless and brutal fucking war that never leaves us.

Wear your scars to build strength within yourself, to take the damn seat at the head of the table of life to show the world, even those not looking, that you are a brave motherfucker.

That you have the courage, and that you are stronger than the world has tried to make you believe.

Use your scars to find your truth. Truth that you will try to stop lying to yourself and you will try to stop lying to the world that you are weak, that the world is stronger than you, that the world has defeated you, that the world will always win, and that you deserve this.

Because, those are all lies. They are all big, motherfucking, goddamn lies. Wear your scars proudly. Stare down your scars showing to the world that you are a brave bitch, and today, and if only for today, the world will not win, the world will not defeat you, and that YOU are going to win today, because anything else would be a lie.

I will fight Jimmy til we are both indistinguishably bloody to say that I am your number one fan, but that is a battle both Jimmy and I would love to fight. I believe in you and I am fighting for you. I am in your camp, I am on your team, and I will always be by your side, even when far away. Any time you feel like the world may win today, you summons your team and we will be there to fucking fight for you. Because we are an army, and even an army of a few, lone, and brave motherfuckers can win the battle against the world.

Miss you like crazy, love you like mad, and please keep fighting Ananda because you should wear your scars proudly and hold your head high.

GrizzlyBearHugs, Uncle Roger.
XOXOXO

Roger Ray Ciphers
Quizzically, some-some the deeper meaning of my proprietary terminology may have whooshed on by you. Sans intention of confusion, here now a truthful unravel of a word or three, just so you know.

Carfentanil is the strongest opioid drug, period fucking period. Abused by addicts, usually as an unknown mix-in cutting drug, often with lethal results. No nickname is known to me other than its bad-boy membership in a gang of hyper-extinguishing life substances referred to as *grey death*. Beyond the might of the highly addictive opioid pill OxyContin, beyond heroin, and beyond the deadly Fentanyl, and at a level all its own is the ultrapotent Carfentanil. Ridiculously powerful and rivaling the poisonous nature of nerve gas, factually over 100 times stronger than Fentanyl, Carfentanil kills on contact. Only touching several grains of the synthetic powder with bare fingertips causes death, hence the need for EMT's, paramedics, firefighters and police to wear rubber gloves when on a drug scene…or else. Cheaper than heroin and easier to manufacture, this drug often arrived from China and served for goodness sake as a veterinary tranquilizer.

Visiting my pal Charles C.H. Stovall at the Madison houseless encampment one night sorta recently, I befriended a down-on-luck neighbor of his, a big guy named Will. Big Will was truly charming, and over-the-moon appreciative for the several pairs of new wool socks I gifted him in the night's air that early December. Without discussion, the facts presented themselves obvious, duh…Will has had a hard life from day one. Seemingly as a birth defect, Will is missing one hand. Will found his way to Madison from Chicago, an unrelenting city for our sisters and brothers lingering at or below the poverty line.

Over our multi-months spent together, none of the 100+ houseless inhabitants of Madison eastside Reindahl Park asked me for money, not a fricking penny, ever. One particular cold and snowy night alongside your bro-bro, conditions presented as proper to hand out some cash, unprovoked. Big Will cried when I put a Jackson in his one available hand, literally, as did ChiTown Chris, Will's Chicago friend, 'litrilly for real. ChiTown cried and hugged both Travis and me on the spot, genuinely appreciative for a few bucks, proceeding to tell his condensed life story to our outside helpful the junior bird Boyd. Doling out money amid falling sub-zero snowflakes, I hoped the funds used for food, or clothing, or bedding but factually *duh*…I knew fricking better. After putting my last donated twenty into the palm of my pal Charles, aka Pops, he frowned at me. Not in a disapproving way, but code for…*let's talk later*. With no one looking, Charles returned to me the Jackson. He didn't need it, not now, he said. That money will just go towards something he shouldn't be doing, he said. He will surely need money later for something else, something real if I'm still offering…but no, no thank you, not now, he said. Totally transparent and straight-up my Birdy, Charles is my friend. Him and I recorded a podcast episode together, and for me it was an education beyond divinity. Mister Charles C.H. holds a management degree from University of Wisconsin, so he's fuck-tons smarter than me, super-dooper fuck-tons, although pal Pops is houseless. Please Birdy give our episode #19 a listen, it's sure-sure to strike a unique chord-chord with you…un-equality, America the equal hater country, addiction, dope, alcoholism, THE Man, awhile as you and I have discussed several times before…*The New Jim Crow*.

The following week I saw Big Will a few blocks away, standing around in front of the eastside *Dollar Store* maintaining a physical stature I knew intimately. Will was hanging out on the sidewalk waiting to score drugs. The next night at tent city I found myself alone alongside Will and I asked what was his poison? With perfectly-positioned pronunciation but to my horror he said flat out, "Carfentanil". *Seriously*, I said…*that's fucked up Will,* I said…*you shoot that shit straight*? "Yes, it's so much better than anything else and I got nothin', so I don't waste my time with anything else", Will explained to me.

Big Will was the first person I met who shot that shit straight, that clinical veterinary tranquilizer shit that is in fact a heavy sedative for rhinos elephants and bears oh my.

Hah…for a hot second to start the concept rattled me, although in lickety-fucking-split short order, I got it, I got it loud and motherfucking clear.

Willing   207

My bird brain bounced back to my shooting years and I absorbed some of Big Will's painful reality there whilst then…when down, the risk doesn't matter. When down…when down and blue and my lying brain tells me I am a loser-loser lowlife loser, and that I am all alone, well…it doesn't matter, nothing matters anymore, it just…doesn't…fucking…matter. To die, oh to die, so I believed for a long time…*to die will be an awfully big adventure.* **Carfentanil.**

Coke. The illegal drug Cocaine, aka blow. Mostly sold purchased and consumed in various powder forms. Made in South America from the coca plant leaf using ridiculously lethal chemicals during the manufacturing process, like gasoline for goodness sake. Originally developed as a medical anesthetic before widely abused and discontinued. Whitey in color while also however rarely found with a slightly pinkish tone, aka Peruvian Pink. One of the most pow-powerful and addictive amphetamine-esque upper speed drugs, second only to Methamphetamine, aka meth, aka crank. Coke ain't physically dependent like its biggest-baddest-speed-brother Meth, or the evil opposite black-haired downer of a stepchild, the downer drug dope, aka sidename for heroin.

When snorting coke, the strength or purity will not be known until we sense the full effectiveness after a few minutes. Besides snorting, coke powder even in chunky form is easily smoked, almost like pot. I used small foil beds to simply heat powdered coke underneath and inhale through a straw, or plainly poked pin holes in a dent-modified soda can, smoking the powdered blow through the main pop-top opening. Sometimes I just spread the whitey powder atop pot when smoking bowls bongs or joints of weed.

Cocaine powder is mostly snorted into the nose with a short section of straw or a small tube, like a hollowed-out pen or rolled-up dollar bill. Many times coke the powder arrives to street level in chunky form, so traditionally a single-sided razor blade is wielded and the chunky is chop-chopped on an impenetrable surface, like a nearby handy mirror off the wall to make smooth consumable powder. Chunky coke does not snort well and can be painful or worse, the coke chunk won't go up the nose and the white chunk mistakenly falls into the floor's deep white shag carpet. The next 90 minutes are spent hands and knees on the white fluffy ground desperately combing white shaggy for the indispensable $2 chunk.

Higher-level drug dealers than me purified powdered coke to produce a void-of-impurities potent form of delivered cocaine called crack, aka *rock.* Crack is high-highly fucking addictive. Crack appears like a crystalized rock and no way no how can crack rock be snorted sprinkled or shot. Crack requires a special glass or insulated metal pipe because of the higher heat required to cook the rock. A smaller and simpler pipe device might not hold or dissipate the heat required to cook the crack rock, and now we are also burning our hands and lips well as our brains. The technical term *crack pipe* describes a more specific pipe built for high heat, compared to a simplistic and many times wooden implement for pot. Pot burns easy and slow while crack burns hard and fast. Once crack is heated proper and starts to burn, we must stay so-so close to thy precious rock.

Crack pipes are small so to conceal, and us committed *crackheads* are found huddled around our precious pipes wherever we go, shielding thy treasure, guarding it, and not letting any of the luscious-no-actually-vicious little smoke escape our mouths, burnt lips and all. The uptown kids or downtown deep-pocket dealers many times sported expensive butane cartridge lighters, exactly like a pocket-sized mini blowtorch to heat the crack fast, while us low budget or downtown ballers huddled around waiting for our two-for-a-dollar *Bic* lighters from *7-Eleven* to warm up and do the job. To manufacture crack from coke powder, we use additional nasty chemicals like ammonia which drives impurities out of the coke, making crack ridiculously potent, almost pure…hence the increased addiction factor.

To inject aka shoot aka bang aka boost aka boot coke, only powdered form is used. A slight serving of the pow-pow is placed into a small cupped waterproof holder object, like a tablespoon or a plastic bottle cap turned upside down. Most my shots were 0.10 or 0.15 of a gram and sometimes up to 0.25 of a gram depending on substance quality and tolerance, costing about $10 or $15 and up to $25 per shot. Using the needle we draw water to fill the small volume low-dose devilish device between half and two-thirds full and squirt the water into the coke-occupied spoon or cap. Using the end of the plunger side of the needle, we mix the solution until the powder is dissolved. A tablespoon not teaspoon is used because the larger volume of solution, and no-way-no-how do we want to spill that shit. If the powder does not entirely dissolve, it means some impurities exist like artificial additives to stretch the drug further, basically diluting the potency of the powder for benefit of additional profits. Traditionally we mixed in profit-stretching additives which is also called *cutting* or *stepping on* the drug, aka cutting-in additives to make the batch bigger. Normally we cut with cheap white dusty substances like inositol or baby powder.

When shooting, all additives and impurities will either dissolve within the coke-water mixture or be left as residue on the other side of the filter in the spoon. Prepping a shot, once the solution is best dissolved, we take a small piece of cotton or chunk of a cigarette filter center, ball it up and drop it in the spoon. The needle is placed atop the small filter ball and the entire solution is drawn into the needle. Now ready to party-party yet the hardest part is to follow, finding available veins near the surface, *hah*…the human plumbing otherwise eluding the malevolent dragon swooping down from above, aka that motherfucker the needle. **Coke.**

Dope. Sidename for heroin and then as it is also regionally, *dope* refers to meth but here inside my small birdbrainish world, I reserve the term *dope* for heroin. Dope powder can be snorted or smoked, but is often injected. Prepping a shot, dope is way more difficult to dissolve than coke. Most all preferred times we hold a lighter underneath and *cook* the dope in the bent-handled tablespoon, before drawing the final rendered solution into the needle. Same-same as when making a run-up to shoot coke or meth and ideally, a drop-in filter ball is used. Thereupon here I hesitantly admit the stupid fucking shit I did when shooting, beyond sharing needles. When not cooking dope or entirely, the substance's resistance to dissolution meant I would waste some of it, that is when rushing to shoot what I could draw through my need-need-needle.

Stoop-stupidly sometimes, I lacked a lighter to heat up the deathly-esque down drug cauldron, mostly when speedballing, and hah when not filtering the fuck up, I might get little objects capable of clogging the needle while trying to shoot the bits into my veins. Oh for fuck's sake not always did I have filter ball material on my person, so I drew what I could get into the needle and just shot that shit. I carried stolen pliable-handled tablespoons and bent them slightly more than their natural curvy-swervy shapes, because otherwise the devices are too wobbly and God forbid that shit might get spilt once sat down. Bending the handle created an outrigger support stand to stabilize the spoon when drawing the mix into my need-needle. Sometimes however inaccurately, the term *dope* is exercised as a comprehensive catch all phrase for drugs in general. See additional dark downer details under heroin. **Dope.**

Eight Ball. An eighth ounce of cocaine. Also applying to heroin or meth, but a term I use referencing coke. Least as it appears to me, the act of snorting coke is often a shared social activity, hence at times we sold larger quantity bags of coke to people planning to share-party, specifically eight balls of blow. I never sold-dealt in heroin or meth, only consumed. Never once did I purchase more than one gram of dope or crank, because of limited at-time funds, plus my speedy desperation to boost that shit into my arm ASAP no matter fucking what. An eighth of an ounce is 3.5 grams, so depending on coke quality, the price would be anywhere from around $300 to $500 for an eight ball. **Eight Ball.**

Fentanyl. The second strongest opioid drug, and the concealed deadly dirty drug killing over a hundred thousand of our sisters and brothers each year in the divided-United States. Fentanyl is fifty times more powerful than heroin, aka 50, aka fucking *FIFTY*. Unaware user-addicts consume the drug most times unknowingly because fentanyl is a cheap cut-in filler material added to heroin cocaine and methamphetamine to echo-stretch the distance of the base drug. Fentanyl nowadays is mostly manufactured in illegal uncontrolled facilities. The recent gamble of the addict because of fentanyl has become frightfully mysterious, and black-heartedly lethal. My dear-dear Joshua Duke informs me that when consuming fentanyl, it tastes like Band-Aids. **Fentanyl.**

Heroin. Sidename dope. Heroin was the grandaddy opioid painkiller downer drug before the fentanyl's crashed the party. In the way-way back and originally, heroin was sold over the counter as a cough and sleep medicine in pharmacies for goodness sake. In overdose situations, heroin slows our beating hearts to a forever and ever bye-bye go-to-sleep-now full-stop. Mostly these party days, heroin kills, *echo-echo*…because of the toxic fentanyl mix-ins. Heroin is a nasty and physically dependent highly-fucking-addictive narcotic, one pushing me down into a frightfully comfortable state, least a while. Shooting heroin produced instant ringing in my ears, an immediate pleasing and weird taste and smell I cannot describe, plus the warm sensation I was swirling down the soft padded drain hole with Alice, chasing after that naughty little rabbit.

Purdue Pharma produced prescription pain drugs and in 1996, dark evil swooped down and landed on earth with the creation of their *OxyContin*, a wildly powerful opioid pain pill. OxyContin is not to be confused with the similar yet slower-acting hence milder effects *Oxycodone*. Supported by the FDA, Purdue Pharma marketed the fuck out of their OxyContin, pressuring doctors to prescribe their new drug gleefully…big-big bottles of forever refill kill-pills going to most anyone with a boo-boo, well, I am exaggerating about that last part a little bit somewhat maybe. After years of these Purdue drug pushers finally creating addicts out of everyday people, *oops*, it turns out this shit is deadly, *but oh well boo-hoo so sad whatever no bother* so says Purdue, *we are not to blame*, and afterward, the drug became highly regulated. Single-handedly, Purdue Pharma's OxyContin created an epidemic, *The Opioid Epidemic*, which has killed over *ONE MILLION* Americans and will continue to kill residually. Purdue then strutted away billions of dollars richer, after paying a relatively mild fine, and no criminal charges were filed. With more than a $10,000,000,000 net worth, the three comma Purdue drug pushers it seems will be no worse for wear, while to this day much of the country continues to struggle in their wake. Purdue Pharma ravagingly fucked us because once their OxyContin became heavily restricted, the pullback left newly-formed addicts seeking an available replacement, so here comes heroin to fill the bill nicely. Dope is a similar high, cheaper and easier to access than OxyContin, so thanks to Purdue directly and however tragic, the heroin trade then exploded.

I have a dear friend TJ, my chapter one Friendwords buddy Tyler Schmidt in this here your book by the way, who served prison time under the *Len Bias law*, after his uncle overdosed in Tyler's Milwaukee college freshman dorm room. TJ's personal heroin habit resulted from his addiction to OxyContin. TJ shares his compounding tragic story within our *LBU* podcast episode #18, and it is a heartbreaking listen no doubt. Both TJ and I lose our shit in that recording and although I cleaned up the edit of TJ's tears, I left mine in.

First-person-personally…after a radical foot surgery gone bad in 2011, the pain left me entirely inconsolable. After barely one night at home post-op in Wisconsin, wife two and I returned and I sat crying out loud in a wheelchair within the Stoughton hospital lobby, demanding they admit me for pain management. The pre-surgery notification had already been fricking made, I am an addict, so pain med precautions must be respected. Two purposeful stainless steel rods protruded from my foot for over a week post-surgery, numerous procedures were attempted, bones and nerves were operated on, yet beyond all that, the doctor did a poor job on several fronts by my measure. Shockingly, and rather dismissively, my doc said *no* I cannot stay because it was *unnecessary*, he prescribed some kind of new super fancy *NON-ADDICTIVE* pain pills instead, then told us to leave. I had no flipping idea what the medicine was, never heard of it before but didn't care, I was certain-certain-fucking-certain-100 nothing would work for me because I knew pills intimately, hence my hospital admittance plea. Completely delirious with pain, I was quite 'litrilly about to pass out, so to-be wife two quickly filled the scrip there whilst then in the hospital pharmacy and we left, me still claiming *no, no, nothing will work*, me still balling like a little biddy bird baby.

When I took that first pill, I knew I was totally fucked…son of a bitch are you fucking kidding me…oh fuck yup, right away I tasted its darkness, straight away I tasted its familiar fucking evil. I would not have filled the prescription or taken that first OxyContin pill if I knew what it factually was, never, but oh no boo-hoo so sad too late…*mmm yummy, tastes just like heroin.*

Heroin arrives mostly in powder form originating from southern Asia, Colombia, and Mexico, yet for many years was primarily smuggled into the USA from Afghanistan. Made from the poppy plant, the rubric then manufactured into opium alongside brother and sister drugs morphine and codeine. Heroin is also sold but less commonly in solid stick-sticky form nametagged *black tar*, which is mostly lower-grade dope for smoking, somewhat similar in appearance to hashish. Heroin gives a ridiculous euphoric-like sensation, however then we are stumbling and mumbling idiots, even when snorting or smoking the shit. When on heroin I got high fast but duh, not in a *get up and do stuff* sort of way, rather in a *I-do-not-care-about-anything-leave-me-the-fuck-alone* kind of way. **Heroin.**

Methamphetamine. Aka meth, aka crank, aka the most evil fucking *drug* delivered to us from the Devil himself. Meth is the granddaddy of the amphetamine speed-upper drug family. Originally street-manufactured using Ephedrine as the base ingredient, aka *Sudafed* decongestant medicine, and as a result the cute little red over-the-counter pill sales are now federally regulated. Ephedrine was mixed and cooked with additional chemicals to produce this, the #1 worst street drug. Slightly similar yet way-worse than cocaine, the up drug meth enhances our pulse, sometimes leading to overdose conditions after cardiac arrest. But oh no for fuck sake, meth runs way-way-far-and-away beyond coke and strikes a unique chord however, chemically juicing up the central nervous system well as creating a physically-dependent addiction not experienced with cocaine.

The California based *Hells Angels* biker gang concocted a new breed of meth back in the day sidetrack-voiding the inclusion of ephedrine. Instead, the nasty cook-mix was fuck-jacked chemicals that not only scrambled our brains and destroyed our bodies but were also highly toxic and flammable, uh yeah…chemicals like sulfuric acid, hydrochloric acid, and motherfucking cyanide. The methamphetamine manufacturing sites, aka *meth labs*, stunk to high heaven and many times caught fire or blew up because of the unstable chemicals inside. Nowadays for all that is god-fuckwrong with this world, fuck-meth is even fricking worse, a crazy all-synthetic street recipe void of ephedrine and no longer utilizing the Hells Angels proprietary ingredients. The updated formula mostly hails from Mexico and the Mexicali mix is called P2P meth, a high-high-highly-sophisticated process producing straight-up fucking brain damage, way worse than all old-school solutions.

The P2P recipe is still an all chemical mish-mash using shit like photo developing solutions and motorsports racing gasoline, yet P2P is less outdoor-air toxic, so the new meth labs are easier to conceal. Old-school popular was cocaine, crack rock, and heroin, them all having their time in the limelight but now meth rules the roost because of its availability, low cost, and highly fucking addictive evil nature.

  Chapter SEVEN

Once more and total-total-truth-100, alcohol is worse than meth but hells bells, alcohol is not candidly categorized as a *drug* but should be so-says-I big dummy stupidhead…fucking alcohol is worse than meth. Alcohol kills multitudes more than meth and is certifiably cancerous to our internal organs, factually-actually worse than *ANY* plain packaged street drug. Friendwords superstar John Stamstad recites within our *Lies Between Us* podcast episode #10 his obscene tale of dancing with the Devil's Water, how it destroyed his stomach, and helped to poi-poi-poison his at-time mental health. By my measure, John's tale is sickening and compounds my commitment to try and never sip the Devil's drink ever again, fucking never ever never. Booze is the societal water of the world and is push-pushed as the norm, much because of its three goddamn motherfucking commas. This top of heap #1 killer alcohol is beyond fucking legal, aka openly fucking available, because of the in excess of *$225,000,000,000 aka two-two-five BILLION fucking dollars,* that alcohol generates in the United States alone…soap box fucking mic drop. Additional 'cipher: *three commas,* aka billion. **Methamphetamine.**

Sans. Meaning lacking, without, or void of. *Sans* is a French word, a saying I encountered once flying 'cross the pond. The question in western Europe inevitably arises, "Sans gas?", meaning would I prefer drinking water that sparkled and contained bubbles like seltzer, aka gas, or would I prefer to have *flat* water? Flat water being water without bubbles, like still calm tap or spring water. I like the *sans* word so I use the darling descriptor in various places. Seems least to me, much of the world prefers bubbling water yet I have and will forever prefer tap water, aka flat still calm spring water, aka water *sans gas.*

Water sans gas related…arguably my preferred fav-fav-favorite place on earth is Canaan Valley in Tucker County West Virginia, aka God's country, aka almost heaven. Once trying to kick the needle, thine eminent supremely fantastical peaceful wilderness I located closest to Baltimore was Canaan Valley, and the region provided a mystical loving comfort I never knew, plus some indescribable attributes. Canaan hooked me with the triple-treble barbs of amazing nature, incredible people, and *the* most extreme mountainbike racing I ever experienced throughout all my years. I first arrived to camp-camp-cookout wake-n-bake in Canaan for a springtime race, event one of a three race year long series as it was. There then and for the following ten years or so, resided a sign atop a pipe flowing out of the mountain in the Canaan town of Davis, a pipe supplying local hoomans with natural spring drinking water. The flowing pipe of heavenly aqua pura still exists and the water is the most superb liquid I have ever tasted. Memorized still are the words from the sign now long gone once hanging over the Tucker County spring runoff pipe…*If you with litter will disgrace and spoil the beauty of this place, may indigestion wrack your chest and ants invade your pants and vest.* **Sans.**

Shadow. Self-defined, shadow validates my hard and dark emotional places. I did not discover the poetic works of *Rumi* until later in life amid my alcoholism, once hyper-studly gal pal studmuffin Sonya Plavcan gifted me my first eastern teachings book, *A Path With Heart* by the masterful American Ph.D. clinical psychologist and Buddhist monk Mister Jack Kornfield.

Critical by my measure to here now mention my Birdy, besides she your strength coach reigning as 10x BJJ World Champion, Sonya is beloved friend family member number seven who saved my life when I was entirely incapable otherwise. Then once reading Sonya's gifted book, I sought out additional pillaring devices. Stumbling through the Buddhism bookshelf area at the Barnes and Noble printed narratives store within East Towne Mall, I happened upon a visually-appealing book, *The Essential RUMI*, and I peeked between its flaps. In true power-shopper persona, I put the book under arm for purchase after only reading one line of one poem within the 416 pages of writings, first penned *seven hundred and seventy years ago* for gosh darn sake.

Rumi is arguably the most successful poet in the world and certainly, my favorite. I read Rumi's artbook of short heart-bled pieces cover to cover in less than two days. Most of Rumi's works are love poems and for me, one stands out, a stratospherically powerful piece and factually, the most supremely crafted collection of words I have ever read seen or heard, ever…fucking ever. The ridiculously powerful piece, my favorite Rumi poem, is called *Looking For Your Face*. When first finding Rumi, I was embedded in my own tangled web of drunken brokenness following the feels of thrown to the curb by wife one, a full 15 years after I got clean from the damn drugs.

My beloved passion for an upcoming newfound romantic dream partner spoke to my broken-hearted inner desire at the time. Truth clear, I hoped for confident indication an honest and new love was even possible for me, because I was entirely unsure of future romance after breaking away from your hot Jersey momma bird. I hoped to be lifted and somewhat carried, awhile blown over by the magical essence of new love. Rumi's writings afforded me that therapeutic faint love visions potential. The while I was angry with my then separated hottie ginger wife who I simultaneously and immensely loved still, but I felt tossed out of her heart, you know, discarded bird…egged tarred and feathered. My heart lost at sea, then knowing I could not go back to our once peacefully harbored love nest, I desired a goddess of goodness, a true partner, a loving soul who would stay longer. My desires aligned directly with the words of Rumi and especially his *Looking For Your Face* poem piece. Within my favorite Rumi poem exists the concept of shadow alongside sunshine, referencing his stationed place however it could be, within his lover's entire being, the bright place and the dim. My adoption of shadow is used within the self-defined location of heaviness thy burden…darkness hardship and hiding.

I seeped myself into Rumi's work, later finding a newly released audio recording from the celebrated spiritual teacher Deepak Chopra, *A Gift of Love- Music Inspired by the Love Poems of Rumi*. I bought the album, CD actually, bought it unseen. Overjoyed with thrill, I discovered the album included *Looking For Your Face*, mouthed by the actor Jared Harris. Jared's reading brings tears to my eyes, and has every 100+ times of me tuning in…his mind-numbing delivery of Rumi's words injecting new meanings into the printed characters, exactly like JR Cash performing Trent Reznor's *Hurt*, aka new meanings. Similarly, Jared's Rumi reading causes hairs on the back of my neck to stand at attention and tears to fall, all in reverence for the extremely powerful and heartfelt read.

Super-surprisingly, one of the other works, actually the shortest piece on Deepak's 36-track Rumi readings album is spoken by an elderly woman, or so I assumed, and immediately I heard something deep in her voice.

　　　　　　　　　Chapter SEVEN

No, no…no longer did I concern myself with Rumi's hearted characters and rather, the depth of the old lady's spoken word took over. Thrice more, like Jared's reading of Rumi before, and like Johnny Cash singing that *Nine Inch Nails* song, especially amid the versioned Cash *Hurt* video…this woman's audible art superseded the entirety of the poem piece itself. Within her vocalization I perceived some unknown versions of wisdom, pain, and love. I cannot properly explain the connection to the old female narration awhile my union was and is, profound. I wondered to self why is this voice doing the reading, of what significance in our world does this woman operate?

Earlier amongst the same Rumi shuffled audio play I recognized several unique and identifiable famous people, but this articulation I never heard before. Already on the album I immediately identified the vocal notes of Deepak himself, Madonna, Martin Sheen, and Demi Moore, yet who how and why on earth is this old mystery woman? Emphatically engrossed, I no way did not want to look, so not to spoil the intrigue. Finally suspense defeated me…I had to know, I had to know her name then research to find some of her likely notable story. Presuming she was an actress, or musician, or something, the heightened status I held of her felt far superior to any paid performer's everyday street life so really, I did not want to know, I did not want my reverence of her voice to be lessened. Still, I moved ahead. I read the CD case and melted, *oh my*…in an instant, *oh shit*, everything made sense…*oh wow, so fricking awesome.* I did not need to research fricking anything…her story, her story beyond imaginability, her story beyond the impact of the sky when full bluebird, she beyond a performer, beyond an artist, a politician she was not, a religious leader no, no, she much more than any of that…she the icon, Mrs. Rosa Parks.

A handful of years ago back from current day, I began to hear the use of the word shadow referenced, I presume to mean the dark side of one's self, or so I believe, I do not know, I may be mistaken. To me…I have one me, one side of me, the one all of me awhile many crevasses within. Therefore I proclaim to no longer have hidden dark places inside myself, I have explored and faced them all. I use shadow to describe the place of fear, fright, terror…a sheltered hideout or any unfavorable emotional condition. **Shadow.**

Sunshine. The good times, the peaceful places in my head-heart-psyche core oracle, well as out and about in the world. The beginnings of my drug addiction mostly created escape to safe haven inside my head, along with varied states of euphoria. Once using LSD and related hallucinogens, I realized the opportunity of self-travel beyond conscious control of mind and body. My 300+ acid trips were mostly entertaining, then at times the strange romp alongside Lucy in the Sky with Diamonds was uncontrollable and terrifying. Terrifying in dangerous and allowing ways, ways I threw myself into situationally from where I almost did not return. Still, I would not categorically label my tripping as a dark experience, more of a tie dye undulating ride. Even the brain dimming narcotic downer pills although mind bending and reducing me to a drooling and babbling idiot, the pill portion of my substance addiction in totality does not carry a grossly dark overtone.

Snorting coke mostly encapsulated a self-defined and placed up-up-up utopian state, until my excessiveness reduced me to a paranoid speed freak, afraid to even look out the window for the cops certain to be coming for me. Therefore to say, my nasal ingested cocaine was still not a lengthily dark experience. The absolute fucking terrifying death pit I resided deep within for more than 8 years however, was the darkness flooding me once first smoking rock. Crack ran into my emotional depths and unlocked the dungeon door to invite my motherly traumas to come play. Learning darkness of emotions first by the hand of my mother, next by holding the crack pipe, followed by the poking of that malevolent motherfucker the needle, and finally the everyday five-year-long liquid polluting of Water from the Devil himself, I possess an absolute comprehension of dark.

Conversely, since I knew dark so well, I learned to appreciate light…the joyful bright times, the beautiful experiences, well as the simple moments residing in nature's peace affording me the lens to identify and substantiate my truthful happy place. Sunshine is the thoughts, feelings, acts, intentions, moments, surprises, and presence of positivity in my life, the concept much prompted by the words of the hopeful Hindu poet Rumi, aka the master of loving sunshine himself. **Sunshine.**

Big Willful Untruths

Resoundingly-100, my number one real world daily sort out are my untruths, aka the lies I spew into my own ear, unto the world, awhile accepting the multitude of falsehood inbounds. Factually-actually I believe proper management of my emotions and actions comes down to one singular fucking thing: my ability to face reality straight-up no filter, period. When not dealing with the true truth of the matter, initially I lie to myself the situation is way-way worse than it actually is, and I'm far-far less worthy than I factually am. When not pausing to sort through truth, shadow rolls in, aka I fuck shit up supremely, inside and out. Yet when committed enough to one-eye focus on it, then disciplined enough to willingly locate reality no matter the toll or tax paid, the sun she comes out, rainbows stretch across the sky, and cute little Fluffy bunnies thy precious begin their blissful play about my feet, even when raining.

Henceforth I run through my found knowings of self…the regarding truth of the lies I tell and accept, which is straight up honestly the core root mainspring of my substance abuse dysfunction.

Lauren my love-my life-my world, thus here I pull apart my legacy lies so to best uncover discern and share my findings to your million-dollar question, WHY was I…*factually still to this day and always am*, a drug addict? I will also puke my guts entirely regarding the second part of your original ponder…*and how did you quit?* Without being highly adolescent about it, I might playfully propose the incidental proposition as…*Daddy, why were you such a liar*, hence the heightened embellishment of my untruths forthcoming, all to best expose the inner workings of my substance abuse.

Perhaps I swirl around the wastebasket brim of irrelevancy and you care not for said detail, thus pleasant-mindedly *la-la-la I cannot hear you* skipping ahead to locate the Roger Ray rhythmic relief zone found a petty ways upcoming, but, *uh*…no. No, and I proclaim fuck to the no my love. No and fuck to the no my darling…thy words-away sort out is a critical share, by my measure. Critical so for you my beautiful Birdy to apprehend the *how* and the *what* of me shaking that naughty little monkey off my back.

Liar-liar bird on fire…*Why and How Do I Lie?*

Liar Number One
Why and How Do I Lie? I Lie to Restore Strength and Confidence
Before realizing such a deep undersea emotional adventure was required, I sat on the surface of assumptive thinking and initially named this first grouping of lies, *Seeking Dirty-Ego Comforts*. After diving four levels sub-surface however, I arrived to find such dirty-ego comforting as my own ignorant primitive assumption. The final naming of what I understand to be strength and confidence untruths are listed here first because these the most recent, this the last big groupings of untruths I let go of, well…the ones I somewhat play-loiter with still, however small and uncommon.

1. The commencing and primitive surface-level list, how or why do I lie in this regard:
    a. I lie seeking pity and sympathy
    b. I lie seeking attention and comfort
    c. I lie seeking praise, and fuel for my dirty-ego
    I believed these dirty-ego descriptors as originating drivers for this grouping of lies. Immediately as noted, *hah*…no, this just surface-level viewings, so I went deeper.

2. Sub-surface level, how or why do I lie in this regard:
    a. I lie because I am scared, I feel or fear becoming lost, I am weakened, I believe myself alone or at risk of being alone, and I am unsure of myself
    No, *no*…that's not really it at all, more exists here.

3. Now deeper, I go deeper and closer to my truth of truths because still the picture fuzzy and I work towards clarity, how or why do I lie in this regard:
    a. I want to stand and travel soundly on my own but think to need a boost.
    b. I elevate by way of lies because I am down or doubting myself. Not needing wanting or desiring to elevate excessively, but overcome a self-defeating low, so I fabricate truth, trying to raise sense and security of self to slight abundance, back to where been before, aka a basic level of sound self-sufficiency
    Well, *hum*…no, that's not exactly the extent of it either, must go deeper.

4. Deeper, deeper still, I go deeper, sensing truer understanding exists, now to the upper abyss threshold, how or why do I lie in this regard:
    a. I lie to gain reassurance from others, wanting to revitalize or regain some of what believed lost, temporarily misplaced, or lacking within myself

b.   I lie trying to dispel fear, shed my sans safety, drop my doubt, abandon my put-
down of self, or unweight my negativity regarding life in general
Oh poopie…that ain't it either, deeper still.

5.   Ok, now deepest…the great abyss. At times I work towards concise all-
encompassing summary statements. Attempting a brief one-liner I landed on the
emotional abyss floor, squirrelling into the deepest corner to find…how or why do I
lie in this regard:
a.   I lie trying to restore strength and confidence in myself

Previous introspection uncovered various emotional scars adjacent to these thoughts, but
much of my discoveries were incorrectly categorized. I lie in this regard, wanting
comforting reassurance that I am ok, and that I *will be* ok.

> *Sometimes I feel incomplete, which can create a downward emotional*
> *slide if I don't first catch myself.*

I might try reaching out, hoping to find a hand to slow my fall. Sometimes I stretch
subliminally or subconsciously using untruths, hoping a hand reaches back helping to
break, comfort, or rescue my reverse tumble. Hum, *think-think-think*…when people reach
out to me, the attention feels good, their notice lifts and helps me feel bigger 'n better than
I do now. So I lied, I stretched the truth, I played the disadvantaged or shit-on victim,
adding 10% making stuff seem better or worse, whichever was in my favor of pity or
praise. When not in recluse mode I want more recognition, more attention, more caring,
more loving, more time, more comfort, and more patience from others to help fill my at-
least slight such void. Maybe I do not allow enough friends in close enough, those who
could help tell me or show me I am ok, and that I will be ok. Or I peck at the fact of
alienating myself from people. Or I just don't possess the social mastery to have enough
of these kind and gracious friends in my life, so I seek it elsewhere through lying. Maybe
this is my tree-of-life type shit, my root-deep beginnings and footings starting to push up
through the dirt and lay exposed, these the earliest makings of me, well…maybe.

I did not sense the confidence of someone being there to help me, protect me,
hold me, lay a soft and tender kiss on my little Roger Ray cheek and make me feel like I
am shielded and ok, that I'm ok, that I'm really ok. Maybe the hollow feeling of missing
known safety and love never went away. Maybe sometimes thy love container runneth
low and knowing I'm low, I lie to help fill it up and feel ok again. Maybe I want someone
to help me think myself forever safe, shelter me least slightly if you will be so kind, and
how about if you pretty-pretty please don't leave, please never ever leave me.

> *Maybe I fear they will leave, and I doubt my own strength and*
> *confidence to survive on my own.*

I meet people who give me praise and are nice to me, and maybe who seem to love me and help protect me. They say so and act so, they love me, so it is so, right? Maybe these loving others claim they are even *in* love with me. Alas as records show, I either cast those in love with me aside, or I doubt their in-love status, or live to disbelieve their love or my long-term sustained and committed love for them, right before their unloving sometimes circles back 'round and joins my questioning, hum…not sure. When I doubt or disbelieve their love, and although maybe they were in full-love with me, once I give up on them, they then give up on me too. Sometimes I get snagged by their manipulation, those once in-love with me or claiming as such, and I latch onto their dishonesty, aka their manipulation, aka their least part-time untrue heart, by my measure, or so I assume, or so I judge, or so I self-righteously crucify-blame.

Most of my lies originated here, to restore or build strength and confidence in myself. Perchance my lies attempt to fill a gap or mend an emotional scar, or potentially it's something else entirely, IDK. Previously I couldn't even catch myself before an added or subtracted self-serving 10% slipped out, but the extra little bit seemed to make things even more spectacularly in my favor. I've since caught myself by slowing down and pausing before much inflation of truth makes it out of my mouth or fingers, and I have operated soundly as such for over twelve years by this time.

Digging into the love element, I lied wanting to be loved. Well, more accurately, hah, I believed myself *needing* romantic love. At times I thought myself not worthy, or good enough, or smart enough, or attractive enough as I needed to be so that someone will love me, least love me for a while based on my outside wrapping. I did not know what I did not know…I knew not what love looked like, sounded like, felt like. Some days I sidestepped such self-deflating notions, but other times when low or blue, I pinned my loser-loser lowlife loser nametag on, climbed back into daytime bed, or shoved more drug-filled needles into my arms. For me, I lived to learn and know that when in love, if sans total truth, I can't make it work, by my measure. Since a year or so before dating wife two, I have mostly kept my nagging negative nametag put away, me slightly amused by my younger self when I thought the need to fill thy voids with lies.

I try to arrive as the comprehensive truthful me, I try to show up as I am, *Run What You Brung*, I try to celebrate wildly my quirks, more tha better, my scars, more tha better, and my imperfections, more tha fricking better, aka weirder tha better. My fear is being normal, aka acting as someone I am not, aka a lie. Oh sure-sure yes-yes, truthful to say my negative nametag came out briefly in the last dozen years, but relatively rare. I try to stay real. I attempt hyper-awareness of true self, and name it when I see-feel-hear or sniff-out such self-defeating and self-blaming mini-monsters scampering 'round amid my shoes. I try to name it so to pause, so to stand taller than said shit. I say out loud to myself and others, "Oh shoot that's a lie, actually, let me correct myself…", or I blurt out to self, "liar", or "lie", or "untrue", or "untruth", or "not true", and I amend.

I try to stay real, even amongst my weirdness 'n wounds. The judgers be damned, this is me, take me or not, aka Fuck 'Em. Mostly in such mind game regards, I learned to lean on thyself first, not relying on romance to complete me.

Not flippantly do I dismiss love, no way, but through love lost, notably both marriages, I found when placing too much weighted bets on love, and when I lose that wager, the suffrage is great, suffrage by my own hand that is, such suffrage by my own hand hard-hard hugely hard. Relying on my friend family and the true relationships with my DNA family I find all the love I *need*, though the while still open to the fanciness of handholdings, featured sunsets, wood walks, fall-asleeps with her on my chest, and some shiny life-shared bits with perhaps one more great love. Some of the biggest stumbles occurred when I put my true self aside, trying to gain connection through grasped romance.

Some of my parts commanding an opinion, a voice…I silenced and sacrificed them because my inner expanse had stretched but not yet filled. I then laid somewhat deflated, all for the benefit of acceptance.

It does not hold, it does not last, it does not work…eventually I need to lay my truthful cards on the table, showing who and what I am, total truth. No commentary, no feelings, and no emotions…truth, only truth, pure truth.

Liar Number Two
Why and How Do I Lie? I lie to Cover-Up, Avoid, and Detour
How or why do I lie in this regard?
1. I lie thinking it better to avoid conflict
2. I lie detouring perceived or presumed hurtful truth
3. I lie by retracting, hiding from, or avoiding undesirable situations

At times I judged my life as working out better or easier if avoiding conflicts. Situations both at home and work arose where honesty was necessary but alas, I assumed trouble would follow once speaking my truth. Not even revealing truth but simply sharing my feelings, thoughts, facts, findings, observations, healthy-assumptions, projections etcetera, sometimes these reveals stirred things up. I once thought it mean or inconsiderate to cause negative emotions within another person. If I shared full honesty, I feared opposition and perhaps even great offense to my truthful words. My lesson learned is not far removed from a continuum I refer to as *The Damn Issue Is Not The Fricking Problem*, aka a proper response matters way more than the original troublesome issue itself. Over twenty years ago I learned and fine-tuned a process to safely lay my cards on the table and I call it the *Lie or Cry* game, ask me about that one if Birdy-intrigued.

This solo one-self…sometimes the pressure clamping both sides of my skull feels too much and I think some quiet alone time is necessary. My get-away and turn-it-off breaks serve me well, I utilize the tranquil moments to think-think-think stuff through. Now and again the stress feels too much, and during my breathers I attempt little as possible, clearing my mind and nudging some of the heavy bullshit from my shoulders. Of course and per always, *duh*, 100% of my defined bullshit is self-generated. For me, I experience both healthy alone time, and un-healthy alone time.

Unhealthy alone time sucks, such sulking hurts greatly and can be hard to climb out of. Having clawed my way out of such deep dark holes a few times before, I try not to cover up from the world too much nor exist as an unhealthy recluse for too long. Covering up under the cloak of dishonesty also arose from something I should not be doing, or felt the need to avoid but didn't, both of which are other problems altogether.

Youthful alone time mostly avoided the truths of my factual world. My judged blaming of adults helped land me in the drug nest, me missing the resulting growth and power from facing non-lethal challenge. Some kind of thing regarding Johnny Powell's drowning pseudomorphed into a feverish self-punished drug lashing, plus some. And then both times when marital shit was hitting the fan, my big boy Trek job demanded I show up each day when not traveling, packed calendar said so. On however occasion, I just couldn't. Such incidences rare…I got snagged not able to handle the totality of my life once at work. For hours I'd sit at Camrock Park work-dressed, trying to understand next moves, or sometimes not thinking at all. Through the windshield I attempted location of a few treasured portions of peace, somewhere out there amongst the trees and the breeze, the birds and the leaves. I wasn't honest with my executive assistants or my teams about such these troubled times, when my heart had fallen out of the bottom of its box.

I needed to sit alone because, I guess…I did not want to appear weak or mentally disheveled in front of my work family, hold them back or get in their way, although I'm sure they probably saw right through me.

I especially should have been brutally honest with my rockstar assistants Abby then Robyn then Kirsten, instead of hiding my horrible distress inside. They would have understood, I'm sure. Thus with everyone knowing why I am behaving as such, I believe the team would have operated more successfully, myself included. When dirty-assuming to hurt someone's feelings, I am lying to self because for me, dirty-assumptions are lies.

I lived to know honesty works every time, depending how effectively I share my truth. Proper delivery of truthful facts and feelings is vital, but to avoid total honesty is a misstep, by my measure. Before accustomed to handling truth effectively, I helped to dig the collective cesspool of globally-habituated lies deeper…spreading thoughts without knowing the truth of my words also means I am lying. Just because I desire correctness, doesn't make it real. The security of feeling good about an unproven spewing might be holding me back from honesty to begin with. Here is where humility kicks in…beyond *knowing* what I do not know, I realize the many more conditions of I *don't* know what I do not know. I do not lie in this regard anymore, I make no time for it. I choose not to make room for the bullcrap, and work hard as hell to remain liable for my own shit.

Liar Number Three
Why and How Do I Lie? I Lie to Please, Comfort, and Serve
How or why do I lie in this regard?
1.   I lie attempting to ease pain or soften suffering

2. Maybe I cannot bring myself to tell the truth, so the relief I intend is actually being incorrectly spewed upon myself…these were some of my dumbest maneuvers

Believing I am helping, minimizing their worry, facilitating less hurt, or plain following orders I lie, or more accurately I used to lie like this style of rug. Especially in front of handgun, I echo-did or said anything possible to avoid harm, and after a while I didn't even realize my behavior was false but rather organically real. Hum…the last time I lied in this regard? I think in 2009 when I was crewing for my gal pal Amanda Lovato at Wisconsin Ironman. Most adulting scenarios of this sort played out with close friends heartbroken either by the hands of romance, or losing someone close to them. Usually, my lies made things worse. I lived to learn and learned to know truth is the best medicine or pacifier. The truth works in the end, placing me where I should correctly be. I found truth to be the best path. I firmly believe, the truth invariably wins.

Our Travis the Boyd faced a related scenario with his pre-birthday 2020 Psychology class homework…a friend is dying and on their deathbed. The dying friend asks for a favor and we have no intention of carrying out the deathbed wish, so the proposition is: would we lie, promising to perform the unrealistic request? I lie in this regard thinking to make things better or easier, because the person will not know the truth otherwise. Like when I lied to Amanda as she sped by on the bike, third place pro-woman, and I gave her a fabricated time split, only to immediately get screamed at by another Team Lovato support crew person, which I deserved. I doubt my lie hurt Amanda on the spot but could have and probably messed her up later, as she calculated time between her and the two leading women pros getting off the bike and going into the run.

My spewed fabrication certainly hurt me right away, because my peer pit crew person Angela then knew immediately…she cannot trust me.

No doubt that an internal component exists here as well, fabricating untruths for the betterment of self. Rarely though do I cross this line…tipping to the point of inflating myself better than I am, unrealistically. Such self-puff-up would fall directly into the category of dirty-ego. If giving myself hope and opportunity, painting an image in my head when a betterment of position is possible but not yet held, if staying on the correct side of truth, such is not a lie but rather…this my healthy-ego hard at work.

Liar Number Four
Why and How Do I Lie? I Lie for Betterment of Position
How or why do I lie in this regard?
1. I lie to connect with people places and things, stuff I need or want, or think I deserve
2. I lie to gain acceptance or furtherance in relationships
3. I lie to gain admission into otherwise out-of-bound places and spaces
4. I lie wanting to fit in, not be omitted, not be odd-man-out, not be the black swan

Wanting such unreachables so bad, I believed no other way existed without stretching the truth far as needed to be stretched. I sought to gain acceptance from others through being an alternative self. By way of lies, the relationship is flat-out untrue to begin with so how will the attempt and effort of building connections initiated with falsehoods add to my long-term success? *Uh like duh*…it fricking won't. More stress within me built up when I did this sort of shit, leading to the production of additional make-my-life-shorter cortisol. Such found untruths risked landing me a reputation as a liar or untrustworthy fake friend and in summary, such misguided pursuits hurt me more than help me. This fitting-in and getting-ahead bullshit becomes publicly evident, contributing to additional unwanted alone time, after being shunned or ousted.

These sort of untruths are long gone but were hyper-present during my ages of 9 to 11 and 12 to 25. From 9 to 11, I intended to be included in neighborhood play. From 12 to 25, I battled to survive within the drug trade. Once clean and starting to make real money at work, these sort of untruths became mostly irrelevant and unnecessary. I found no reason to lie in school, unless concerning drug deals. I enjoyed only a few friends in school and was rarely there, so my interaction with people was minimal.

Once in high school, I befriended the toughest and most loved guy in the academic complex…varsity football team center Darren Bosserman.

When coattail hanging with big bold beautiful legit bad-ass Darren, I worried naught about fitting in…he was hyper popular. Actually for the first 15 years of my life, Darren provided me with more emotional protection and shelter than anyone else ever did, my parents included, by my measure. When I exited school abruptly in my shorty-short junior year, I did not speak to any of my high school classmates again.

Oh wait, that's not true…I still chat a little on Facebook with a girl from our shared high school mechanical drawing class. I had a crush on her, Cathy Molfetas. I built up the nerve to tell Cathy how much I liked her, then she asked what I wanted to do about it. Not prepared to answer, I never thought it through properly. Distance between Cathy and I then grew, right before I dropped out. Hah, I should have known better, especially because her boyfriend probably would have kicked my ass supremely, I knew him rather well…varsity football superstar center Darren Bosserman.

Liar Number Five
Why and How Do I Lie? I Lie to Gain Respect, Power, and Money
How or why do I lie in this regard?
1.   I lie wanting others to perceive me as generally knowledgeable, artificially so
2.   I lie, keen to compete and be better than others or better than my natural self
3.   I lie desiring notice, recognition, promotion, or compensation
4.   I lie attempting to keep people from fucking with me

The foundational intent within this section is not entirely bad. Recognition is positive, and encouraging, supporting my healthy-ego. Reinforcement that I am worth one or two shits in this world is a good thing, long as I remain on the east coast of truth.

Earlier in life when unrealizing how much smarter the majority of people around me were, I made shit up. Quickly I learned most people knew more than me, certainly after my self-expulsion from school. Much these untruths occurred in my youth, during the ages of 13 through 21, the height of my drug dealing. When selling buying or negotiating, I attempted intimidation which most often did not work for me, I held not the chops. Once every so often I effectively presented myself as a badass motherfucker but sometimes my short-held dominance backfired entirely. Within the trade, the incoming confrontations elevated rapidly, often into a no-win pissing match of sorts.

Trying to maintain a heightened position, not letting them knock me down too much, I lied my ass off attempting to maintain leverage.

The fuck-bulk of trouble amid my untruthful pissings was remembering what lie I told last to whom. In short order, the dishonest wranglings became a real damn circus. Everyone selling or buying volume was highly guarded concerning the matter of getting robbed, or doing business with an undercover *narc* officer. Over 100 occasions when picking up, delivering, or paying shit off, I did so in the shared presence of handgun. The existence of handgun fell on me as a legitimate threat, *panic-pshaw*, I scrambled to get the hell out of there fast as possible without bullets flying my way, aka fuck the truth.

Venturing to gain acceptance, respect, and afforded opportunities, I hid my weaknesses and ignorance, which actually made me dumber, both internally and outside my squishy human shell. I lied to fill in or round out a conversation, present a belief, message of power, or even a threat. I might grab onto untruths supporting the fill-in tales I told. Tragically at times, here is where facts lost grasp in current reality. Desiring my wants and advancing my initiatives, I selected bits and pieces of some truths and deselected others to better make my case. Selective facts and partial truths are not accurate so therefore obtusely outright lies, by my measure.

Liar Number Six
Why and How Do I Lie? I Lie to Hurt, Harm, or Retaliate
How or why do I lie in this regard?
1. I retaliate after feeling unfairly injured, physically or emotionally
2. Once feeling blue, I push myself lower and closer to legacy but fake pain levels
3. I judge blame and assume others as core-stupid, in addition to their stupid behavior

I lash out, though it's been awhile, mostly when struggling with appalling unfairness or disapproved action. The straight-up righteousness dynamic began to crumble for me over four decades ago. Within the drug trade I felt the need to explode on people when ripped off or dealt with wrongly, like Rodney…me trying to inflict damage, or collect quickly what owed to me then I jetted. Comprehensively this tough guy crap backfired, hah…both my weak wings and DNA ran upstream to such downward actions. Since unearthing my root problem on the foundational floor of right versus wrong, my targeted judgment instead shifted to unfairness.

Chapter SEVEN

Initially, I lash out silently within my heart, intentionally thinking negative thoughts constructed with blames judgments and assumptions, aka lies, lies, lies. If my emotional hotheadedness is still boiling and bubbling over the top its cauldron, I electronically or telephone contact or say shit that either is not true, or spew crap I truly do not feel. The last bit of such judgements I normally release are that of resentment, which for me have no further to go. Once on a joyride with resentment, this emotion either begins to consume me or I release it. For me, the only way I let go of resentment is forgiveness.

My forgiveness does nothing for the other person, but rather releases the burdened array of the 200-pound backpack I carry, that which is stuffed full of resentment rocks.

Considering now the one in the mirror…I became skilled at hurting myself. Attempting a weird deflation of humility, I minimized my importance, value, ability to contribute, or even participate. Often I sank quickly to the bottom of the lying well, flooded with self-doubting abuse. Too often I preferred misery over smiley, because I expertly blanketed myself with more blame and harm than I dared to throw over others. My early childhood plays a leading role here…when camping in Florida with BigBird I solely pushed Patricia Lou over her final crack-up cliff's edge, aka bye-bye Mommy. Then verifiably alone, I had no one else to cling to, I had no one else to blame. My world then became so small that I was the entirety of the emotional pin cushion real estate available.

Beyond my antisocial self-harm habits, there is the ugliest and untruthful model of my dirty-ego, thinking myself better than others. Sometimes this ugliness arose, even shocking me, especially concerning those I dislike. Of course my dislike is an assumption judgment and blame game, downgrading those my sisters and brothers with great pleasure, me spewing lies to try and even the scale alongside this person, even the lies I silently think in my head. The sort-out is my devout *Trifecta of Ugly* actualization. When I *judge* others I am lying, because I see not their scars. When I *blame* I am lying, because I know not from where they came. When I *dirty-assume* I am lying, because their shoes fit me not, I have not bled their wounds, this their own shit and all of which drives their physical actions as displayed. If anything, I judge their shown behavior, not their person because I know them not no one. Judge-blame-assume, aka Trifecta of Ugly…long as you don't get in my face or threaten one my sisters or brothers, I am better off, much better off, taking the low road, turning around rudely and walking away without a single word said or barely another thought thunk. This walk-away may appear to others I am the asshole but, in an attempt to retain my own truth and values, I am better to avoid and abandon their stupid behavior immediately. Mostly I have let go of my own stupid Trifecta of Ugly judge blame and assume gameboard behavior.

A byproduct is the viable divide truth creates, cutting deep and pushing people apart. I've both unknowingly and knowingly done this, formerly through general conversations when my filter is turned to low settings. Low filter means I speak more with truth and less with heart, although not my nature. Thereupon low-filter, I inflicted extra pain and drove some people away.

Certainly during the years writing this here your book, as my dictioned creative mind billowed and my false kindness tolerance factor dropped to a thus-far low tide mark, I found myself speaking openly and rubbing some people the wrong way. Well, as it is, sometimes, and as it goes, sometimes, so sorry yet not too-too sorry, still I choose truth.

Liar Number Seven, *last one*

Why and How Do I Lie? I Lie When Relegated Outside of Reality

How or why do I lie in this regard?

1.   I unrealistically wish and pray for shit to change on its own, aka magical turnaround, awhile stagnant bird, aka me not stepping the fuck forward to do the work required
2.   I am lost emotionally, distanced from my true self or my genuine here and now
3.   I am stuck believing the non-reality true, due to poor mental health or external forces
4.   I feel or think to be standing in the midst of the worst thing of my life, often aka a lie

I sling these untruths still…does this make it *best saved for last,* or *worst saved for last*? IDK. Mostly, these are the fantasia-fabricated untruths I tell myself. Before age 21 and set out unto the world under my own power, I echo-knew the pestilence of finality coming my way. Such statement was not a fabricated fear or worrisome wonderment, but rather a calculated forecast. Facing such harsh end of lines truth at the time and by my measure, I collected my shit, got the fuck up off my ass, and went out journeying upon the land to find the truthful resonating peace within me. I lived to learn and mostly maintain a calm sense of security after moving home from Colorado. My Rocky Mountain learnings taught me…*things will work out, shit comes together in the end, I won't be left with nothing or stuck without a roof over my head, least not for long.* This viewpoint has served me accurately for decades, thus helping alleviate much worry from my shoulders and brain.

Recently, my position finds me stuck in a lower activity level, meanwhile depleting reserves at the same time. This is a lie I am somewhat suffering from right now, suspending realities of my cognitive and fiscal ailments well as being open to new love, to instead write this here your book. For the last few years, the practiced self-trickery tells me something is just going to *happen* or *come along*. I have not been out there in the world kicking ass and bouncing about per normal, work-wise anyway. Facing the reality of my inconsistent business consulting revenue, the failed challenge to make my new garage remod business profitable, atop the mountainous task of unsuccessfully reentering the corporate world without a four year degree, I ignore many of my bleak true facts. Where this your book project takes me I have no flipping clue, 'prolly nowhere, but I know it's the right thing to do because it could help one of us, it could help one of our stuck sisters or brothers see a slight sunny path, aka my future and fiscal means be damned, aka fuck it, aka just go, aka just fucking jump, aka huck and hold.

At times, rare times…I avoid thinking about shit I prefer not to think about.

Part of this *scared to look at it* affliction is the naivety of what lurks out there, just waiting for someone like me to come along. Naivety concerning appearingly-good people doing bad things, most of which I am pretty good at identifying, least when paying attention to it. I too am capable of doing horrible hurtful shit but mostly keep myself within the guardrails of socially acceptable behavior.

I maintain my devilish claws within, I believe myself no different in this regard. While the what…when backed into a corner with no way out, I am capable of acting in a way categorized as flat-out fucking vicious, I know so.

Though as of for long time now, even when provoked prodded threatened beaten or cut, I mostly do not strike back. I naturally choose to not do such horrible things, things I could do once recognizing I am of means, but rather let the other person with the upper hand victimize me. I am surface nice, aka not mean on the outside. I mingle appropriately by my measure amongst the rest of the other eight billion rat-humanoids on earth and mostly, I try to get along. The issue here is being able to live through the shit I have no idea about yet, which isn't a lot. To withstand the hard shit not yet on my radar, because although dreaming about forever-sunny possibilities, the reality of much more evil things happening seem foreign, yet this another lie I convince myself of, because any fricking thing is possible.

Much of my successful practice to rejoin reality and deal with the totality of my issues are my personally fabricated everyday tools. Basically, I map out my unfiltered truths alongside my worries or fears, often dispelling the untruths and realigning myself to the here and now. A bonus round of the truthful reality check versus my untruthful fabrications is the challenge of TimeBombs. Within multitudes of occasions spanned across my days, I have said silently or out loud to myself, *this is the worst thing that's ever happened to me*, and the majority of times I was lying. After one-too-many clamorings claiming the hardest rain ever from the sky was falling upon thy head, I called bullshit. Documenting the eleven worst happenings in my life that *could* possibly occur upcoming, forced ranked, I also added three or more immediate resulting actions I would attempt if said TimeBomb blew up. Initially the list held horrible things that *might never* and I *hoped never* happen, but were *possible*. Quickly I realized myself only tending to one side of the trauma garden. Adding associated, however slightly converse horrible things that *most likely YES will* happen barring a miracle or freak occurrence, I added the subtitle…TimeBombs, *ticking and otherwise*.

I intend to generate my own momentum. To this intentional end, I avoid *wish* and *pray* in my personal dictionary. To and for me only, *hope* and *faith* are ridiculously powerful forces capable of helping to change and save my life because I believe at times, that is all that did, and can. Mentioned amid my bird blabber elsewhere…*echo*…hope is a superpower.

Shining the Light New

There is no keeper of truth

There are no watchers of lies

We bumble and mumble at will without compass, all on our own

The barrage of small life and big world lies…they relentless

Overpower me they might

Overpowered me they did

Never can untruth within me and upon me change, so I thought

I began to conform, bowing down to the lies, until I didn't

Until I wore new eyes, then seeing a new path to a new way

A passage unobscured…brightened by new light held by new hands

New hands shining the light of my total truth alone unto the world

This my way…this my path…this my truth.

Changing the (Un)Truth

Perhaps uniquely, oddly, and even inappropriately, I distance drugs apart from alcohol. My alcoholism began 15 years past clean from drugs, then once three years past sober from the Devil's Water I lost grip of my mental health and was clinically suicidal. Although perchance I should stop here and not bore you with my additional out of orderliness, I feel the issues are in fact related.

Presumably then, the notion of eliminating something undesirable from my life although a challenge, I believe such the competition possible. In association, I kept moving in the direction of betterment even after some certifiable hard and scary fucking shit, specifically the confidence strength and momentum collected once putting drugs behind me. Extended drug use scrambled my brain, the Devil's Water then poisoned this bird's cognitive sense. All substances required me to lie so to maintain my usage. Once feeling lost and alone, my damaged un-thinking dragged me down the fuck it all sharp-rusty-metal-edge-exposed death rabbit hole. So to quit substances I had to get real. To face my mental anguish and right this bird brain I had to stop lying to myself. And then left was perhaps the most dysfunctional dynamic yet, the untruths of the world.

Quitting lies is different than quitting drugs and alcohol however, much different. Leaving substances behind involved my collective efforts of want, willingness, choice, discipline, avoidance, build-up of self, letting go, and filling in some holes once poked in and leaking from my core oracle. If wandering into a location where drugs or alcohol are present, I can leave under my own power without touching them, if I am truthful enough, brave enough, willing, and committed enough.

Back in the day, much of my lying was because of the drugs. Lying because of the drugs was because of me lying to myself.

I think much the bottom line concerning the drugs was my fright, I felt wronged, I regarded myself small weak and exposed, and my self-confidence was so low I thought I needed *something* to comfort me. Ideally I wanted *someone* to comfort me, but these resources were not available.

External lies are sometimes unavoidable, especially when I share my bed with them or we are related by DNA. Lies have existed profoundly in my life, both received and delivered, since before the days my memories began. Barely could I imagine even where to start…how do I begin to alter the lies I spew? How do I possibly begin to manage or even navigate the projectile falsehoods flying in and aimed at my head from the outside organic world?

I observe untruths, both the ones clear as the high noon sun and others billowing around disguised as everyday normalities. Incessantly the dishonesties of the world come after me…various times I effectively avoid lies, yet alternatively and often, their devilish craftiness reigns supreme over all mere mortals, myself included.

Once initiating movement towards authenticity, the intentions and efforts of honesty engaged every area of my life. Although needing to sort out the trickery pre-monopolizing available space for growth in the truth room, after getting rolling, my positive momentum snowballed fast.

Digging in and directly drug related, the wretchedest untruth struggles in my life, *echo*…arose during romantic relationships. Much as I try to do shit right…openly share my beliefs thoughts and feelings, and keep my pants on outside the relationship, alternatively several of my partnered girlfriends, and certainly both my wives, seemed incapable of telling the truth when it mattered most by my measure. Although the previous sentence is a total-truth share observation, it's simultaneously an assumption and judgment…I am no-way not perfect and I stumble too, yet however forever faithful.

Questionably, perhaps much of my inner angst percolated up from my misaligned or unsettled heart, well maybe, quite possibly maybe…just sayin'. My love attempts were my hardest missteps to manage, that is until tougher things came along. Still, at the time, I thought myself incapable of living outside an active romantic union, a notion that proved itself to be one of my biggest lies I told myself ever. Here now some supporting honesties on the matter…the romance dance with truth.

For quite some time and on a specified level, seems the more I worked towards truth, bouncing back were stronger and bigger still, more lies. Likely, my untruth awareness became so heightened that the projectiles of romantic dishonesties came flying in aiming to blind me, then dart-boarded themselves straight into the end of my nose with excessive visibility. Identifying perhaps my most damaging substance-absorbed untruths as fear and loneliness by way of love lost, here I linger longer in an attempt to explain my position on romance, whether this makes me either an expert or a failure, this bird not at all entirely sure on the darn heartbreak matter. Henceforth immediately I paint my romantic emotional truth portrait on the relationship canvas in color, although the text here still appears black on the white page.

Say what dad, what in the fucking shit's sake hell are you fricking talking about?

Ok thy precious, I rhetorically hear you. Let me spell it out my Birdy, well…here immediately upcoming I attempt to exercise my theoretical and proverbial storied paint brush, speaking of malicious knives, emotional two-headed monsters, my imaginary shield that is my heart's defense, and my sword which is my courage and intentional willingness to move forward and fight for what I believe true, all regarding lost love and my fallout substance infliction, 'cause elsewise I bird-lack the damn diction. Using these mystical objects, I attempt better delivery of my core oracle heartbled feelings. Zero fabrication here…no lies, but rather slightly fantastical word colorings instead of monotone put-you-to-sleep quantum physics textbook-like typed character pukings.

Untruths within my erratic teenage life began to suck blood from me when an early girlfriend had an affair with her work boss.

The pain I bled from the betrayal came close to killing me. I was shooting at the time and the vicious unfairness boiled spoiled and bubbled within my heart. Barely plausible, but hah…I then spun further out of control. Heightened self-abusive drug use resulted and the malice suffered by my own hand verifiably scared me.

Running from the strong breeze of disingenuous devotion, next a Pandora's box opened to the likes I never heard of and validly, only the devil may care…my unconcerned breath continuance teetered daringly atop life's high-wire, no cable, no net.

Facts-first and previewing the emotional coloring book on matters upcoming, this death walk ventured far past willingness to accept my own end of life if it comes by way of the needle or Devil's waterbottle, influenced by my lover's betrayal. I felt so unfairly hurt that I was not only indifferent for my personal well being, but spying the suck-the-life-out-of-me forces coming my way, I self-abusively wanted them to injure me much as they could, if you pretty-pretty please.

The dagger of cheating romance plunged deep into every critical organ of my body, until the blunt wall of the knife's handle guard bottomed-out against my skin from the kill-you-now force. Never could I imagine she was capable of such a thing, first not only the dagger of betrayal, but second the ridiculous weighted coercion applied…now her upper-hand multitudes stronger than mine. The large eight-inch defrauding blade buried foremost within my lung number two, twisting ninety-degrees each way for effect…*twist-twist*. Purposefully the lung first, so my frantic fright in full effect…desperately gasping for air and reaching for life as the known but cloaked murderer came to play. My yesterday lover's cheating game unknowingly intent to place me six feet under, not only this long-ago time and along the way but later twice more, yes my darling Birdy as you know all too well, by the hands of wife two and wife one.

Lung two irreversibly damaged, the death blade of betrayal torn away then onto the next lung one…maximum damage, *twist-twist*, my liver, *twist-twist*, kidney two, *twist-twist*, kidney one, *twist-twist*, my spleen *twist-twist* and ripped away just because and why not, oh good, more bonus hurt…her misty eyes twinkling softly.

My love's untruthful kiss swoops in, looks like seduction…barely brushing my quivering lower lip the taste oh so familiar, this her slow faintness. I start my reconsideration…well maybe *ouch dammit* she bit me and bit me hard, my mouth bleeding too, the dark red droplets flowed from her smirk in unison, perhaps it seems this our last goodbye, however the aggravated smooch that it is. An acquainted but sinister *I love you* whispers flirtatiously into my ear but, well, here it comes…yes-yes finally, oh good yes please do it, be still now and forever my barely beating heart, I see her blade get cocked…plunge, *twist-twist*.

On my way down I try mumbling but she waltzes from the murder scene, paying no mind.

My blood splashed across thy love's killing room floor, her trophied dripping blade forcefully wiped clean both sides, afront her jeans like preparing for soon another slaying. Again attempting concluding words out loud but cannot, I am dying this instant…not so sure but hum, sounds like she is whistling, maybe soft singing, a slight gleeful tune. Within the bare feeble pop noise of last breath bubbles I eek out, "…thank you, ending my misery, love you I mean what the fuck?".

The first episode of this paint-by-word-colorings daytime drama aired when I was 19, then showed on and off for another 34 seasons until the near-death-by-cheating-love gameshow was finally cancelled. Once fabricating the conscious image of my factual future, I began not only confronting the reality of my death row street illegals, but realized this lying drug dragon a two-headed monster. Head and neck one of the Siamese beast being my addiction… the self-abusive drug roulette game, the substances, the volume, the frequency, and the malevolent needle itself. Head and neck two of the dragon being the *why* of invented frolicking with drugs from the start, and to continue forward as such otherwise, aka the lies, lies, lies.

Yes Lauren my Birdy as you asked of me to tell you…I see it was my much-much empty voids at home, the house fright and wobbliness, the lack of practiced I love you's, and the self-blame becoming of my running, aka my disconnected self-deceptive lying. Straight up moreover, my waffled feelings of giving up, the stall of trying for betterment of life, that shit arrived on scene to come play with me since I was four years old. My advanced feelings then became thoughts, but smartly refused travelling silently to *The Other Side*, aka the quiet side, aka the dark no-nothing side of lifelessness. I stared down lies with violent defiance, trying to defeat them yet still not understanding them, both the *why* and the *how* of the drugs along with an arena of partnered untruths.

I struck my right knuckles best I could upon the chin of my darting darkness within, meaning I was fighting my internally-generated untruths.

Lashing out at my lies with a quick second punch of my other fist, I realized this goes back to the motherfucking beginning.

My slightly-grown up shade grey of sensibility hesitated and just then, the heart of my four-year-old self was ripped wide open. I backed way up, insightfully knowing this a long-standing ravaged resentment for losing my mother to the monsters in her head. Before I knew even what my feelings and thoughts were saying, the realization arose of my earliest pain paving foundation for my lanes of legacy hurt, traveling up to current day. I never knew such candid clarity lived inside me, until starting to face my truth once barely out of my teens.

With both hands then hammer-fisting simultaneously upon my weakened self, I faced my truth of truths of the time. There I saw clearly, I knew such as so for fact…I will not survive like this, small meek and scared…I will not survive by the unhelpful hands of myself. So there then my journey began, I started living more aligned to my truth, least trying to point myself that way…I got real, least I tried.

Readied for battle, least I tried. My shield my sword gripped firmly by one hand each, I entered the lair of the lying beast. Oh the smell...the stench of the undone the untrue and all that is false in the world. The monstrous demon was crafty beyond belief...exceeding every earthly measure. Her horrific putrid gleam, her unfairness and for goodness sake she wore two operational heads. Firstly I knew not how to even face one or the other. Every day my near slaughter, I barely escaped so bloodied, so war-torn...I battled the two-headed land serpent for five years. Finally I slayed that motherfucker the reptilian underlord, or so I thought. Its head one, the neck and face of my substance abuse laid severed, lifeless on the cave floor, once and for ever ending my drug abuse. The beast however, its untruthfulness, its lying side, its depthless why of the fraudulent me existed far beyond this physical world. Hah...with a brief screech the old rank one scurried off into an unreachable arm of the cave then laughing, its second head of deceit knowing to taste my blood again soon, again and again for the next two-plus decades as I battled with untruths in and out of my life.

Finally, I decapitated neck two of the-now double-stumped-neck dragon. The drugs long ago conquered, then my truth futures mostly within my own hands. I decided...I would deliver and receive only truth, period. Once deciding, I recognized the war never over but on the day I moved out and apart from wife one, I began to live anew, winning the battle, severing the second head of my truth dragon...the devilish falsity within, the fables I toss, and the lies I allowed others to cast upon me, or so I believed. Although challenging myself intently over the next decade, I finally stabilized my balance, then not accepting untruths from the outside world in general.

Leaving your momma, I accepted the somber fact I may never hold another love's hand again if I guard my heart from betrayal like I wanted to. Exiting our family's once-comfy nest, foremost I committed myself to truth first, knowing that in the long run proper family love required real togethering.

Although considering the hurtful complexities of fleeing the marital nest, I first chose love for you- my offspring- my brood- my love- my life- my world, attempting to lead by moral example. While the while, simultaneously my personal truth reversed rapidly once I spied our broken home and picked up the Devil's waterbottle...but, but honestly it was my inability to suck up and bury the lies as suggested by wife one thine baby momma.

Truth is Truth
Recalling untruths, following the dishonesty unveilings and bare-all showings...the damage already done, too late to save the gosh darn thing trying so hard to gain or preserve in the first place. In my experience both as giver and receiver, a small to moderate lie carried for a short while is forgivable and tenably, forgettable. *Hah*...but an untruth concealed for an extended period, even the seeming insignificancy of handful of days, is rarely forgiven or forgotten. To clarify...a small untruth carried over an extension can, and often does still, inject great harm. To me, the previous mention of longer-held pint-sized untruths is accurate because at the time of uncovering, the longer duration means the deeper the dagger of doubt once the fabled cover-up is revealed. The fallout result is a level of hurtful betrayal and shocking deceit that is rarely shed entirely.

But dad...how so, why so?

Well, let me here try to explain effectively my precious...a small slip of omitted honesty can be regarded as the most earth shattering hurtful lie ever experienced, because us hooman's operate from our personally-calibrated emotional measuring systems. Learning hand-first, the most challenging dynamic of managing untruths is the fact that this here human absolutely sucks at mind reading. Although my intention is to share, sometimes I am vague. And when listening, sometimes I am rather distracted. My general orientation these here days is supreme focus, otherwise I lose track of what the hell is going on, aka that snarling junkyard dog of down-wrong dirty assumptions has big teeth and that fucker bites hard.

Time she precious...time she fragile.

I try not to end up in such a scramble because rushing and hurriedness creates self-trickery. When time-challenged I attempt shortcuts and hah, shortcuts are factually dishonest workarounds. Every minute, every hour, every day, every week, every month, every year, and every decade I spend speaking and acting falsely is time I will never get back. Both the overblown pretending and embellished striving, they neglect that which I hold so dear...those fleeting and treasureful moments of life's beauty sans filter.

Near my end of days, I might recount the many wasteful hours spent, especially dawdling amid unhealthy pursuits. My frightful risk is the waste of time, the chanced opportunity of hopeful dreams never becoming reality, most of which evolves into regret. I lived to learned this truth...endless are the pains challenges and heartbreaks that help me learn and grow. However, for such self-driven momentum to generate, I must be present for my own life, I must be available, I must be awake, I must have eyes and heart open to truthfully receive that which waits, that which physically sits afront me.

There is No Try, There is Only Do
Excuse me Master Yoda, I need to drop this your class. I somehow landed here in the wrong Jedi training group, so sorry.

To try…maybe the word *try* does not sound reassuring to you my precious darling.

Maybe *to try* sounds weak to you, unsure, or uncommitted. For me, I echo *try*, because after immeasurable challenging situations, I have experimented and learned to know this as my own truth…there is only try. I try because otherwise, I am dealing in the mixed-up and fabricated world of unrealistic absolutes, period.

I screw shit up all the fucking time and there are certainly many more fuck ups to come. Through the while and by my bird measure, emphatically I am diametrically opposed to the notion *there is no try*. To and for me, resoundingly, *try* is a cornerstone of my truth operating system. Amid my proprietary diction and gabby glossary, when I state with inevitability that I *will* do, when I *promise*, when I say with devout certainty most any singular fucking thing, I am lying.

I shared with a beloved gal pal recently my planned intent to do something, ride my bike for an hour so to get my body moving, after almost three weeks stationary writing this here book. She said, "There is no try, promise me you will ride your bike today". Oh boy, I felt sorry for her…she just cracked open a can of terminology worms. I became enthused to explain, and was slightly defensive, but I did not cross the line and she understood my position. We both said we love each other and hung up still friends. I can only promise three things, period, these my concrete certainties.

1.   I promise I will die
2.   I promise everything changes
3.   I promise to try my best try

That's it, that's all, because shit unravels often and without pronouncement. If promising to ride my bike like Splendid Staci wanted me to, my words of certainty would be nothing but lies. I cannot promise I actually *will* ride my bike today, no not any day, I know better. Unexpected crap and priority shifts happen hourly, stuff I did not plan for, did not see coming, or could ever imagine as possible.

Hence my attempted aversion to fixation on results because I hold no Godlike controls, I can reasonably manage only intent, and not for-certain outcomes beyond my concrete three. This now here a *life critical 100*…and when doing more of what I say, thus avoiding complete misses, I gain pillaring confidence and emotional stature, or as my beloved Friendwords Joshua Duke Sansing famously says, "Walk tall fuck 'em all".

When speaking falsely, when not doing what said or promised, even when speaking to only me, the chipping away of self begins, and eventually I crumble.

Aiming to tower taller than my pain, my fear, my aversions, my problems, my addictions, my complacency and my challenges, I factually do so when truthful. When pinned to the deck by hard expectations of outcome, often I break loose and am blown overboard, then left to the shark feeding frenzy of my own falsehoods.

When promising, I frequently create unrealistic expectations likely to blow up and make matters worse. I quickly learned not to promise, not to lie, aka not to promise lies.

Sorry Master Yoda, for me there is no promise to do…I will and can, only try.

Clean Not Clean
Possessing nothin'…'cept horrified desperation
My butt covered mere underwear, only then some socks too
Frantically fleeing shitty brown duplex, frantically fleeing fast as I could
Howling my precious where have you gone, no-no precious where could you be?
Maybe abducted then tossed, maybe ran off regardless, now lost
Absolutely terror defined, absolutely fucking losing my mind.

My two preciouses, my only forever true loves Birdy and Boyd vanished, I lost my kids. My pinnacle worst nightmare came to life in an instant that morning.

My kids once here but now, nowhere to be found. Oh no, wait…are they somewhere else today? I thought-thunk them here last night, were they even here at all? I can't think straight. I need to calm my frantic breaths, stop shouting to the world from my sidewalk, put some clothes on, and sort this shit out. Compounding the confusion, but truthfully creating the panic was my new pathetic practice consuming massive amounts of tequila, presented to my willing hands by newfound friend Senor Jose Cuervo, available wherever the Devil's Water products are for sale.

My over-consuming occurred nightly, for months by this time. Once you and bro-bro were sheltered safe under your sheets and off to dreamland, the sealed almost half-gallon premixed lime margarita package-good emerged from the kitchen cabinet, ready to party and refusing to leave 'til emptied. Your precious innocent sweet noggins crushing little pillows, while poppa bird challenge drinking against his monsters trying to escape big pain.

My love abounds for you and your bro my preciouses…my Birdy, my Boyd. My love for you two unwavering, forever lasting, and stronger me myself I alone could be. My love for you both individually and together is boundaryless, possessing zero hesitation and zero fear. Any executioners in my way to safeguard my preciouses, come on and try me motherfuckers, you better bring every single fricking thing you got.

Unbeknownst to you is the strength aura you transmit to me that magnetically connects us. The second I saw your cute swirl of hair but not yet the rest of you, I walked taller. I was stronger because of your baby bird feet existing on this earth.

Because you were here and I made you, I had to do better…I had no choice. I had to try harder…I had no choice. I had to protect, care, love, laugh and provide…I had no choice.

If married to the one and only woman I ever offered my hand to now stepping out, I would not have gone back to the drugs for comfort or escape. The cushion of time away from my former precious aka the drugs, was a hidden springboard for me to dive into the best-self pool of life. I would not give up my best-self stoop for a mere love, not even for the mountainous higher great love she is. I would not exit my best-self pool because I knew to dip a toe into any shallow puddle of street substance comfort meant certain for me to drown there. For me to even smoke a little pot, half a joint, attempting to take the emotional edge off, I would drown, aka I would die. And drown I would not fuck-to-the-no-100, I have two mini-me baby birds to raise, both still in the nest and it is my job to teach them to fly. Protect them best I possibly could, this now the entirety of my life purpose, aka…I have no fucking choice. I would not have gone back to drugs but likely, without the existence of you guys I would have drank myself to death…yowzah, did I really just type that? Hum, interesting…this is new. I've never been down the drunk Roger Ray rabbit hole before but take my hand little Birdy, let's tumble together.

Never before had the Devil's Water consumed me…alcohol was not a problem with me prior. I hated the taste of all Devil's Drink, yes, all his flavors ever touching my lips…blech. Whiskey, wine, beer…yuck, yuck, triple yuck. So I did not see the threat, my father did not drink, no one ever fell out of my family tree and died of liver failure resulting from years of alcohol poisoning.

What forcibleness could drive my hands to drink myself to death without you and your brother in my life after tall hot ginger's affair? Well, hum…great question. Principally, simply your existence took away my option to leave your presence…I had no choice. Hum-hum however straight-up and still, unpacking now the feelings of marital damage, how deep did it cut? What was so horrible for me to surrender to the poisonous Devil's drink? What authoritative preeminence was capable of creating such core oracle hopelessness? What put me so close to waiving the white flag of my continuance?

I was feeling hurt, injured…unloved. I felt hollow, frail…a shell, and missing my insides. Yup-yup straight up, a bag of bones and skin that was me. Missing my thinking brain I was, and also displaced my kind heart I did. Pain? Yes that too, much-much searing heart pain. Fear? Accurate. Doubt in myself? Yup, horrible encapsulating doubt, not entirely sure what I did or did not do so horrible to drive her away from me. Unable to see a get-over-this period in the long-term future? Correct. Numb? Certainly. Uncaring for anything, conscious uncaring? Totally. What about discarded? Check, total truth, absolutely discarded like a bag of stinky garbage on trash day. Not able to envision purpose after the trystful upheaval? Without a doubt. Lost? Unequivocally, but not just disoriented lost. Unstable, decentralized, dismantled, sold away then scattered about lost. Lost like about to fall off the corner of a curb into something without a bottom lost, um, yeah…lost like ridiculously precarious lost.

Ridiculously precarious lost…dropped on the side of a four lane highway with another four lanes on the far side going the other way. It seems late evening time standing alongside the highway, most all light is gone and no more brightness exists overhead but skimpily, a mere faint glow.

The roadway is frantically hurried, crowded…all are angry at each other and angry at me the stranger. I see no exit ramps in either direction, no signs for upcoming escape routes anywhere. I cannot stick my thumb out for a ride or even wave for rescue, I have no idea where I would ask to go, I have no idea where I am. From where did I come? Amnesic…and where am I trying to go? I do not know, I have no earthly idea…entirely oblivious.

Still lost, it seems darker now. I cannot begin to understand the location of West. Where now did the sun just set, what is the brightest part of the sky, from where are the nominal remnants of light originating? The slight light will orient me west. Oh but wait, is it dusk? Maybe it is morning. If I can look to find the soon-to-rise sun coming from the east I will be able to travel, least I will know my direction. If I could establish base orientation, I will be ready to flee this paralyzing position aside these lanes of rats a racing.

Barely shuffling in place, my elbows shelter atight my slight side ribs. Instinctually these here my hands sprawl, my nails curve inwards to clench the opposite sides of my upper framed torso…I huddle within myself. I can hardly move. Oh wait, oh no, I think there is less light now, will the faint flush soon slip through my fingers off the left coast, then to be trapped here within only these feeble arms of darkness? I cannot gain my bearings, strange I'm unable to identify this here odd somewhere. This and here seems a place I previously missed during my many world travels. I must leave the litter-filled roadside soon or I will surely perish. The breath is swiftly vacuumed from my chest, an incurvature almost lays me down, my tears begin their painful descent.

Frantic to flee, I am frozen…my feet a shuffle yet affixed. It smells, like no stench I know, the subordinate gas and diesel fumes are almost asphyxiating. The shards run and jump to latch on and line my sole bottoms. The highway concrete side walls are too high to climb, hah, and besides, my shoes now layered with glass bottle bits. If I could jump out, where would I go? I do not have even a starter clue…blisteringly consumed by cluelessness.

More lost…however invariantly, I cannot, I cannot, I cannot understand which way I am standing. The frenzied movement beside me now shines no light at all, are they lost too? Chaotic the road is now staggering silent, thus thrice the danger. I cannot hear the flurry one way or discern the wall nearby the other. The twister of wind from the nearby frenzied traffic tornadoes all around me and unrecognizable is the originating direction of its rat rage. Maybe I am going deaf, I can only scantily hear. I can hardly see, am I also going blind? Am I pointing towards the traffic? Or the wall? I dare not stick out my hand trying to feel the close-to-me cement vertical surface, a speeding truck mirror may take it off. Trying not to lose my balance and fall where I stand but with barely eyes to see and but one slightly working ear, how can I begin to walk? I might go the wrong way, my face might hit the wall or my legs taken out by a hurried hostile auto and the rest of me too. The hand of an unseen force is felt upon me, holding me and stealing my senses…rattled, baffled, *lost*.

I am filtering these understandings and trying to sort-out as I clack so pretty please with jimmies on top my precious, bear with your BigBirdy. Hum, what is the not plural summary feeling descriptor of consequential harm from the unfaithfulness?

                    Chapter SEVEN

Hurt, unloved, hollow, frail, and without center. Pain, fear, self-doubt, unseeing future, numb, uncaring for any and all conscious things, and discarded. Seeing no open and available purpose, abandoned on a foreign roadway, precarious, about to fall and plunge within the bottomless. Then lacking discernable light, then going deaf, targeted as the other stranger danger that is me…the stranger in town and feeling in danger. I was angrier and angriered at, clueless, disoriented, bearingless, mildly asphyxiated, and unable to climb. Directionless, scared to walk, afraid to run, barely able to stand, frightened to kneel, unable to lay down, and trapped. Void of understanding, almost or about to be handless and maybe even legless. Rattled baffled and lost…imperceptive. Hum, yes of course, all that. But there is something else…darn it, gosh dang, there is something more, something to properly pinpoint and vividly expose my emotional position once wholly wrecked.

Well, I guess, let us see clearly through the mystical fog…*discarded* is maybe the strongest target-center feeling mentioned during my rattle it off by the side of the rat race road session. I think discarded seems most correct even beyond hopeless fearful pain. Sprinkled atop discarded is likely the pointless future and unraveling of self *oh fuck ouch that hurt- bloody hell damnit all and back,* for holy fuckballs sake, two of my long ago pains and entombed-down self-definitions just poked up out of the ground. Oh man here we go…fuck-so, what capable internal forces existed, possible for me to drink myself to death after the implosion of the marriage, if not for you my darling baby birds my brood my love my life my world?

First of second…I felt discarded, akin abandoned. After decades avoiding my little Roger Ray experiences, not denial but avoidance, later during dissection I understood the time from when my mother left, followed by being dropped in Detroit, and finally my father going to night school for five years, well…I understood this as feeling abandoned, aka discarded broken bird boy. The span of time between my mother's monsters first appearing to me and BigBird completing after-work schooling added up to eight years, Roger Ray ages four through twelve. I felt nothing but unsafe from when my objective truthful memories began, but perceived a sense of calm security atop my consciousness after the age of thirty. Hence maybe this a farce, maybe I was still scared when upon the day me and your momma's marriage blew up. Bullshit, is this bullshit? Maybe. I like to think this *still scared* notion a huge stretch, but I'll size up the suit to see if it fits.

Feasibly I pushed through all the discarded and abandoned shit, never really sorting things through as once thought, hence driving the undesirables into my subconscious do-not-open hurtful memories vault. Imaginably I still held a deep rooted core unsafety factor. Once poked hard enough and my heart bleeding out onto my love's killing room floor, perchance all I could feel was unsafe, well, that is as the emotions dust may settle to show. And if so, I should be banned from all romantic relationships, certainly marriages…just sayin'.

Second of second…I saw nothing but a dead end pointless future following the affair, after attempted but unsuccessful reconnection of truth efforts, by my measure. I sensed an unraveling of self-worth, akin to a lowlife piece-of-shit loser junkie.

The hopelessness of my addict status fifteen years earlier was a self-evident crystal clear reality.

So, my worst self is a lowlife piece-of-shit loser junkie, me who through trial triumph and trauma has learned to stand tall with my head up and chin out. Slightly bold, aka healthy-ego, slightly a show-off, aka dirty-ego, resoundingly present, honest, and doing better these days than my worst lowlife loser self. But without a pinch of doubt, I am still a junkie and will forever be. I wear this nametag and carry a matching business card proudly, my scarred descriptor of truth offering me a view and vantage point most people do not have and never will. This does not make me better, fuck to the no way, it only gives me different lenses on life to look through and I am thankful to have them. This is not a play on words or a self-defeating sympathy attempt, no, I am only sharing myself unfettered…here the one and only truthful me, as only me truthfully is. True-true, current day I do not practice as a piece of shit or junkie or lowlife, much as I am many other things though the while. These are all pieces of me no doubt, exactly same-same the fact I am an alcoholic, albeit twelve years and I believe sober forever more.

Junkie…explaining my position, or perhaps spilling my contents on the definition of junkie, to me junkie means unearthing my entire sub-surface system, like pulling my own proverbial roots out of the ground, and now residing in a pot sold at market…a pot, a cheap pot, not even a clay pot, but an almost-bucket-like plastic tub. Someone else owns the almost-bucket-like tub now, the tub-pot is not mine, the plastic tub owns me and someone else owns the tub. Myself is held captive within the tub, and cannot travel or even speak to what or where or how I desire to reside, if even on a windowsill. I am not me, there is no more me, I am practically nothing, I am…I am barely a speck of sept-aside dirt, I am a junkie.

The planter tub defines me and restrains me now, I am nothing. The junkie thing momentarily exists in the space of the ever-lasting soil within a never-to-decompose cheap plastic brown tub. A tub houses the linger-longer junkie nothingness residue, maybe only a faint red bloodstain inside the brown tub, below the dirt line and camouflaged to mostly indistinguishable levels. The nothing non-being me is frail, surviving only for now but not much longer and shoved into the dirt, the junkie thing in the dirt which will die soon enough and die for any reason, die at any ceremoniousless time. Too much water, I die. Not enough water, I die. Too much light, I die. Not enough light, I die. Like a bipolar unsuccessful gardener…no clue. *Junkie*.

Lowlife loser…unmasking thine unallowed reflection in the pointless life mirror, explicated earlier is lowlife within thy precious' Ananda brave bitch reachout, so here now only a slight touchpoint.

Chapter SEVEN

I am a loser-loser lowlife loser and this game designed for only others to win, I am not allowed to win, me unpermitted from arriving even miles near the front. Last, always last, DFL- dead fucking last that's me. Despite any desire, attempt, or hopeful plan that could be self-defined as somewhat however crafty, I will always lose no matter the advantaged position I start from.

I am smaller than my opponents, I am smaller than the game, I am smaller than every nano smidgen on earth. The world awhile all its inhabitants are bigger than me and all they do is win. All I do is lose. All I will ever do is lose. I will never win, ever. I am underneath all, I lay below every atomic particle, living and otherwise. I am amid dookie dirt, I am beneath nothingness, I am that which you wipe your feet upon, hah…my existence is but wasted thought time. An irrelevant over-used disposable doormat that's me, an adjoined toxic waste soil substance disregard. I am force-fed weak juice every single day, I have no choice. My wings as begin to heal, they are re-clipped before even afforded a slight opportunity to stand upon the edge of the nest and try to fly, but I may just jump anyway oh well whatever who the fuck cares anyway nobody.

I arise each day for what purpose, so no one else needs to lose? Seems the fuck so. Because that is my role, that is my place, that is my job…loser, loser piece-of-shit lowlife loser. The world is bigger, the world is stronger, the world is better, brighter, hopeful, and able. I am none of those sunny things. I am not able, I am a piece-of-shit loser lowlife loser. *Lowlife loser.*

Sum-Sum Summarizing. Post-drugs and with specificity, them being the start anew days throughout my late 20s and mid 30s…I moderately faced and stood shakily toe-to-toe with the abandonment resonating within me, yet however I held not the cognitive orientation, comprehension, or terminology. I operated rather randomly and clueless, hence…I tried. Direct intentional and mindful thoughts about my parents and grandparents mostly produced acceptance, forgiveness, and letting old pained emotions go. I was not necessarily stuck on the hurt anymore, so I believed.

I called bullshit there too, would any Roger Ray futures depress negatively because of my old abandonment shit? Analyzing options, I hedged regret and rather invested into continued talks and attempted quality time, with both my parents and grandfather Thurman best as time allowed. The gambled forecast was the feelings sort-out once my parents one-day died. Rather certain to handle my father's death ok, because later into my 30s we began mending the father son emotional fence, just before BigBird died in his 71st year. The true wildcard however, was my mother. Although spending time with Patricia Lou and we spoke on the phone when I could find her, your Grandma Pat was still emotionally unsteady. After three-plus decades of heightened fright with my mother, I remained on pointed guard until the day of her lonely-lonely death, four years after my father died. Once the docu-veri-facts alaid my hands of wife one's stepping out, all this shit flooded me once more, me the tossed-aside lowlife piece-of-shit loser.

Go-Time…the heinousness began, the battle between my angel and devil within. Uncontrollably, scant functional guidance preexisted because I had you my darlings underwing, yet the conflict raged on for five years, aka me party-drinking with His Darkness before sober.

Hence my highest height to date, sprouting to tower taller over that which tried to pin me to the floor, aka the damn drugs and Devil's drink. Magic decoder ring clue on the matter and being crystal-crystal-100…when referencing the combativeness, shadow, and His Highness The Prince of Darkness, indubitably I speak to this horde of one, aka thy glaring reflection in the fog-free mirror.

Surface Spewed Untruths

Always, never and associated absolutes when I speak them are lies.
Promise and *swear* when speaking with certainty of tangible earthly outcomes are lies.
I cannot do it is most times a lie. Maybe *I don't think I should do it now* is more truthful.
I'm not good enough is a lie.
I'm ok, I'm fine, is a lie.
No one cares is a lie.
I don't have any friends is a lie. Even if appearingly so, I mostly close-off prematurely.
They won't understand so why even try is a lie.
Things will never change is a lie.
It will never happen is often a lie.
I know I'll get fired if I try that is a dirty assumptive judgment, therefore a lie.
I know I'll get fired if I try that is a lie, but delivery of said *try* is critical however.
I'll never get ahead is a lie.
Nothing will ever change is a lie.

The simplest thing at work was assumed as off the map, like talking with my boss revealingly. I feared sharing even minor truths, divulging slight story of struggle, or asking for fractional help. I stretched presumptions to worst case, panicked about getting fired today if saying anything beyond scope of current work. I covered up, hid, sheltered, and defended from co-rat workers. I sat still so not to bring attention to personal or departmental problems, I felt at great risk, and I dirty-assumed myself vulnerable.

> Drugs clouded my truth and once poisoned with such falsehoods, I believed myself smaller, weaker, and much less than I was.

I darted from offered opportunities because floundering on the downside of selfhood, well, that is…until I didn't. Once starting to flush drugs from my bloodstream, I learned to say *yes* at work, say *yes* to life, and the up-ladder rungs came fast. At the height of my global executive status, I faced my core truth yet again, and quit my job. My boss Jb had praised me gloriously for a decade before I resigned amid my alcoholism. Believably, because of my honesty damn the sacrifice, Jb rushed in full force to help, ridiculously affording me every possible resource at his disposal. As the case may be, he embraced my virtuousness…Jb denied my turned-in two weeks' notice and rather held me lovingly tight in his own way, standing alongside me to stick in the middle, facing my pained truth and not run away. Straight-up 100-100…to and for me, if not able to be truthful at work, I am employed at the wrong fucking place.

If honest at work and it blows up in my grill, I am employed at the wrong fucking place. My commitment is truth, and if my truthful hand is unable to correctly operate the doorknob, then fuck it, it's not my goddamn door.

Standing Over the Pain
Each my self-reinventions were birthed after deep and uniquely-focused introspections, sometimes the proprietary periods lasting years before true change began.
Each life-defining moment resulted because of one common theme, one shared problem…I was stuck. Realizing my stuckness and after trying other varied solutions, I could not create lasting positive change. So once stuck, without anywhere else left to go, I found the only remaining path available to me.

The one verified thing in my life stopping me, holding me down, and blanketing me with emotional suffering, are the untruths I tell myself.

I become stuck when not knowing or accepting pure truth. Only once facing the absolute facts within my current reality can I hope for change. Only once pausing or stopping with adequate conviction, time, tools and focus am I able to learn and know my truth. Only once facing my truth without emotions, judgments, assumptions, blame or resentment can I proceed. These were neither quick nor easy to solve challenges. For decades I stumbled through life needing or even wanting such change, but stalled on performing the proper work required. Once making time to do the work, awhile calibrated with adequate dedication and willingness, I understood my laser-focused effort as hyper-essential in order to accomplish said change and frankly, in order to survive.

My precise commitment was necessary, but not always yet had I *wanted* alternative life conditions badly enough to truthfully alter any damn thing. The tenacity required to resolve my stickiness constituted as critical, because I learned in some cases, there existed a necessity to get that shit right the first time. I assembled maximum strength on occasion, because of forecasting myself unable to pause again with adequate time or assertion to fix the same issue a second or third time. I determined my only down-stuck escape route was led up and out by the leading light of truth. I made the upcoming life-altering movements and in summary, I lived to learn and know my proven formula for achieving intentional surrogate results. My Roger Ray rudimentary equation for change:

> Different Thought Process
> + Different Tools
> + <u>Different Efforts</u>
> = Different Results

This here now is the what, how, and why of my propulsive life leaps, relatively speaking.

ONE. The first big conscious truth I faced to help reorient myself towards the good was…my mom, my dad, my big sister Laura and my brand-new little biddy bird baby sister were gone and never coming back. Dropped in Detroit, then asking to know if or when my family was coming back for me, I was nothing but angrily dismissed. Not hearing from my father for almost a year, I faced the truths of life on my own. Only after standing nose-to-nose with my truth, and not running from my bothers could I settle into my reality. Well, but I did not like my real world, no not at all. My life felt horribly unfair, like being punished for breathing. I wanted to run sans care for what happens next. But no, I paused, I did not run, I did not cling magnetically and stew on the incogitable, no, this was no longer about me. My life was no longer about me, my life was then for someone else. My job was to protect my best friend middle sister Beth, using every micron of my actuality. Although the truth convincing me to live for the benefit of Beth's well-being was a fabricated falsehood, the exercise saved me. The process of facing reality, even if motivated by an ignorant lie, helped me change my life orientation towards the better.

  I was five years old.

TWO. The second big conscious truth I accepted before able to face my current world and keep going was…my mom was gone and never coming back. It seemed impossible to me, trying to live without a mom. I did not want to even play with my reality, I wanted to trade it in for a new one. I hated my truth, confused and scared imagining how life was supposed to work without a mother, and with only a yelly father who was hardly ever home. Looking back, I was mad. I was mad at everyone and everything, I was mad at the world. More than mad at the world, I hated the world. I resented everyone and everything. I felt punished but no one would tell me what I was doing wrong. I had to shut up and read the books or else, do the homework or else, and not allowed to be sad or mad, or I would be yelled at and punished. Life felt ridiculously unfair. I did not understand what was going on. I grew confused and angrier trying to unriddle this crap. Then standing alone with my truth, dealing with only the current reality underfoot, such grounding helped me get up and keep moving, regardless of my sadness and madness.

  I was eight years old.

THREE. The third big conscious truth I convinced myself of to start living a better life, trying to exist easier and smoothly fit in with the world around me was…start carrying my knife everywhere and be more of an asshole. I recognized clearly the drug hustle was not going to end, and if not sticking up for myself more effectively and soon, I was going to get stabbed or shot. School became more troublesome and whatever the academia issues amounted to no longer fricking mattered, I knew the worriments could neither get resolved nor continue much longer, so I hung such irrelevant musings in the back window. I must prepare doing a better job selling drugs, I had no choice. I did not try to put the bigger picture in focus, or challenge if oriented in the correct direction or not, no time for that shit. Besides, seemed like zero options existed, I never even considered myself to have a say, so, I put thinking aside and showed up to do the damn work.

After getting beat up a few times and robbed a few times more in somewhat short succession, I exercised my best educated guess and knew in my forward vision this crap was going to get much worse. I was horrifically underprepared for additional faceoffs, so I knew adaptation was called for. By embracing my truthful reality whether I liked it or not, or if best for my overall successful future, I reoriented towards a more sustainable life, albeit life as a drug dealer. My holstered folding knife afforded me hidden confidence, however misguided the strength it was. I lived to learn and find fortitude wherever, whenever, and however possible to journey my intentional direction, no matter how fucking bloody battered and broken.

      I was fourteen years old.

FOUR. The fourth big conscious truth I realized entirely, the one thing allowing me to survive, orienting me towards the sunshine and help me live my one and only best life was…move out west and live in the mountains. Only once facing my deepest and darkest truth, entirely hidden otherwise, did I recognize my inability to stay away from the needle. I knew intuitively I was not strong enough, and major distance was required between me and my known shooting community. Simultaneously, I was not able to minimize or even vent my mounting internal anger. I saw no end in sight with the lies and excuses I myself amassed, until unearthing the need for a hard geographical relocation.

I grew sick and tired of the judgments, the blaming, and the unforgiveness building up inside me. After searching my truth of truths and failing elsewhere, I afforded myself the gifted chance of true change amongst the high-altitude snowcaps. Challenging as the move was emotionally and logistically, I left, I fricking left, not once looking back.

      I was twenty-one years old.

FIVE. The fifth big conscious truth I learned to know and lived to understand, allowing me to move forward in the best possible life direction was: quit drugs with finality you big fucking dummy and trade that shit in for a hopeful professional athletic career. After a turbulent five-year de-escalation, I knew in order to leave all drugs behind and have it hold, I must clench a superior passionate purpose to get away, stay the fuck away, and not rebound. Fog-free and sans-hallucination I viewed that only within the supreme self-discipline lay waiting for me as an athlete could I be held sound and safe enough, hence insulating me from the creep of drugs. Within a 24 hour period I left behind every single fucking thing I knew in my world that served me awhile hurt me…the drugs, the pain, the lies, the fears, the indifference and the self-doubt, then charged full force forward on my bike. No, I was not slowing down, no, I was not looking back, no, no way forget it.

      I was twenty-five years old.

Surface-Level Living

Let me silence the hurried noise of life. Let me smartly do as I intend, avoiding what ought be evaded. Let me ask befit questions, patiently listening. Let me learn to achieve the truth within truth itself.

Coveting the collection of peace tolerance and honesty, oh my dear me I learn they subsist below realms rightly gottable… outlying where I breathe, no place I can see, the deep abyss.

Nonsensically I loiter fidget on the surface, mind seeking. Then knowing, I do what I must. Studying the swell… she comes in, she recedes… quick now quick, avoiding the nets, I jump.

The nets they snag me… God no I may drown here. I wriggle I squirm then praise it all, I am clear. Dive now dive, heading for the shadows… down, down, down. This deep I visit but cannot stay, no breath only near-death for me here. I dive multitudes each day, weeks now, fleeing the netted traps, foraging for truth. I struggle my continuance one more try, I tire. My body depleted, my heart defeated, my breath taxed and beyond, exhausted and almost gone.

Miles behind me, the world over my head, I accept my perilous weakened state. I hesitate… think it best to cease the effort, stop the try, only then the suffix… sacrificially float on by. Abruptly then that moment, unbelieving the absurdity, an exquisite patch of light shines upon me… I flinch bewildered. An in-fact shock wave… utterly irrational. I have seen no light here before, fact one none… thought deep below only no-nothing light, just done.

Reddening tears drown thine eyes blues, instantaneously I know all I need. Barely lasting of breath I spin fast… must surface. Up-up-up… go, go, go, up to the fulltime light. I hold tight not a loose-jointed cache showing… I hold tight deathly tight my truth, here now my knowing.

Remove thy barriers, go where I must. Truth engrossed, first I must breathe. Finding truth I must risk not breathing. All which is left, only truth… I see as so, I know as so, I have no choice.

The shadowed abyss gifts me truth, my truth gifts me light.

Savior

I hold not, nor can I impose my nonexistent superpowers of change over any my sisters
or brothers, despite my desire to intrude…me trying to *fix* or *save* people. Yes of course
the intent and attempt to help is an otherwise desirable trait. I lived to learn and know
that when stuck, I need to hold myself accountable to sort out the *fixing* part on my own.
Many times I languished deep within the moments when I cannot effectively navigate
life. True-true, during my *I need help* emotional down times, I do not always ask for
support, nor now and again can I admit anything is wrong at all. Even when others see
my pain, I might deny my suffering, sick of hearing myself complain, cognizant everyone
has their own shit to handle or I'm too proud to admit I cannot do it on my own.

Sometimes I silently hope for the simplest yet most complex of all
support…please just hold my hand. Please just hold my hand and allow me to be the one
to let go first. Such hand holding could help lift me up and out of my mini hell, at times. I
think I need to know I am ok and that at the end of the day, if I still feel ruffled or unsure,
a hand is there for me. Here between lies the truth…not always can I have such hands at
my beckoned call, not always exists the necessary tough love from others when I do not
see clearly, and the challenge of my habituated aloneness day and night will be fixed by
no other. Romance or not, I hope for occasional support to help me make and find my
way through the crappy hard shadow times of life, times holding me back from the
sunny better days coming ahead. My living to learning to knowing has produced the
straight-up realization such balanced calm is internal, or least it my challenge to open or
ask for help, if even for a slight hand hold or a glorious GrizzlyBearHug from Travis the
Boyd.

Lust to Lament Lingers

My healthy-ego operates only from truth. Truth of the ever-present sun, truth of
possibilities, and truth of the try. When truthful, I feel see and think many things are
possible yet still unproven, so not yet are they fully believed. Once accepting my truths of
possibility, I push away with both hands from the mirror to *try*. Must I hold a definitive
meaning of life to start living? *No.* Must my short-range paths, orientations, and planned
results align perfectly with my long-term needs and desires? *Not always.* I proved many
times my excessive evaluations become tangled semantics because I am certain to face
change regardless. So, if quite probable the sticky webs lay waiting ahead of me at eye-
level anyway, why delay more? Infinite variables loomed before me and once I began to
believe one or two were possible, I began my run at the throne to become the king of self-
certainty, aka the lord of inner and outer truth by my measure.

Fueling my healthy-ego, I start by taking the first small step, gaining strength
and courage along the way. Early each day I plan my do's and don'ts, then I start. I know
change will occur so I plan blank openings, leaving room for adjustments, thus
accomplishing most of my three or less highest priorities. Only once beginning does my
future become clearer, if even only for now. I might ponder too much, akin to stuck
gazing deeper and deeper into my mind's eye through the mirror. Deep thinking helps
me live more precisely and yet, taking anything too far is too far, this my truth.

So, trying to do *something* with my life, I attempt to keep relatively short my lust to lament lingers, then get up and begin the doing. I do not need a perfectly laid plan before starting, mostly because I lived to know one of my two life certainties will adjust my route and even my destination…change.

Trying to retrain this brain I retain the pain left behind from them there the lying times.

These Here Nowadays

To me and for me, eternal happiness exists not. This marketed and packaged promised land futures, the sustained aura of happiness, well…to me and for me is an impossible myth. Pain and suffering comes hard fast and often, this truth undeniable. When unprepared for life's incoming pain tide, I uncentered, I fell, grasping to grab ahold of whatever I could find to arrest my fall, which included drugs booze and hopelessness. Through factual living then learning, I grew to know the self-evident truth of my biggest challenge is effectively navigating my struggles.

Through introspection, helping others, and letting go, I arrive safely into the calm harbored waters of my life, yet not by chance do I reach the proverbial pier.

Only by way of carefully mapping course, stocked and prepared for every imaginable challenge, contingency plans in place for my missed assumptions and unplanned rise-ups, my precise intention ablaze, my unquestionable willingness steering the ship, most days wearing the badge of courage to not fucking quit, only then will I make land at my destination, even when blown precariously off-course for years. Then and only fucking then do I stand in these here shoes, pausing with clear mind to bask with the sun on my face once the clouds clear, preparing towards the better once more, before the next storm rolls in. These here nowadays I am at peace and mostly remain in the middle, living within truth, existing outside and apart from any single regret across my days, awhile eyes wide open.

Wrap'round

My desired motorcycle racer embodiment was a relatively short-lived dream yet still, never before had I inflated any life aspirations with such death-defying drive and enthusiasm. When about the time drugs entered my world, trying to live as perhaps I might desire, for a short time I thought myself good enough to race bicycles, until I factually attempted. My body led me to the kids-size bicycle motocross track, wanting to do something, wanting to do something physical, wanting to do something competitive, wanting to do something that could help me get somewhere away from here, wanting to do something I might be ok at, but ah, hard no…I sucked at that too, so I quit.

                    Chapter SEVEN

Drug Addict was the first of an upcoming powerful string of self-imposed labels I hung on myself with negative connotation. It took six years for the creep of shame to cancer-in upon me, by way of the lowlife loser junkie identification placard I wore once shoving the needle in my arm. Early drugged, I had no vision, I was only escaping. I had no dreams, no premeditated plans existed for my entry into the dealing trade. Once the heavy abuse shit kicked in, there was next to none no more play, no more bikes, no more motorcycles. No more games, no more skateboards, no more frisbees. I zombie-focused on the job at hand, get more drugs, do more drugs, period. I utilized drugs to steal myself away from the world, steal myself away from myself, and steal myself away from school. Little did I know the *dropout* label would stick with me rather profoundly for the rest of my life, then cause immediate and negative judgments from others long as I allowed that shit to bother me. Only once quitting my awesome two-decade big boy job at Trek Bicycles would I begin to use my dropout status to my advantage. No longer would it be a pin of shame and dysfunction. I grew and learned to wear it as a badge of honor, feeling strength within myself for what I have overcome, and what I have achieved despite my past decades of quitting, stupidity, and mangled speedbumps.

Clawing Atop the Walls of Thy Self-Dug Death Pit
Pain oncoming is my most self-evident personal truth of all, such veritable honesty empowering me to stand taller over my addiction. Drugs controlled me because I enabled them, until I didn't. Yes it took five years to kick that shit once *decided*, but then I learned to comprehend a remarkable strength within. The recognition arose I am factually tougher than ever known, I can do similar hard shit again, and I will, because I am capable.

I was about two months in when it hit me, the one singular condition more over all others that kept me from relapsing. When about to abandon the Mister Clean ship, I glared vividly within the truth of going back to using. Similar to my cooked-up funeral day vision, I did the math. Sickening was then the notion, *blech-hurl*, of cashing in and rejoining the roulette table. I did not want to give up my accumulated days, no way, they meant too much to me, factually they meant everything. For my first 20 years clean, I always knew my number. Even right now I can cipher it quickly...34 years and 27 days clean...April 4th was when I smoked my last skank bong hit in my buddy's condo. If crumbling, then my next possible day clean would be day #1, if still alive. I just couldn't bring myself to lose the days I had collected and start all over again, I just couldn't.

Much of my additional manageability is labeling what I see when spying such shit through my truth goggles, then I name it. I address it out loud, so to pause, so to self-inflate, or per minimum, not let it deflate me. Arguably my most vital physical operation is regulation of breaths. If losing control of my breathing, my ability to process and proceed is hampered greatly. I learned this straight-up fact during athletics but now use the practice extensively to regulate stress, pain, fear and frustration. Lastly I have become rather mechanical, I had to…I had no choice. Utilizing my proprietary utensils within my carry-everywhere physical three-ring binder, these are the daily processes, rituals, routines and practices which maintain my guardrails so I don't drive off a cliff, or least detour crashing into a big old oak tree. My implements not only pave my way but help to jack me up when I flatten, help me see when all light is gone, and help me rejoin course when I exit too soon or late.

Trauma is an enduring hurt, a lasting pain, something not easily shed, if fucking ever. I believe to have long-ago formed a practice of self-blame and shame, trying to somehow counterbalance my loving connections with others, or rather lack thereof. Attempting to exit this self-pummeling playing field, I tried to make my way 'round to find a slow-down softness, then even a kindness, collecting clarity, and even move to reign as puppeteer over my personal operations, aka properly enacting most of what I think say and do…well, least I try. Me myself alone I travel my single solo one path, no matter how often others try to fricking steer me a different way. I cannot decode my pain, no one legitimately grasps my fear nor can ever comprehend this the deep-rooted multi-tentacle hurt I carry except for, *hello-hello*…me myself.

I value greatly my comprehensive substance abuse experience. Impossible to say how different I would be today if not for my downward bird druggie self but for sure I would not be the same me. I gained while simultaneously lost pieces of self by way of the drugs and Devil's Water, but overall the pick-up appears as the captured self-reliance and pride, well as the after-life survival reflections. Although taking years to recognize the value of accepting my purposeful experiences as-is and the associated benefits to both myself and others, it is however a participation I now find power in, great-great power…total truth.

Curator of Pain

I maintain a true-true objective technical reality. Which is a factual, I can prove it, show-me-on-paper reality. I have an emotional reality that is subjective, based on feelings. My emotional reality can neither be proven nor shown on paper, yet times too far often, I reside there, stuck in my bird brain, full of stress, fear, what-ifs, and downright dirty lies.

> I create my own pain, certainly my worst pains, the crippling fantasized fears fabricated nowhere else except in my own head.

Even after the bleeding heartache has somewhat lessened, I carry still, my 200-pound backpack. My pack of petrified pain burdens me, heavies me down, hah…despite me knowing way better.

I feel the weight growing minute by minute yet refuse to drop my sack of sadness. I carry the packaged hurts, I senselessly let the absurdity cut me time after time…my bled frights soak its straps. My rucksack I lug it everywhere, creating residual pain and suffering long after once leaving the crappy emotional tempest behind.

The chaotic life is the one I choose for myself. If too busy to do something, it is because of my choices to make that some-thing a supreme priority, or fucking not.

Let me try to live a life of purpose and be intentional with my pursuits. I should live with purpose instead of living by accident, trying to not fumble through my days and years as things just *happen* in my life. There will forever be surprises, there will forever be urgent issues I must tend to.

I get to choose what is truly urgent, what is most critical, and how I spend my time.

Here-here little dear darling doggie…I try to spend my remaining moments well, by my measure. I try to shed that which holds me back from the life I want, holds me back from the life I desire. I try to anticipate the unique challenges and best I can, try bulking bigger and standing taller than the shadow stalking me. So, here my intentions, this my explicated life process, here my enunciated tries, and still…am I doing it? Am I using what built, am I walking my talk, aka are the dogs eating the dog food? Is what I have formulated correct and valuable to me, does it work, aka does it serve up as appealing yummy doggie treats, specifically, *mmm*…Scooby Snacks?

Yes I believe so, yes I understand what it is that I intend, and yes I objectively monitor what it is that I do. Yes I say, yes I see as so, I am doing exactly what I know is correct for me, this here your book…to share, to encourage, to help however plausible. You CAN do it, you CAN DO anything you can dream, I am here, FOR you, I am here, WITH you, we CAN do this together, we fucking CAN. We can…from blame and shame we can shed that stinky skin, we can start anew, we can stand tall over all that which held us down prior, we can persevere, we can survive as we dream to dream, we can, we fucking can, I know this to be pure fucking truth fact one fucking hundred. I believe in you, I am fighting for you, I believe in us, I am fighting for us, we are a fucking team and I fricking love you one hundred-100.

Damage…the collateral damage as a result of this here my addict narrative commitment I see none…fuck the money, damn the house, fuck it just fuck it, the fricking job, and mostly, fuck that speedway of them rats a racing, fuck it all because only this verifiably matters, me & you & you, period fucking period, by my measure.

Scorecard

By technical accounts there have been more hits, more moments of pain, and more years of suffering than times of sunshine across my face, rainbows ablaze, and bunnies 'round my feet. Be as may, I learned this life of mine a nonstop collection of rises and falls.

The energy and choice to face life head-on, leaving the pain behind, that shit arrived only from deep within…the courage to keep rolling forward meanwhile my wounds inside and out still healing.

For years long, far past clean, the mind numbing desire to high-dive back into the drugs, or just let go the wheel, both for the singular purpose of ending my miserable suffering was hyper prevalent. I learned to smile between the pain, if even a smirk or a contrived grimace of optimism, despite the bleed-burning below. Once tuned into the truth of the hurt locker, I found crippling pain does *NOT* last, it *DOES* pass, it *DOES* fade, and it *WILL* lessen. I recognized not to sit too long licking my wounds…do not wait too long sad and blue because of the darkness I just survived. I assembled the knowing to get up, get going, and go nuts in the sunshine, even when it is raining.

The most extreme physical expenditure, when my heart rate is 200 beats per minute or more, fades quickly when I slow even minorly. Suddenly, extreme pain is lessened. My heart rate would drop from 206BPM, my maximum heart rate ever recorded, down to under 150BPM in less than one minute. Anything under 180 beats per minute for me was sustainable and although challenging, 180 was bearable. And when my body was at 180 or less, I could think, and learn, and experiment, and come back stronger because of the pain and hard work I was *WILLING* to go through. It a similar situation with my emotions and tasks…it gets better, no matter what…it fucking gets better. This pain, whatever I am feeling, it too, shall fade and perhaps even pass.

Only through the hard does something softer come. Only after a harsh winter do wildflowers rise up and bloom in the spring.

Some folk I know cannot settle with such enduring pain…laboring hard and willing to suffer to reach a better place. Whether physical, emotional, or mental pain, it equally hurts like hell. If learning how to face it and even deal with it, least sometimes when quite frankly there is no other option, I think such provocation most always worth the suffrage.

Yes I hurt, sometimes badly. I cried, for years. I mourned my void for decades, *but*…but I learned to be willing to live through it, thus understanding I *DO* come out of those pained times in one piece. Only when facing the hard stuff and finding I do survive that shit, only then did I learn to truly live. Even when at my worst, when I am more miserable than I have ever been in my life, there will be moments in the day when I would forget briefly about my pain, when distracted. If aware of it, I saw that I was still among the living, that I am not totally broken, although it feels that way.

Over time the learning came that I can put things, mostly, back together again, even after the death of my parents and close friends, you know Birdy, like losing your amazingly awesome coach Glenn, like me losing my best friend, me losing my best friend Glenn. How then do I say, well, still I must, um…super sadly, some people do not make it out of their troubles alive. Some are hurt too much by the trauma, the fright, and the worry. Some poor souls let this hard shit control them for the rest of days instead of facing it, dealing with it, and tenaciously working through it. Not everyone wants to face that shit. Not everyone is willing to stare that crap down, or even rise to try. Not everyone steps off that fucked-up witness stand keeping both legs. Not everyone wants to sweat and bleed and cry. Not everyone feels they can do it alongside all the other stressful shit in their life, so they stray the attempt. Not everyone feels they have enough fight left in them and, well, um…and I have learned, well, least to me, that…that this is entirely ok…it's ok, it's ok, it is really, really, really ok. I try not to judge others when their pain or fear consumes them entirely. I help best I know how and when it does not work for them anymore, I hold onto unconditional love and support for them, no matter fucking what.

Face it. When bad shit came for me, well, I did not always feel so strong…I didn't always want to, or know how to, face it. Face it…only possessing the willingness to do whatever it takes to make it through and back to the sunshine did I recognize my opportunity to live as myself. This hurt, this pain, it came for me, and will come for me again to be sure-sure-100. This hurt, this pain, will come for me once more, sit down on top of me, leaving a pool of blood behind when it runs off looking back, joking and laughing madly. The understanding at first eluded me, the incomprehensibility that something so wrong, so horribly hurtful, hateful, evil even, exists in this world.

Bravery. Bravery, and then there is my bravery…can I, and will I…will I always be able to gather myself and rise up, lifting and letting the salty tears fill my mouth, yet still with arms wide open, ready for the next glorious blast of beauty that will certainly radiate down upon me, filling my heart and making for a life well-lived, if willing? Willing…willing, will I be willing to hurt and carry such hurt? I hope I can continue to face such odds going forward. I am not always so strong, although I now know much more of what I am capable, this my truth. Pain. Pain…a pain that will soften and in reality, the only thing left behind will be the memory and maybe a scar. A memory and a scar, not leaving me crippled by the big hole in my heart I felt before. I *am* alive. I am *still* standing, I am *ok*. I want to be willing, willing to face it, endure it, and repeat, and repeat, and repeat. I hope to have the strength. I hope to withhold the bravery, the courage, the grit, and the guts.

Taxes. Echo-echo…change and death are the only truthful certainties I know, besides my try. Some people say taxes are a life certainty yet to me, taxes are a technical reality of living within the grown-up competition of rats a racing, not a guiding certainty. Everything changes, everything. Even if visually untouched, everything ages thus changes. I will change, proactive change will be required of me, and me required to keep changing. I hope to work with change and not fight it, because pure stagnation will drown me. Although not knowing when or how my last day will come, I wish not to drown if you pretty-pretty-please with sprinkles on top, although I may still owe that one to Johnny Powell, not sure…maybe.

Doubt Not in Hope and This Truth

Our journey grand, but alas…no picnic

The clouds, they stalk us.

And yet, the sun she is ever-present, lurking behind the darkness

The black sky dumps tears atop our head, yet she shines still.

The sun, she is there, burning bright…she always there

This no fable, mere no metaphor no riddle, this total truth.

Do not await the trip off the tarmac to see it, to know it as so

Hope we all feel her warm and loving rays, more than not.

Strive to remember, she is there, always there, the sun

She warms us, casts light upon our world, even when dark.

That is, when we choose to feel her, choose to see her

Doubt not in hope and this truth…feel the sun, despite the clouds.

Inner'ear

Certainly when in altercation with ailing mental health, burdened with hardship and wrestling with addiction, the value of loving and engaged humans around me is immeasurable, well as the critical nature of foundational introspection. Often I journey into my head, into my heart, 'tempting to unravel thy oppression holding me back.

I go often deep within, sojourning to understand, attain comprehension and ask…how do I best live the life I desire instead of just dreaming it?

So to somewhat summarize this PAB shit, hither here my infantile introspection outline:

1. Authoritative change requires my best try, my best effort. My best effort demands the willingness to endure no matter the unyielding challenge, fucking period.
2. Aside, not mistaken to linger longer, not stay too long buried inside of my emotional brain, chanced to unwittingly get caught in the endless web of thoughts and feelings.
3. Sorting shit out best I can, I get going in my most presentable direction, knowing all-all too well the hardest component of doing anything is, just…get…started.
4. Once doing, I try my intentional best, not crucifying myself when unexpected results follow. Soundly I try to find peace in the truth I did *something*, least I tried. Like hiding the drug spoon from thyself, or skipping every other acid trip, aka *something*.

I try to get up and get going, living joyfully within the presence of others. Others who bring more harmony, beauty, and love to my life than able to do on my own. Yes for sure, the complex life math puzzle game also includes the critical time of being alone in silence, thinking and letting go, and this too like human connection, is a balanced non-negotiable.

Stuff of Intention

Not because of dumb luck or through some moderate-sized miracle will I succeed. I must act responsibly, with resolve and a fun fluidity to live on purpose as I intend, forever changing direction as I play the life rollercoaster puzzle game. One morning postdrugs, I lay in bed listening to heavy rain nail upon the roof. My schedule of the day included an intense three-hour bike ride and as reinforced by my alarm clock currently in snooze mode, the time to ride was, *now*. Mid-day I would begin my other payroll work, and no opportunity awaited me to tonight ride after clocking out from the bike shop. So, I needed to get up. But I didn't want to, I wanted to go zip-zero nowhere, I wanted to stay in bed. The good-mojo feels of my face-forward desires, aka riding regardless the damn rain, that shit escaped me entirely. Although yes I wanted to improve my fitness, go on to log better race results, and live up to not only my personally-defined potential but my commitment to sponsors, *meh*…I more so wanted to stay in bed. Trying varied approaches to rise, the same scenario reappeared weekly with no new findings on display, until they did.

Intently I exchanged drugs for a mountainbike race career. If not performing to my gauged best effort on the bike, was this worth it, and would it last? I had to make this bike thing work, had to. More-more better…one cold wet morning before resetting the clock-clock numbers for two hours later, I thunk something brand new.

Fact, each time I ride my bike, my bird brain feels better. Even if my bike breaks or the weather challenges me or I get hurt, it is a good ride. Weather never stops me, I have the gear. Fact therefore, every ride is a good ride. Every ride is a good ride. Every ride…is…a…good ride. So, if every ride a good ride, why not get up? Well, duh…the attractiveness for staying in bed was way more appealing than thinking about the hurried breakfast and changing my clothes and slathering on sunscreen and packing my nutrition and filling my waterbottles and inflating my tires lubing my chain checking my suspension and walking the dog and facing the weather.

But, but what if…what if I don't ponder the irrelevant? What if I laser focus on making it to the bike, getting to my start of good ride? What if I fixate on the one singular critical, zooming past the rest, would that work? Maybe. So I tried it, and it worked. I tried again, and again, and it worked every time. Then til now it still works, I one-eye focus on getting to the curb. If I can get to the curb, once I start, the ride will be a good one. Once pushing that first pedal stroke, the weather no longer matters in the slightest, factually nothing matters, long as I get to the curb. In many other situational areas of my life I utilize an associated approach…unravel unhealthy assumptions, maybe re-engineer things backward or otherwise, so to overcome a slight dilemma which might be disguised as a huge ordeal. In such life-all regards, once started, I am then on my way, doing *something* instead of decided but sitting still, so I do most whatever necessary to just…get…started.

Allowing Room for My Spark to Rise

As an active addict I fabricated myself stuck, stuck doing something not good for the long-range me, stuck in some undesirable circumstance chosen forced or found. At times I could escape, and at times I became however as it was, unstuck, least a while. And for the times when able to break free, per partially, when able to get up and begin to try and get started, how for shit's sake did I break away?

Did I find hope and did hope allow me to escape being stuck?
Did I find faith and did faith afford me a way out?
Did I find inspiration and did inspiration motor me away from what I disliked?

What got me up, what got me started?
What got me going, what got me going in a direction of betterment, by my measure?
What clarity can I identify to help lift me and guide me in my stuck future?

I unstick when I pause, I unstick when I stop.
I unstick when I think deeply, and write that shit down.
I unstick when I dig and burrow within my truthful self, traveling far subsurface below.

I journey into head and heart searching for my truth.
Challenging my truth, I face harshly my current reality, only then able to see truthfully.
I try to commit myself and test my found truth, so as to hold my truth proven.
I live to learn and find the trust in the truthful reality I embrace.

　　　　　　　　Chapter SEVEN

Only once going deep, deeper, and deepest can I see.
Once finally seeing, at first I do not always believe, aka no faith in myself or my seeings.
Trying to trust truth, I dream of better outcomes, using my courage and willingness.
Not yet did I always believe the slightly fabricated vision, aka my betterment of self.
I lived to learn I do not have to believe in all things known or unknown, when stuck.

I paused, I dreamed…I learned to know that *maybe*, maybe something else is possible.
Maybe I attempt or experiment with new-to-me possibilities, maybe not.
Once going back, and going back, and going back to depths of self, I finally saw it.
I saw it, oh my word yes…possible, most anything I could dream to dream *is* possible.

Once finding feeling seeing and accepting fully…the knowing of
possibility allowed room for my spark to rise.

Once realizing the truthful reality of possibilities, I built hope and I built desire.
I built a picture of truthful hope and honest desire I wanted to see myself within.
Once imagined, I built that image as my new reality…it *is* possible for me to arrive there.
It is possible…I *can* do it…I can do it and I *will* try to *try*.
I will try because it *is* possible and I desire it.

I once looked and waited for reclamation from ruin, I waited…nothing, nothing, *nothing*.
Yes hands aided me, helped me, yet at the end of the day, left here alone was only me.
Then the next day, only me…and the next…and the next…*and the next*.
Me…*me alone*…left with my thoughts and nervously fidgeting with these here idle hands.
My mischief mind and hands, hurting me when not on my intentional path, and willing.

Fact, I saw. I saw…in my truthful reality a stillness, no movement, barely a sound 'cept
when stopping so hard to listen and let it be. I then sensed…the thump, thump, thump
reverberation set halfway back my chest skin, set forward halfway afront my spine. No
one, nothing else existed in this scened arena…me, just me, just me, just…me. Just me
there in my seeing, thus just me here in my shoes, thus just me here in my truthful reality.

I know for *fact* the only sentient being possessing the power to move me, is me,
only…me.

I factually found to live learn know and understand the truth within myself, because myself is all I truly know, all I can prove, see, hold, taste, smell, touch, all that is true…purely
me under my own power is…the…only…truth…I…know. I gave up the undesired and
unwanted in favor of the sought, because I could not have both simultaneously.

I gave up my present to gain a future, a living future, and through
truth I realized the only future worth pursuing is one pointed toward
the good.

I abandoned what I was trying to leave behind. I traded up for something else, in theory something safer, sustainable, and desirable. I presented myself the opportunity of my future because only I could, only I could, only I could…with…these…here…hands.

Proprietary Pissings

I am only minorly original. I uncommonly value the substantiality of not enduring the additional years held captive and seeped deep in scholastic book theory. Yes of course I withstood a barrage of cast-upon conjectures as I bopped around but I enthusiastically proved each concept handfirst. Tested them I did, through daily experimentations instead of blindly accepting the curriculummed-notions as assumed facts or truths, without the latitude to live learn and know the propositions honestly.

> Before giving credit to additional outside influences however, I must first make mention of another one…me.

Beyond reason I believe to give more thought to this here functional life, certainly more than the average bear or bird, such work gifting me numerous valuables. I merit the notion the wherewithal and the aftereffects to engage in such self-inquisitive sessions to places which quite frankly, scare the fuck out of me. I also honor while honestly revere, that which I avoided or simply did not do, hah…some oblivious side-stepped blind wanderings which otherwise may have killed me. Outboard, and strange as it may seem, but I am appreciatory for the over 300 doses of LSD consumed in my lifetime. The hallucinogenic implements allowed me to not only experience see feel and know deeply, but journey to a held-aside connected mental landscape otherwise unobtanium to traditional conscious or subconscious states.

So here now I recognize and pay honor to all within and without…if, if really, if real-really dealing with the brutal reality of known facts, if casting aside the drama fear and dirty-ego, splendor has a chance to occur. No fricking way will what I select to manifest bubble up randomly and-or by accident…my intentional commitment is needed, well as everything else I fucking got. Learned honestly along the way, I try to be ready for most everything. Awhile, I am truthful to know storms will occur during my journey, challenges and barriers will rise up no doubt, even an occasional iceberg in the middle of the night, all such hazards forcing me to constantly adjust.

> If acting properly, I achieve more towards what I am oriented.

Daily I show up to the outside front of house curb with a plan. I do not aimlessly wander, I do not float along wherever the winds of whimsicalness might carry me, willy-nilly speeding slow or trailing fast, travelling short or long intervals at random but rather, I set out hyper-intentionally and adjust as I go. Only with a map do I have the chance to arrive where I am going, the roadblocks detours and work-arounds be damned.

                    Chapter SEVEN

The Weight

We struggle own struggles

Suffer days past

Tears our tears ours alone

No one sees what we feel

Not our pain nor our shiny

None our passions move others

Barely some days we know us ourselves

Let us stop... let us pause

Let us think... let us feel

Let us face days past... let us cry

Let us dream, let us rise... let us try

Let us not, let us not, let us not fucking quit.

Choosing to Sit, Choosing to Rise

The Europe ski trip when twenty years young legitimately changed me.
My high-alpine Swiss venture provided a taste, a peek, a spark, a lift, and a push.
I lived to know I am neither small nor meek amid self, I am no way not so weak.
I traveled to learn the world ginormously bigger and better than ever dreamt, ever.

If I want to do something…
If I want to change something…
If I want to learn something…
If I want to see something…
If I want to go somewhere…
If I want adventure…
If I want something different or new…
Only within will these things be presented to me.

If I want, I must provide.

I must rise up, I must rise up, I must rise up under my own power and go.
If wanting a fuller and truer life than a settled or disgruntled one, I must travel.

Once, I believed I was stuck.
I was not stuck, I was afraid, well, um…I was unmindful.
I cannot see how I will ever be truly stuck, unless I decide to be.
And if I decide to sit settle or stew, it must be myself that sees it, and changes it.
I believe I will be as alive or dead as I decide to be, yes, yes, yes, this I believe.

This Here Twisty-Turny Life

Despite the trials of heartbreak, aside the triumphs of victory, I construct my world big or small, bright or dark as I make it. As I make it…even when proceeding swimmingly, sometimes I'm down and blue. As I make it…even when bleeding broken and abandoned, my courageous willpower is able to pull me up, brush me off, and speed me off into the sunshine frolicking, if I choose. As I make it…the world travel, the skiing, the physical blows, the drugs and the defies, all existing as major parts of my fantastical life history.

Bizarrely by my measure, even the slightest alteration, the littlest twist or turn, both the intentional ones and the uncontrollable ones, any of them capable of shooting me off on a radically different trajectory. Thus my learned hardcore opposition to go back and change anything happening or not happening along my journeyed path. No way would I want to risk, chance, or sacrifice who I am or where I am now, no way, it could have well likely turned out so much worse. The jobs I didn't take, the risky maneuvers I pulled away from at the last second, the love interests I did not make a play for, all that and the wrapped up rest of it equally contribute to my current existence. My current existence…my place on the board of the rollercoaster puzzle game, aka the twisty-turny rise and fall of this here bird's life flight path.

Thus perhaps the contemplative massive…the realization that pain changes me for the better. More than joy, pain is capable of altering this here thumping heart and bird brain for the better. I believe such amassed resolutive strength is the wound remembrance, the pause it demands of me and the profound work it requires of me, to make my way through to the shiny side, to make my way through to the light.

For every down, an up follows, always, always…*always*. When down, even if pierced and pinned under the prolonged heel, such catastrophic poked hole eventually fills in…*always*. Perhaps to appear again at another time, as another sorta indentation elsewhere, only then to be filled in again and again…*and again*.

The hard stuff, existing as the stronger remembrance.
The resistance…my best lesson.
The adversary…my best teacher.
The hard stuff is the stuff I remember, the stuff burning alongside waking me.
The hard stuff leaves a scar, the easy stuff does no-way not.

Only when standing face to face with the truthful reality I had grown horrifically self-abusive with the needle, only then…only then could I make room to imagine any tomorrows.

Turning away from the mirror, I disoriented. My head afog with some sort of off-centered unknowing, I tried to calm, I tried to settle. All I thought I knew, and all I believed to have missed, was now held aside. Beginning over almost from scratch, I prepped to start anew. A large blank peach-cream colored canvas was raised onto the awaiting easel and affixed, I readied fresh paints. I removed the expensive brush from package, grasping it between my thumb and index finger intently yet with a softness, my second finger soundly rearward, stabilizing with precision the instrument of all days to come, and I began.

Ok, now what?

Now what…without anything stopping me, where do I go from here?

What do I do now, and what do I not?

My brush instinctually hovered momentarily over the pallet board's heavy corner, *Black of Night* as it was. Precisely like touching an unseen blazing hot wood stove in the dark, my hand jerked away frantically. I looked off elsewhere for but a moment, biting my pained lip and when turning back, my brush had already picked up *Canary Yellow* and formed some sort of sunburst, centered soundly amid the brand new me.

Perhaps, perhaps…perhaps my sought recollection of self is needed because of unsettling forces like fear and pain, this multitude of darkness leaving my foundation fractured. Not always do I need such back to basic introspective comfort practices, no, sometimes I absorb to accept all that is, and is not. I might think intently or not, I might breathe intently or not, I might relax intently or not. Often as I have lived to learn know and find, the possibility exists for me to enter such peaceful and calming states anywhere anytime. Why do I perform such slow-down pauses of true truth only truth? Well, let me attempt here a crystal-crystal fucking clarification.

Even when engaged fully with something, I feel somewhat unoccupied. Even when surrounded by people, I feel somewhat alone. Even when satisfied and complete, I feel somewhat anguished.

Do I experience these feels always or often? No. Am I coming-out to say I am bipolar? No I mean to say that when rolling along soundly, I might lose sight of the reality pain-be-a-comin'. I mean to say that when face down in the mud, I am still ok, I am ok, I am really ok. I mean to say I may forget to recognize this shit I'm standing amid ain't so bad, and it will turn out in the end, turn out ok…turn out somewhat ok one way or the next, least it won't kill me, long as I decide as such.

     Chapter SEVEN

Even when not feeling said conflicting or opposing notions, I step aside for a few minutes and either shed what burdens me or enjoy the engulfment of here now and nowhere else. When I open as explained, I feel completely and truthfully. When I stay busy, *this rat be a racing*, I get distracted by frights and worries, doubts and wonders, old pains and future fears, most of which are untrue abound my here and now real world.

My commitment and ability to go deep, feeling fully, being truthful, writing that shit down and doing what I believe to be correct does not occur invariably.

Sometimes such cleansing intentions, my attempts and efforts...include sacrifice great sacrifice, but what then a more worthy endeavor I know not none.

Without the practice to entirely utilize my senses both surface level and hidden, I can neither determine my personal truth, nor even begin to make sense of myself.

This centering allows me to return back to the me I am, without permitting the noise of who I am not to continue.

By way of truth, exploring who I am and am not, well as an understanding of what I am willing to do or not, I gain my clarified foundational drive, my proprietary engine, my core oracle, my one true central operating system from where all that is good has an opportunity to materialize.

If I want to accomplish something, if I desire to go somewhere, it's first on me. I must also share these my hopeful wonderments with others so they can help me or per minimum, clearly be put on notice to get the fuck out of my way.

<u>**Index, the What and Where of Them Pages**</u>

Notes to Self: Do what, and do not? Write that shit down...

Notes to Self: Do what, and do not? Write that shit down...

Notes to Self: Do what, and do not? Write that shit down...

www.ingramcontent.com/pod-product-compliance
Lightning Source LLC
Chambersburg PA
CBHW072212150726
48002CB00005B/1777